## *Praise for*
## Be Not Afraid

"As people of faith we are challenged to adopt a profoundly different understanding of security from that being sought through a 'war on terror.' In *Be Not Afraid*, Tom Cordaro articulates a compelling alternative that deserves our thoughtful attention. His book is worth reading; his proposal worth taking to heart."
*~ Marie Dennis is Director of the Maryknoll Office for Global Concerns, Co-President of Pax Christi International, and author of the 2008 book* Diversity of Vocations.

"With gentle authority Tom Cordaro gives back to readers Jesus' words, 'Be Not Afraid.' His study of the 'signs of the times' today, viewed through the optics of social analysis and theological reflection, provides critically needed comfort and instruction to those seeking true peace. *Be Not Afraid* is an encouraging and distinct contribution to contemporary Catholic social thought about the peace of Christ enlivened in our hearts and in the world, a peace which can be found only in justice. This resource should be on the nightstand of all who yearn for communities of compassion, peace, and justice."
*~ Donna Toliver Grimes is catechist, a member of the Pax Christi USA National Council, and a JustFaith graduate who resides in Washington, DC.*

"*Be Not Afraid* is superb for classes/universities, study groups, communities, organizers, and anyone interested in a broad, faith-based approach to today's issues. Both starkly realistic and grounded in hope, this book proves an understanding of both our times and of the many people seeking a way forward as human beings made in the image of the most Holy One, the Just One, the Compassionate One, and the Peaceful One. What if we—all of us—were made for peace and not for tearing each other and the earth apart? This book looks at our world with wide-open eyes, but also asserts clearly that freedom and life are at the heart and soul of our world; it is time to go to our roots and resurrect our original human dignity and promise as the people of God."

~ *Megan McKenna is a theologian, storyteller, writer (the latest of her thirty-four books is* The Hour of the Tiger: Facing Our Fears), *and professor of scripture, justice, peace, and spiritualities that cross cultures, religions, and peoples' experiences. She is also an Ambassador of Peace for Pax Christi USA.*

"Tom Cordaro is one of the broadest and deepest thinkers in the faith-based peace movement in North America. In this book he assesses what is new and what is old in the shifting paradigms of globalization, terrorism, and the war against the poor. Our dominant ideologies and policies in the U.S. are underpinned by deep and ultimately theological narratives about the world, which can and should be analyzed, critiqued, and revised. This is a thoughtful effort to do just that, and I commend it to both young and veteran activists who are endeavoring to engage this historical moment."

~ *Ched Myers is Co-Director of Bartimaeus Cooperative Ministries (www.bcm-net.org), an author, and an activist theologian.*

# Be Not Afraid

To Dawn —
Thank you for your
work for justice.

Tom Fowler

# Be Not Afraid

## An Alternative
## to the "War on Terror"

Tom Cordaro

Pax Christi USA
Erie, Pennsylvania

Pax Christi USA, Erie, PA 16502
© 2008 by Pax Christi USA. All rights reserved.
Printed in the United States of America by
Signature Book Printing, www.sbpbooks.com.

Bible quotations from *New Revised Standard Version*,
New York: American Bible Society, 1989.

*Library of Congress Cataloging-in-Publication Data*
Cordaro, Tom, 1954-
Be not afraid : an alternative to the war on terror / Tom Cordaro.
p. cm.
Includes bibliographical references and index.
Summary: "Examines the dominant U.S. narrative about terrorism told
after September 11, 2001, its historical context, and its relation to the War on
Terror and outlines a faith-based, democratic alternative narrative for the
United States that is centered on peace rooted in justice. Includes recom-
mendations for individuals and communities"—Provided by publisher.
ISBN 978-0-9743804-6-9
1. War on Terrorism, 2001—Moral and ethical aspects. 2. Terrorism—
Government policy—United States. 3. September 11 Terrorist Attacks,
2001—Religious aspects—Christianity. 4. Terrorism—Religious aspects—
Christianity. 5. Peace—Religious aspects—Christianity. 6. Peace movements—United States. I. Title.
HV6432.C68 2008
261.8'73
2008026808

Project Credits
Copyediting and developmental editing: Shannon McManimon
Cover design: Michael A. Jones
Indexing: Shannon McManimon
Layout: Shannon McManimon
Proofreading: Barbara Richardson, Barbara Roseborough, and Tessa Ryker
Reference checking: Angela Cordaro

**Pax Christi USA**
532 West Eighth Street; Erie, Pennyslvania 16502
phone: 814-453-4955; fax: 814-452-4784
e-mail: info@paxchristiusa.org; Web: www.paxchristiusa.org

Pax Christi USA item number 523-500

# Dedication

To my mother Angela,
who always saw more in me
than I ever saw in myself.
She knew I would write this book
long before I ever put pen to paper.

# Contents

# Introduction

As a child, I loved war movies—particularly movies about World War II. My father, a Marine and a veteran of that war, was wounded in the battle for Saipan, so of course I was very interested in knowing more about this heroic struggle. (I was also drawn to World War II movies because my father was very tight-lipped about his personal experiences of the war. I recall only a few times when he talked about his experiences—and then only vaguely. He died when I was fourteen years old; it could be that he was waiting for me to get a little older before he told me his story.)

Besides my personal interest in the epic struggle of World War II, I think I was attracted to this period in history because the dividing lines between good and evil were so clear and understandable. In almost every movie of that period, the "bad guys" were undeniably evil. The German bad guys were often led by a black-booted general with a monocle; the Japanese military leader had a stoic discipline and stern, piercing eyes. They had no second thoughts about using torture. Invariably, they would utter that all-too-familiar line: "We have ways to make you talk!" And you knew right then that our brave heroes would undergo horrific treatment.

Another common story line involved prisoner of war camps. The highest ranking U.S. or British officer would protest to the prison commander about the ill treatment his men were receiving, citing the rules of war in his defense. The evil German or Japanese prison boss would respond with a sinister laugh: "In this place, your rules mean nothing!"

The bad guys were the ones who would pick up civilians suspected of being in the resistance and take them away, never to be seen again. Men (and sometimes women) were loaded into trucks while their children and mothers cried and pleaded for their release. The bad guys were the ones who rounded people up and held them against their will—without charges or due process of law. Eventually, a relative of the detained person would sheepishly go to the office of the prison commandant, pleading for information about a child, a spouse, or a parent. The evil commandant would cruelly dismiss the relative: "I have no information about this person; he (she) is not in this facility."

As a young boy, I absorbed the historical telling of World War II from these movies and other sources—how we fought the Nazis and the Japanese imperialists in order to create a world safe for democracy, and free from torture, secret prisons, and the denial of basic human rights and legal protections. The accounting of the Cold War further reinforced this story of U.S. struggle against evil. The communists of the Soviet Union were evil because they did the same things as the Nazis and Japanese. In secret prisons, they locked away opponents of the regime who were deemed a threat to the nation. They regularly denied their own citizens basic human and civil rights in the name of security and public order. They were not above the use of torture to get information they thought crucial to their national security. We, on the other hand, were the global champions of human and civil rights; we were a beacon to the world of the commitment to the principle of the rule of law.

To be sure, this U.S. telling had a lot of problems. When constructing a national narrative, it is easy to divide the world into absolute evil on one side and absolute good on the other. But history shows that when it comes to conflict, no side is completely good (the United States held Japanese-Americans in concentration camps during World War II without due process or proof of guilt); no side is completely evil (during Nazi rule, many Germans resisted Hitler and his policies, often at great risk to themselves). During the Cold War, we in the United States claimed the mantle of defender of human rights, but our record of supporting brutal, anti-communist dictatorships around the world often made a mockery of these claims.

But national narratives have less to do with historical accuracy and more to do with constructing national identity and enshrining the values and principles that a nation holds dear. From the beginning, our U.S. narrative always held that we were not perfect in living up to our own ideals. Yet we were committed to closing the gap between our professed principles and our actions. In this sense, the United States of America has always been a work in progress.

However, since the terrorist attacks of September 11, 2001, something has gone wrong with this description. The Bush Administration said that with the terrorist attacks of 9-11, everything changed. Many in the United States are beginning to understand just what the administration meant. In essence, it means that to protect our liberty, we must forfeit some of it. To protect our values and principles, we must violate them.

With each passing month, one new revelation after another seems to contradict what many people believed foundational to our national narrative: the president signs a directive approving torture in certain circumstances; the Red Cross accuses the United States of secret detention centers which are declared off-limits to inspection; hundreds are held at the Guantánamo prison without access to lawyers or courts; U.S. military personnel at Abu Ghraib and in secret detention centers in Afghanistan torture prisoners; the president admits to setting up a program of secret wire-tapping of U.S. citizens without a court order; thousands of Muslim Arabs and South Asians in the United States are rounded up after the 9-11 attacks and held without charges; the FBI is given broad powers to spy on U.S. citizens without showing reasonable cause; the right of *habeas corpus* is set aside. In the past, the brutal face of U.S. power was usually directed at people around the world who dared challenge U.S. economic or cultural domination. Now that brutal face was coming home.

How is it possible that so many U.S. citizens would come to accept things like torture (under any circumstances); secret prisons; spying on citizens without reasonable cause or court order; holding any person (citizen or not) without charges and without due process of law; and giving the government broad powers to violate its citizens' privacy? The answer: *fear*.

The attacks of 9-11 were meant to terrorize us so profoundly that we would lose our sense of security and well-being. In that sense, the terrorists succeeded beyond their wildest imaginations. Many people in the United States have been so traumatized by the al Qaeda attacks that they have been willing to give up their civil rights and abandon their civic principles for a promise of safety.

But these terrorist attacks alone do not explain the willingness of so many in the United States to forfeit the most sacred values and principles of our democratic republic. The other factor is the Bush Administration's decision to construct a narrative of the 9-11 attacks that deepened the sense of terror that Osama bin Laden and al Qaeda sought to instill. By framing its 9-11 narrative in terms of a "War on Terror," the Bush Administration sought to put this country on a permanent war footing where peacetime notions of civil and human rights, of treaty obligations and the rule of law would be put aside because, as the administration often claimed, this war was different from any other. While some take solace in the fact that—for now—the iron fist of power in the United States is aimed at Arabs, South Asians, and other Muslims, many people wonder if perhaps the Bush Administration's "War on Terror" is meant to change the fundamental nature of our democratic republic. Many are concerned that the Bush Administration's rewrite of the U.S. story is deleting many of the values and principles (such as civil liberties, the rule of law, and universal human rights) that U.S. soldiers and sailors fought and died for in World War II.

If we desire true peace and security, we must understand the world we live in—and the stories we tell ourselves about that world. We cannot comprehend the terrorist attacks of 9-11 outside of their historical context, a context that includes the framework of globalization.

This book seeks to understand the globalized world we live in, how it led to the terrorist attacks, and then how and why the Bush Administration's 9-11 narrative gave rise to the "War on Terror." Understanding the psychology of fear is crucial to this task. The book then offers an alternative that can free us from our constant state of terror and allow us to act more effectively to address the real threat of terrorism, as well as embody our highest ideals and values. Doing so means building peace as an enterprise of justice. We will also explore what the Christian faith has to say about terrorism and fear. And we will examine the role each of us can play, both as individuals and as members of communities. In spite of all that we seem to have lost, we need not live in fear. There is reason for hope; God's promise, revealed through Jesus, can help us build a new future.

Part One of this book begins by putting the terrorist attacks of 9-11 into a broader context. It looks at the attacks and other crucial issues through the framework of the economic, environmental, and cultural forces of globalization. Additionally, Part One describes terrorism and its various forms, focusing on the psychology of terror, the effect that terrorist attacks have on the people they are meant to influence. Part One also looks at what the Bible says about the psychology of terror. Finally, it introduces the importance of narrative in the psychology of terror: How do the stories we construct to help us cope with these terrorist attacks affect our lives and our choices?

In Part Two, I take a closer look at the 9-11 narrative constructed by the Bush Administration and compare it to the one constructed by Osama bin Laden and the al Qaeda terrorist network. Both have been constructed in a way that makes them mutually sustaining—each designed to keep the U.S. people in a state of terror. While al Qaeda's motivation for sustaining the terror of people in the United States is obvious, the rationale for the Bush Administration's desire to do so is not. Part Two examines possible explanations for the Bush Administration's motivation. I close this section by offering a set of principles and values that can provide the basis for constructing an alternative 9-11 narrative that rejects the rhetoric of the "War on Terror" and offers a more effective way to combat all forms of terrorism.

Broadening this analysis, Part Three suggests that to sustain an alternative 9-11 narrative that moves us away from the framework of the "War on Terror," we need to connect it to a larger U.S. account. Part Three offers two visions of peace with roots in this larger U.S. narrative: peace as enforced order and peace as an enterprise of justice. I argue that to effectively combat all forms of terrorism, we need to abandon the notion of peace as enforced order and embrace the concept of peace as an enterprise of justice. In doing so, we are not abandoning our U.S. story but are instead rediscovering an existing tradition that has been disregarded and ignored. This part of the book calls for re-visioning our U.S. narrative so that it is more faithful to our nation's founding principles and embraces those religious or ethical values that call us to protect those who are poor and disenfranchised and to work for peace with justice.

In the final part of this book, I move from the macro-level to the individual and communal level. Most of us do not hold positions of power that would enable us to reshape foreign policy. But there are things that we can do as individuals and in community that can contribute to constructing an alternative to the "War on Terror." In particular, there are spiritual resources, common to many religious traditions, that enable us to overcome our fears and keep us from being victims of the psychology of terrorism. This final part of the book also emphasizes the need to form communities capable of resisting the power of the dominant narrative and its culture of addictive consumerism.

Although this book is written primarily for U.S. Christians who are troubled by the Bush Administration's "War on Terror," I hope that many of its themes and arguments will also appeal to a wider audience and contribute to the public discourse on the "War on Terror." This work is so important to the survival of our republic that I feel obligated by my commitment to the Gospel and my love of this country to contribute to a more rigorous public dialogue, despite the limitations of my own experience and understanding of these complicated issues. For far too long, we have allowed media pundits, paid consultants, and talk show hosts to monopolize the public square. It is time to start thinking and speaking for ourselves. This book is a small attempt to begin that process.

# PART I
## Reading the Signs of the Times

*[Jesus] also said to the crowd, "When you see a cloud rising in the west, you immediately say, 'It is going to rain'; and so it happens. And when you see the south wind blowing, you say 'There will be a scorching heat'; and it happens. You hypocrites! You know how to interpret the appearance of earth and sky, but why can you not read the signs of the times?" (Luke 12:54-56)*

It is the challenge of Christians in every age to raise their eyes, ears, hearts, and minds from their everyday tasks to understand what God is doing in the world. With twenty-four-hours-a-day news channels, the internet, and countless other voices bringing us more and more information about our world, we seldom take time to understand what it means. The difficulty of this task should not deter us from engaging in the effort.

Certainly, personal worldview and ideology, race, gender, economic and social status, as well as our personal theology and moral standards, influence how we interpret and understand what is happening in our world. While this cannot be avoided, to keep us honest, we must acknowledge our own limitations as well as our gifts. As a white, male, middle-aged, middle-class, First World progressive Catholic Christian seeking to embrace the Gospel of nonviolence while struggling for justice on the side of those who are oppressed and marginalized, I understand the limitations I bring to the task of reading the signs of the times. If the Gospel tells us anything, it is that truth is perceived better from the margins than from the center of power and privilege. Nonetheless, I believe that each of us can contribute to the collective discernment process.

## SIGNS OF THE TIMES:
## READING SEPTEMBER 11, 2001

The horrific terrorist attacks on the United States on September 11, 2001, stand as one of those markers people use to divide history. Politicians, pundits, and social commentators speak of things as "pre-9-11" or "post-9-11." Given the scope of these attacks and, more importantly, the consequences resulting from them, it makes sense that the attacks of 9-11 are understood as an important historical marker. The problem comes when we fool ourselves into thinking that these attacks represent some historical break with what preceded them.

If we think that 9-11 "changed everything," or if we fool ourselves into thinking that the attacks represented something so new that the past cannot provide a sound basis for planning future actions, we make it impossible to understand the meaning of these events. If we embrace the "9-11 has changed everything" approach, we have no way of putting these attacks into their proper historical, political, economic, and cultural contexts—which is crucial to effectively understand and respond to the continuing threats of our world.

As tragic and horrifying as the terrorist attacks on 9-11 were, they represent a continuation of forces already at work in our world more than they represent a break with the past. Therefore, before we can articulate an alternative approach to the "War on Terror," we need to put the terrorist attacks of 9-11 into a context that will help us understand their meaning. We also need to examine what the Bible offers. This is part of what it means to "read the signs of the times."

# CHAPTER ONE

# Globalization:
# A Framework
# for Understanding Our Times

As a peace activist, I operated for almost twenty years out of a Cold War framework. Since the Cold War's beginning, many U.S. peace activists (especially those of us who were white) had interpreted almost every issue in terms of this overarching, bipolar superpower struggle for domination.

With the horrors of the war in Vietnam fresh in our minds and the nuclear Sword of Damocles hanging over our heads, many peace activists in the 1970s and 1980s viewed the world through the lens of the geopolitical struggle between the Soviet East and U.S. West, fought primarily in terms of military power. We tended to divide issues neatly into three categories: international, national, and local. International issues took precedence; national and local issues (like the lack of affordable housing, poor education, and underfunded anti-poverty programs) were usually described as consequences of misplaced national priorities resulting from the Cold War arms race and U.S. military intervention.

For instance, we understood U.S. education issues within the context of the wasteful military spending of the Cold War. We said that it would be a great day when schools had all the money they needed and the military had to hold a bake sale to build more weapons. Many of us felt that the economic, social, and political problems within the United States could not be addressed successfully unless and until we put an end to the stranglehold of what former President Dwight Eisenhower called "the military-industrial complex."[1] As a consequence, for U.S. peace activists engaged in the struggle to end the nuclear arms race, to stop U.S. military intervention around the world, and to reduce military spending, every other issue was secondary.

When the Soviet empire collapsed in 1989, that traditional frame of reference began to unravel. Many of us began to feel overwhelmed by what seemed like dozens of unrelated issues vying for our attention. On the one hand were issues related to crushing Third World debt; on the other hand many environmental crises cried out for attention. Trade agreements that threatened jobs in the United States and communities around the world were being negotiated. At the same time, the U.S. military waged a war against Iraq and was imposing deadly sanctions on the Iraqi people. The United States also sent troops into Somalia and Haiti in what were called "humanitarian interventions," and we had waged an air war in the Balkans against the Serbs.

Our sense of being overwhelmed resulted not only from all these issues demanding our attention, but from not having a way to understand and link them together in a way that made sense. In the past, the Cold War had provided many of us with a way of understanding how all the challenges facing us fit together; we knew what needed to be done. Now we had no way of sorting through all the issues, no means of determining which issues were most important, or why some issues needed to be addressed first. We needed a different conceptual framework for understanding our world and working for its betterment.

One can use many frames of reference to read the signs of the times; one can choose different lenses to interpret and organize the seemingly disconnected events and forces that shape our world. While it was challenging to come to grip with its implications, one frame of reference that I find helpful is the process of globalization. While many of the forces at work in globalization have been active in the world since at least 1492, the globalization of the last thirty years has accelerated a simultaneous process of integration and disintegration on a worldwide scale not seen before.

This globalization provides a new conceptual framework for understanding our work and our world. A Pax Christi USA (PCU-SA) statement, "Towards a Globalization of Solidarity," described the primary dynamic driving the process of globalization as

> a simultaneous expansion and compression of time and space. On the one hand, globalization has expanded connections between people and places around the world in ways not earlier known to humanity. At the same time the speed of these interactions has been dramatically compressed. We can e-mail someone on the other side of the planet in less than a minute, and we can transfer money across the world in seconds.[2]

When looking at the world through this process, we can begin to see how many of these issues we face relate to one another and how every person on the planet is affected economically, socially, culturally, and environmentally.

## THE ECONOMIC IMPACT OF GLOBALIZATION

For those (like me) who became active in the peace movement during the 1960s, 1970s, and 1980s, globalization poses an important challenge to the way we think about our work. Today, the East/West geopolitical divisions of the Cold War are receding in importance. In their place we see the ascendency of the struggle between the rich North and the poor South, fought primarily in terms of economic power. Globalization plays a major factor in this development. Furthermore, particularly due to economic forces, distinctions between international issues and local issues are becoming increasingly meaningless; the local is the global and the global is the local. The same economic, political, cultural, and environmental forces at work in South and Central America are also at work in South Central Los Angeles. And many times, the same corporations and their subsidiaries are the primary actors in our local communities as well those in Mexico, India, or Egypt.

To understand this interconnectedness, we need to examine how economic globalization plays out; we must also understand the gap between the promise and the results. The promoters and protectors of current forms of globalization held out to the world the promise of ending global poverty. The type of globalization championed by the world's richest and most powerful economic interests assumes that removing barriers to corporate trade and investments, while reducing government spending for social needs, is the best way to do this. This assumption is associated with an economic theory called neoliberalism.

Although the term neoliberalism is not often used in this country, South America and other parts of the world commonly use it. Elizabeth Martínez and Arnoldo García have identified some of its main characteristics. The first is the primacy of the market; that is, private enterprise should be free from any state interference, no matter how much social damage it might cause. The ultimate goal of neoliberalism is total freedom of movement for capital, goods, and services. The second characteristic of neoliberalism is the need to cut public expenditure for social services (like education and health care). Neoliberals believe that any act of the state that interferes with the dynamics of the market in deciding winners and losers reduces the market's efficiency; and for neoliberals, efficiency is the greatest good. Deregulation and privatization are two other defining characteristics of neoliberalism. Government regulation should be minimal so as to not diminish profits. All state-owned enterprises, goods, and services should be in the hands of private investors.[3]

Neoliberalism is more than an economic theory; it is also a philosophy. It champions the ideal of individual responsibility over the notion of the public good or community; it sees the world in terms of market metaphors. In answer to the existential questions, "Why are we here?" and "What is the purpose of life?" the adherents of neoliberalism believe that humans exist for the market. The existence and operation of the market are valued in themselves, apart from any social, ethical, or moral standards. Despite the promise of globalization and the economic assumptions of neoliberalism, the current forms of globalization have, in fact, increased the gap between those who are rich and those who are poor, and consigned billions of the world's people to poverty. When countries are pressured to organize their markets and economies along neoliberal lines, many of the poorest people find they cannot compete with producers from richer nations, especially in the agricultural sector where farmers in rich countries are often subsidized by their governments. And when social services provided by the poorer states become harder to access or completely nonexistent, these people are left to sink into abject poverty and misery.

The neoliberal principle of unfettered markets and the free flow of capital across national borders so as to maximize profits have linked the fate of low-income workers in poorer countries with the fate of low-income workers in the United States. This dynamics and its effects on people's lives are illustrated in an article by William M. Adler entitled "A Job on the Line." Adler tells the story of the intersecting lives of two women and one job. Mollie James was an African-American woman who worked for thirty-four years for Universal Manufacturing Company in Paterson, New Jersey. Although Universal had always turned a profit, they moved the plant to Matamoros, Mexico. After losing her job, James, at sixty-eight years of age, could barely make ends meet.

In Mexico, the workforce at the new plant was almost entirely women in their teens and early twenties (most plants along the border will not hire anyone over age twenty-seven). One of those workers was twenty year old Balbina Duque. Duque's probationary pay was slightly less than $26 per week or about sixty-five cents an hour. Even when she worked an eight-hour overtime shift (which she did two or three times a week), she found it impossible to make ends meet.

Further, the city of Matamoros gets no tax revenue from the border factories, but is responsible for providing services to the workers. Yet workers' wages are so low that taxes collected from them are practically nothing. The roads are unpaved, houses have no running water, nor does the city provide garbage pick-up or sewage.

Adler concludes:

> The job in which Mollie James once took great pride . . . that both fostered and repaid her loyalty by enabling her . . . to provide for her family—that job does not now pay Balbina Duque a wage sufficient to live on. Embedded in that central fact, and in the intersecting lives and fates of the two women who held that single job, is a broader story about the fundamental changes currently remaking the global economy. . . .[4]

Mollie James and Balbina Duque have never met. They speak different languages and live in different countries, but the economic forces destroying communities in Paterson, New Jersey, are the same forces at work in Matamoros, Mexico. The Mollies and Balbinas of the world, along with their allies and supporters, share much more in common with each other than they do with their own political leaders or bosses. And the neoliberal economic policies, rather than benefiting them as promised, move both deeper into poverty. The economic forces of globalization have concentrated wealth and power in the hands of the few around the world and in the United States, while driving the working poor (and increasingly, the middle class) deeper into poverty.

What does this mean? According to a study of 2005 Internal Revenue Service data, in a single year, U.S. income inequality grew significantly, with the top 1 percent—those with incomes of more than $348,000—receiving the largest share of national income since the Great Depression. While total income for those in the United States increased almost 9 percent in 2005, those in the bottom 90 percent saw their average income drop slightly. The gains went largely to the top 1 percent, whose average income rose to more than $1.1 million—an increase of more than $139,000, or about 14 percent.[5]

But this wealth gap is often hidden. Like the daily struggles of billions of poor people around the world, the struggles of those who are poor in this country remain largely under-reported in the media. Until events like Hurricane Katrina. Nothing in the past twenty years has laid bare the ugly realities of poverty and this wealth gap in the United States like the waters of Hurricane Katrina that washed over New Orleans and the Gulf Coast in 2005. As images of people stranded on rooftops and abandoned at the Superdome filled our TV screens, many in the United States looked on in disbelief, "Was this the United States of America (the richest country in the world) or some Third World country?"

Shock and disbelief were directed not only toward the totally inadequate response by government on all levels. Many people also saw, for the first time in decades, the fragile and precarious existence of people who are poor in the United States. Many of my neighbors living in the affluent suburbs of DuPage County, Illinois, (and I suspect this was true across the country), were in disbelief that so many of "those people" didn't have the good sense to get out of town before the hurricane. It just did not occur to them that people might have so few options due to poverty that they would be forced to try to ride out a hurricane, even when living below sea level. Why did the city leaders of New Orleans have such inadequate plans to deal with the evacuation of the tens of thousands of poor people with no transportation out of the city? Could it be that this community of poor people had become virtually invisible to their richer neighbors (except perhaps as the cast of characters on local evening news reports of carnage and crime in neighborhoods into which most of them would never venture)?

Like the economic fate that befell Mollie James and Balbina Duque, the outcomes suffered by the poorest people during the natural disasters of Hurricane Katrina and the Asian Tsunami of 2004 were made significantly worse as a result of neoliberal policies that placed the primacy of the market above the well-being (and even survival) of people. The pain and suffering they experienced as a result of the failure of their governments to adequately respond to their needs clearly demonstrates that these poorest survivors of Hurricane Katrina and the Asian Tsunami share more in common with each other than with their political leaders. Both have been consigned to live on marginal lands that are more susceptible to natural disasters. Both were victimized as much by their governments' inadequate responses and decades of misplaced political and economic priorities as they were by natural disasters.

In the richest country in the world, we do not have equal access to the wealth globalization produces. And we don't have to look too hard to see this wealth discrepancy showing up all over, not just when extraordinary natural disasters strike. The 2005 United Nations Human Development Report identifies places in the United States that are as poor as the Third World. The report shows that child mortality is rising in the United States and is now the same as in Malaysia. The U.S. child poverty rate is now more than 20 percent. Blacks in Washington, D.C., have a higher infant death rate than people in the Indian state of Kerala. Throughout the United States, black children are twice as likely as white children to die before their first birthday. Those who are Latino/Latina are more than twice as likely as those who are white to have no health insurance.[6]

These statistics reveal another factor linking those who are poor globally and in the United States: the majority of those hardest hit by the negative effects of globalization are people of color. It is no coincidence that most of the world's poor are people of color. Centuries ago, pseudo-scientific and socially constructed notions of race helped justify and legitimize the subjugation and plundering of non-European people by white Europeans, setting in motion patterns of global wealth distribution. Today's neoliberal economic policies (designed largely by white people) have replaced the now-discredited ideology of racial superiority and inferiority (at least in polite conversation) with a legal and economic framework that champions a (supposedly) non-racial ideology of "free markets," but which nonetheless ensures the same patterns of wealth and power distribution.

Looking at the tremendous impact that globalization has on economic development, world trade, and the gap between the rich and the poor, the driving force behind the present forms and structures of globalization is clearly the maximization of profit, an insatiable desire for control of, and unfettered access to, the world's resources (including people for labor and as consumers). Current forms of globalization are also driven by a constant need for growth, which reduces the human person to a mere consumer, a commodity, or a tool of production.

## The Impact on Migration

The economic impact of the current forms of globalization can also be seen by looking at migration. While immigration is a hot topic today in the United States, its causes are only rarely discussed. When you mention immigration to most in the United States, they think about it locally or nationally. But this narrow view keeps us from seeing the bigger picture. In announcing the formation of a United Nations Standing Forum on Migration and Development in June of 2006 then-Secretary General Kofi Annan pointed out that international migration was a key component of the globalization process that is both a positive force for development and a challenge.

In 2005, 3 percent of the world's population (191 million people) lived in a country other than the one in which they were born. The United States led the world as a host country, with thirty-eight million migrants constituting almost 13 percent of its population. However, the share of migrant population was larger in Australia (19.6 percent) and in Canada (18.9 percent). In regional terms, Europe's migrant population of sixty-four million was almost 50 percent greater than the forty-five million in North America. Western Asia also hosted a considerable share of the world's migrants, totaling twenty-two million. These migrant workers sent home to developing countries an estimated $167 billion. For many poorer countries, this remittance constitutes a major source of earnings.[7]

Why do people leave home and then send money back? This question is usually ignored in polarized immigration debates. The mass migration of people around the world is, to a large extent, a direct result of the current forms of globalization, especially in the United States. The economic elites of signatory governments developed and negotiated global trade agreements like the North American Free Trade Agreement (NAFTA) and the World Trade Organization (WTO), writing the rules of international trade to benefit those who already have the most economic advantage. Emphasizing "free trade" (as opposed to "fair trade") means that the economically powerful win, while those with no economic power are crushed. While global free trade agreements go to extraordinary lengths to protect the free flow of capital across borders, the movement of labor (workers seeking a better life in other countries) is tightly controlled and in some cases criminalized. This clear advantage of capital over labor at the international level drives the problems associated with immigration in the United States.

To understand why undocumented workers migrate to the United States, we need to look at the "push-pull" dynamic of immigration. Many Mexicans are pushed into migrating to the United States by economic forces. As an Economic Policy Institute Study in 2006 pointed out, since NAFTA took effect, employment in Mexico has become even more precarious. Of all new salaried positions generated between the second quarter of 2000 and the second quarter of 2004, only 37 percent have full benefits, and 23 percent have no benefits at all. Meanwhile, the agricultural sector has suffered a large and steady loss of employment. The share of the population engaged in agricultural activities fell from 26.8 percent in 1991 to 16.4 percent in 2004.[8] Many of these small farmers end up in the slums of large cities like Mexico City or cross the border into the United States, looking for work.

The "pull" of immigration lies in the U.S. need for cheap labor. The availability of low-wage workers from Mexico has been used for decades to benefit the U.S. economy at the expense of immigrants. As *The New York Times* reporter Nina Bernstein wrote in her article "100 Years in the Back Door, Out the Front":

> Nearly every immigrant group has been caught at that crossroads for a time, wanted for work but unwelcome as citizens, especially when the economy slumps. But Mexicans have been summoned and sent back in cycles for four generations, repeatedly losing the ground they had gained. During the Depression, as many as a million Mexicans, and even Mexican-Americans, were ousted, along with their American-born children, to spare relief costs or discourage efforts to unionize. They were welcome again during World War II and cast as heroic "braceros." But in the 1950's, Mexicans were re-branded as dangerous, welfare-seeking "wetbacks."[9]

What the "push" and the "pull" of immigration in the United States have in common is higher profits for the economic elite and more economic insecurity for the working poor. Wages are driven down on both sides of the border, and a lack of discussion of who actually benefits pits workers from one country against the workers of another. Yet wage earners in the United States actually have more in common with undocumented workers from Mexico than they do with the economic and political elite in their own country. And, due to the economic policies of neoliberalism, everyone's job standards and rights are under attack.

## THE ENVIRONMENTAL IMPACT

As we've seen, globalization as it currently plays out has enormous economic implications for humans. But, driven by the same profit motive, it is also devastating our planet. Just as the economic impacts are often deliberately hidden or used to pit people against each other, the current forms of globalization have often sought to downplay environmental impacts or to hide the connections. And just as economic policies consign millions to economic insecurity or an early death, these effects are killing our planet.

Again, a story may best illustrate the connections. In the *Chicago Tribune*, foreign correspondent Evan Osnos writes about the links between goat herders on the Alashan Plateau of China, cheap cashmere sweaters for big box stores like Wal-Mart, and dust storms of pollution stretching around the globe. This story starts with a U.S. desire for cheap cashmere sweaters. In less than ten years, goat herders on the Alashan Plateau increased the number of goats producing the expensive wool. But while U.S. consumers can now purchase sweaters for as little as $20, a centuries-old industry in China has been transformed into an environmentally destructive business in pursuit of higher profits. China's enormous herds of cashmere-producing goats have slashed the price of sweaters, but they have also turned China's grasslands into a moonscape, unleashing some of the worst dust-storms ever recorded. This, in turn, contributes to heavy pollution falling from the skies over the United States and most of North America.[10]

In a Christmas-shopping season editorial about this story, the *Chicago Tribune* editors underscored the economic and environmental connections:

> In a global economy, it is difficult to comprehend all the backstories behind the products we are now wrapping with care and stuffing under the tree. . . . All of

us who drive or eat or dress up—in other words, all of us—share at least a little responsibility if the products we consume cause environmental problems. . . . the U.S. is the world's largest consumer market. The buying choices we make send ripples across the globe, sometimes with unintended impact on human and natural resources. . . . We consumers decide which of these backstories trouble us enough to influence our buying habits. That is the power and responsibility to consider as we swipe our credit cards this holiday season.[11]

Yet if you were to purchase or receive one of these cashmere sweaters, you would most like not know about the devastation of the Alashan Plateau, the impacts on Chinese goat herders, or the dust-storms of pollution—even in the air you may breathe as you unwrap the sweater.

Cheap cashmere sweaters and other consumer goods are not the only source of pollution that poses a challenge to our future on this planet. Greenhouse gasses produced by fossil fuel burning are having a dramatic impact. For decades, scientists have been sounding an alarm about global warming. However, just enough doubters (many funded by energy companies and their lobby groups) have convinced governments to delay action while calling for continued study of the problem—effectively stopping any action that might begin to slow the process and heal the earth. The economic pressures of the current forms of globalization do not take into account what we are doing—perhaps irreversibly—to the planet.

These environmental impacts are widespread. The PCUSA globalization statement points out other environmental dangers:

The globalization of diseases; the introduction (by accident or by plan) of non-native species of plants and animals into foreign ecosystems; the destruction of biodiversity in food production; the corporate patenting and genetic manipulation of life; pollution; depletion of water sources; expropriation and exploitation of land and all types of life forms without regard to their ability to survive; and the practice of toxic dumping in exploited countries and in communities of people of color are just a few of the ecological consequences of the current forms of globalization. It is also growing increasingly clear that the planet's ecosystems cannot sustain the current forms of global development. Current models of development are destroying many habitats leading to an alarming rate of species extinction.[12]

As this statement points out, the environmental effects (like the economic ones) of globalization fall disproportionately upon poor people of color who seldom benefit from the technology that generates toxic waste, but often pay the environmental price. This dynamic has been called environmental racism. Most of the waste generated by the rich ends up in the backyards of poor people of color. For instance, in 2006 the Panamanian flagship *Probo Koala* unloaded more than 550 tons of toxic waste at Abidjan port in the Ivory Coast in Africa. Emissions from that toxic waste killed seven people and poisoned thousands. The deadly cargo was shipped to Abidjan from Amsterdam.[13]

Environmental racism that makes impoverished communities of color around the world dumping grounds for rich nations also occurs in the United States. *The New York Times* reported on a study by Harlem Hospital that found 25.5 percent of children in Harlem had asthma, many previously undiagnosed. No well-documented local asthma rates above 20 percent exist anywhere else in the nation.[14] The major populations in Harlem (in northern Manhattan) are African-American and Latino. Six out of eight of Manhattan's diesel bus depots are located in northern Manhattan, as well as two of the city's largest sewage treatment plants, powered by huge diesel engines running twenty-four hours a day. The area is also flanked by highways and two major bridges over which trucks (also running on diesel) deliver goods into Manhattan.

The relationship between this pollution and respiratory diseases like asthma was described in a 2002 resource paper presented at the Second National People of Color Environmental Leadership Summit:

> Ozone and particulate matter have been linked to the development of asthma. The levels of these air pollutants are higher in poor communities of color. Ozone forms when stagnant air polluted with vehicle emissions is subjected to heat and sunlight. Ozone can form and when it is inhaled it can directly damage the lung and aggravate respiratory conditions like asthma. Particulate matter is believed to behave in a similar manner in the body. These chemicals and other chemicals in the environment can cause lung passageways to become narrower and to fill with mucus.[15]

According to a 2007 study, California has the nation's highest concentration of minorities living near hazardous waste facilities. Greater Los Angeles tops the nation, with 1.2 million people living less than two miles from seventeen such facilities; 91 percent of them (1.1 million) are people of color. Statewide, the figure was 81 percent. Though about one-third of U.S. residents are people of color, more than half of the people living near such facilities were Latino, African-American, or Asian-American, according to the report. As Robert Bullard, sociologist at Clark Atlanta University in Georgia and lead author of the study, points out, the reason is simple: "The most potent predictor of where these facilities are sited is not how much income you have; it's race. . . . You don't have many of these facilities in West Los Angeles, and you don't have many minorities in West Los Angeles either. . . . You've got both in Vernon and surrounding neighborhoods."[16]

## THE SOCIAL/CULTURAL IMPACT

Producing goods and services has effects on the earth and its inhabitants. And the profit motive of the "free market" also depends on these products—specifically, selling them. To make a profit, the players in the world market must create a demand for a product and then sell that product. Over and over again. We tend to forget that these products, exported to the world, come with their own inherent social and cultural values. Combined with the cultural values that are used to market these products, we begin to see what a powerful cultural force globalization can be.

For example, even though the United Nations World Health Organization put restrictions on how infant formula is marketed in poorer countries, corporations like Nestlé still aggressively market baby formula to poor mothers by touting it as the modern, Western way to raise healthy and strong children. This is in spite of the fact that medical studies show that breast milk is far superior to baby formula. Nestlé provides free samples to new mothers and encourages them to immediately start using it. Often by the time these free samples run out, the mother's breast milk has dried up. In addition, in poor families, the formula is often mixed with contaminated water or is diluted to last longer. Both of these practices lead to increases in infant deaths in poor countries.

In addition, our entertainment industry, one of our largest worldwide exports, carries enormous power to shape values and affect cultures around the world. A global culture, dominated by the West, has emerged and is spreading to almost every corner of the planet. As the Pax Christi USA statement on globalization points out:

> Embedded in this global culture is the assumption of the superiority of Western culture, a culture forged and carried forth by the power of whiteness, patriarchy and colonialism. It is a culture marked especially

by signs of consumption. . . . They provide worldwide cultural aspirations, especially among the young. But because of the growing gap between rich and poor, these often-unattainable aspirations result in frustration and social disintegration in poor communities. The cultural hegemony of the West (and the U.S. in particular) seems to also break down forms of art, music, and even language in local cultures.[17]

In his book *Jihad vs. McWorld*, Benjamin R. Barber describes this cultural aspect of globalization as "McWorld." Barber points out that "McWorld" is about expanding global markets. But it is also more than that:

McWorld is a product of popular culture driven by expansionist commerce. Its template is American, its form style. Its goods are as much images as matérial, an aesthetic as well as a product line. It is about culture as commodity, apparel as ideology. . . . Music, video, theater, books, and theme parks—the new churches of a commercial civilization in which malls are the public squares and suburbs the neighborless neighborhoods—are all constructed as image exports creating a common world taste around common logos, advertising slogans, stars, songs, brand names, jingles, and trademarks.[18]

Another impact that exporting social and cultural values has is to create counter-cultures of resistance, which take many forms around the globe. The most militant forms of resistance often come from radical expressions of religion (both in the United States and around the world) that flourish when a religious group perceives itself under threat. The more threatened a particular group feels, the more militant and even violent its resistance becomes.

This is particularly true for the communities in the Middle

East and in Muslim countries around the world, who experience the phenomena of McWorld as a direct threat to their cultural and religious identities. During the Age of Enlightenment and for hundreds of years after, Christianity and Judaism in Europe negotiated their place within the growing secular, scientific culture. (A look at the so-called "culture wars" in the United States, however, shows that this negotiation over spheres of influence is far from settled.) Unlike Christianity and Judaism, Islam was never given a chance to negotiate its own terms of accommodation, and unlike the religious leaders engaged in the culture wars in the United States, Islam has no seat at the table to negotiate with the powers that shape McWorld. U.S. governmental misreading of this frustration in the Muslim world, particularly in the Middle East, has come at a terrible price. Failing to recognize that the values embedded in the current forms of globalization are not culturally neutral only heightens cultural misunderstandings in an increasingly small world.

## AL QAEDA: A PRODUCT OF GLOBALIZATION

The terrorist attacks on September 11, 2001, were both reacting to the current forms of globalization (and the inequalities it has produced and amplified) and made possible by the process of globalization. In many ways, al Qaeda represents the globalization of terrorism. In the past, terrorist organizations were local or regional phenomena. Over time, Osama bin Laden began to see himself as the head of an international jihadist[19] enterprise. His Islamic Army Shura served as the coordinating body for an alliance of groups from Arab nations such as Saudi Arabia, Egypt, Algeria, and Morocco; from African nations such as Nigeria, Chad, and Uganda; and also from South Asian states such as Myanmar (Burma), Thailand, Malaysia, and Indonesia.

Al Qaeda's organizational breakthrough was its ability to "go global" with terrorist attacks and recruitment by using the very tools and infrastructure that make globalization possible. The internet and e-mail were crucial tools in planning the attacks of September 11 and in spreading the ideology of al Qaeda. The same financial tools that make it easier for corporations to transfer billions of dollars from one country to another also allowed the hijackers and their financiers to get the money to carry out the attacks of 9-11. The greater ease by which people can move across national borders because of globalization was crucial in getting the terrorists into this country. Finally, one of the greatest symbols of globalization, the jet planes that make global travel possible, was transformed into weapons of mass destruction.

Al Qaeda not only used the tools and infrastructure of globalization to launch the attacks on 9-11, but also chose a target that was an important symbol of globalization: the World Trade Center in New York. Targeted not simply because it was one of the tallest buildings in the United States, the World Trade Center symbolized the current forms of globalization that dictate the future of billions of people around the world. Home to nearly 500 businesses from around the world and employing some 50,000 people, the World Trade Center represented everything that the architects of globalization had in mind. Housed in the twin towers were numerous international banks, oil companies, media conglomerates, investment firms, and commodity and futures trading companies. In fact, the New York City World Trade Center gave rise to the World Trade Centers Association (WTCA), linking approximately 300 World Trade Centers in ninety-seven countries that facilitate international trade more efficiently. As WTCA visionary Guy F. Tozzoli described its purpose, "The practical day-to-day commerce and business conducted in and through world trade centers transcends narrow nationalism as well as ethnic and political barriers of the past."[20]

To the supporters and sympathizers of al Qaeda, many of the Western-backed rulers of Arab countries throughout the Middle East operate more like CEOs of private companies than political leaders of their countries. Many Arab Muslims believe these autocratic oil rich Arab rulers are more interested in their global investment portfolios than the welfare of their people. In an audio recording released in December, 2004, Osama bin Laden revisited one of his most frequent arguments for jihad by lashing out at the Saudi royal family: "Millions are suffering poverty, while riyals [Saudi currency] pour into the hands of the Saudi royal family."[21] He also lashed out against other Arab rulers accusing them of being puppets of a "crusader-Zionist alliance" led by the United States that seeks to steal Arab wealth and occupy Muslim lands. For many Arabs, the World Trade Center represented economic humiliation of their people. Al Qaeda terrorism is an extreme reaction to what many Arabs in the Middle East see as a world order designed to exploit and demean them at the expense of the Western architects of globalization.

## THE WORLD WE LIVE IN

As we've seen, the policies and practice of neoliberal globalization do not benefit everyone equally. Often, the economic and political elite benefit more than the people of their countries— sometimes even at the expense of the people. Unless we can step back and look at the economic, social, and environmental impacts, we cannot begin to understand our world and the lives of those who live on this small planet. Whether we are aware of it or not, globalization affects what we eat, what we wear, where we live and work, what we do for entertainment, our health, and even how long this planet may be able to support human life. For those of us who work for peace with justice, the processes of globalization can connect seemingly disconnected struggles. And, as we will see, globalization can also help us set the proper context for understanding the challenges posed by the rise of global terrorism.

# CHAPTER TWO

# What is Terrorism?

Terrorism has probably existed as long as humans have. To understand what we are talking about, it is helpful to have a definition. This is more difficult than it may seem, since many definitions exist today, and they often come with specific political and/or ideological agendas.

People often define terrorism in a way that includes their enemies and excludes themselves. As the saying goes, "one person's terrorist is another person's freedom fighter." To King George III and the British people, George Washington was a terrorist; to those in the colonies and the resulting United States, he was a founding father of the republic. If the colonists had lost their war of independence from Great Britain, Washington might well have ended up as nothing more than a historical footnote, an eighteenth century terrorist leader who came to a bad end. (This illustrates the difficulty of identifying terrorists throughout recorded history; history is often written by the winners of conflict who have their own agendas in naming terrorists.) Ultimately, every definition of terrorism suffers from some degree of political or ideological bias; and, once you offer a definition of terrorism, someone will soon find an exception that doesn't quite fit the rule.

Keeping in mind these pitfalls and recognizing that I cannot offer a definition of terrorism that is completely free from my own biases, I offer the following description (not quite as "definitive" as a definition) for this discussion: Terrorism is the use of violence and/or the threat of violence against civilians in order to change their behavior or beliefs for the purpose of achieving political, religious, ethnic, and/or economic objectives. I prefer this description because not only does it include specific acts of violence, it also includes the psychological dimension of terrorism. In this description, I describe violence as the use of coercive force to injure, kill, humiliate, intimidate, and/or subjugate another person or group. Finally, I describe a civilian as anyone who is not a member of a national security force (military); a domestic security force (police); nor engaged in armed struggle. (Those engaged in national and domestic security, as well as those engaged in armed struggle, accept the possibility of becoming victims of violence. Civilians, for the most part, do not have that expectation.)

Experts in terrorism often categorize terrorists by tactics (e.g., suicide bombers, truck bombers, hijackers, random shooters); by choice of weapons (e.g., conventional, chemical/biological, nuclear/radioactive); or by objectives or motivation (e.g., political, economic, religious). I would like to suggest a different set of categories: terrorism of the strong and terrorism of the weak. By suggesting these two kinds of terrorism I am not implying that one kind of terrorism is good and the other is bad; terrorism of any kind is a crime against humanity and can never be justified. Yet differentiation is important because it distinguishes between institutional actors as distinct from terrorists who do not have access to institutional power, allowing us to use a power analysis.

## TERRORISM OF THE STRONG

In general terms, those employing terrorism of the strong aim to preserve the status quo or to strengthen and deepen already existing power relationships. Terrorism of the strong uses violence and the threat of violence to terrorize civilian populations into accepting their place in the social, economic, cultural, and/or political order.

Because those who engage in terrorism of the strong often have at their disposal many social, economic, cultural, and political levers of institutional power, they can commit their acts of terrorism under the guise of legitimacy and legality. This might explain why the FBI's definition of terrorism includes the caveat that terrorism is the "*unlawful* use of force or violence."[1] (Emphasis added.) Or why the U.S. State Department's definition restricts terrorism to "sub-national groups or clandestine agents,"[2] conveniently eliminating the possibility that nation states, like the United States, might be guilty of terrorism.

Many of these terrorist leaders wear suits, are powerful members of governments, and may sit on corporate boards. Their foot soldiers wear uniforms and have at their disposal the planet's most powerful and technologically advanced weapons.

The specific forms of terrorism of the strong correlate to the institutional levers of power they employ to carry out their objectives. Often, multiple levers of power are engaged at the same time, making it difficult to clearly distinguish one form of terrorism from another. However, to better understand the unique aspects of each, I will distinguish between three forms: military terrorism, economic terrorism, and political terrorism.

### Military Terrorism of the Strong

Military terrorism employs the powers, personnel, and weaponry of a legally-established military to carry out its objectives. One recent example of military terrorism was the U.S. military's

Operation Shock and Awe bombing campaign at the start of the current war in Iraq. Even U.S. military leaders admit that Operation Shock and Awe (which included launching 300-400 cruise missiles into Baghdad on the opening day of the campaign) was meant to terrorize the political leadership and the civilian population of Iraq into a quick surrender. "There will not be a safe place in Baghdad," said one Pentagon official at the time. "We want them to quit. We want them not to fight," said Harlan Ullman, one of the authors of the Shock and Awe concept. Ullman went on to emphasize the aim of an overwhelming attack: "So that you have this simultaneous effect, rather like the nuclear weapons at Hiroshima, not taking days or weeks but minutes."[3]

The U.S. military did not attempt to account for the civilians killed during Operation Shock and Awe, but anecdotal reporting compellingly indicates that a large number of civilians died. This points to another characteristic of military terrorism of the strong: evading culpability for civilian deaths by appealing to the moral principle of intentionality. Because of the bureaucratic military command structure (the institutional degrees of separation between the decision to kill and the act of killing) and because of the availability of high-tech weapon systems that allow killing from a great distance, those who practice terrorism of the strong can kill large numbers of innocent civilians while claiming to not "intentionally" target them. Additionally, they may never have to come face-to-face with the consequences of their actions.

In fact, those who engage in terrorism of the strong often argue that civilian "collateral damage" is an unintended consequence of carrying out military objectives. This is why many who engage in terrorism of the strong include the notion of intentionality in their own self-serving definitions of terrorism. For instance, former Israeli Prime Minster Benjamin Netanyahu defined terrorism as "the *deliberate* and systematic murder, maiming, and menacing of the innocent to inspire fear for political ends."[4] (Emphasis added.) This of course means that the killing and terrorizing of civilians in the Palestinian Occupied Territories by Israeli jet fighters, helicopter gun ships, and search-and-destroy operations is not terrorism because only terrorists are "targeted." If terrorist acts only include the deliberate killing of civilians, then the Israeli military is exempt. The moral calculus of those who engage in terrorism of the strong allows killing as many innocent civilians as necessary, so long as one doesn't directly target them.

But if the determining factor in defining an act as terrorism is its impact on civilian populations, then the attacker's intentions are irrelevant. It does not matter to the civilians terrorized by Operation Shock and Awe that they were not "intentionally" targeted—the effect was the same. The intentions of the Israeli military do not matter to Palestinian families when their neighborhoods are bombed; they experience the terror and understand its meaning. Hiding behind the moral principle of intentionality might soothe the consciences of those who engage in terrorism of the strong, but it does not make them any less terroristic.

## Economic Terrorism of the Strong

While military terrorism of the strong can be directed at economic targets for the purpose of coercion, economic terrorism involves using the institutional levers of economic power to injure, kill, humiliate, intimidate, and/or subjugate a civilian population in order to influence their behavior or change their beliefs. Economic terrorism may not have the immediate impact of a bomb, but it can be just as effective.

Faced with economic terrorism, civilians are often bewildered because the terror's source may not be apparent or easily identifiable. In some respects, this can make the experience more terrifying than military terrorism because ordinary people may not fully understand how to respond, or they may be powerless to do so. They may not know what they can do or where to focus their anxiety or fear. Those who engage in economic terrorism of the strong often seek to instill a general sense of pervasive uncertainty, powerlessness, vulnerability, and insecurity in order to more easily manipulate or control a civilian population. Economic terrorism is often employed not only to get civilians to change their behavior, but also to keep them from doing anything that might challenge the status quo. Often, economic terrorism of the strong is employed as a means of population control.

One example of how economic terrorism of the strong can terrify and bewilder at the same time is the ten-year campaign of economic sanctions imposed on the Iraqi people after the first Gulf War. In their hurry to contain Saddam Hussein and ensure reparations for damage inflicted upon Kuwait, the United Nations Security Council imposed upon Iraq some of the strongest, most comprehensive economic sanctions ever created. Among other things, these sanctions blocked the import of replacement parts vital to restoring the Iraqi electrical grid and water treatment system. The sanctions also blocked the import of medicines and medical supplies vital to public health, as well as chemicals like chlorine which are crucial for water purification.

The devastating effect of these economic sanctions on the lives of ordinary Iraqis cannot be fully appreciated unless they are seen in light of the U.S. bombing campaign launched against the Iraqi civilian infrastructure during the first Gulf War. This combination of military destruction and devastating economic sanctions is an example of how terrorism of the strong can employ multiple levers of power in a coordinated effort to maximize pressure on a civilian population.

For instance, during the first war, the Pentagon intentionally destroyed Iraq's water-treatment systems. *The Washington Post* noted that Pentagon officials admitted that, rather than concentrating solely on military targets, the U.S. bombing campaign "sought to achieve some of their military objectives in the Persian Gulf War by disabling Iraqi society at large" and "deliberately did great harm to Iraq's ability to support itself as an industrial society." One Pentagon official who helped plan this bombing campaign against critical parts of the Iraqi civilian infrastructure was asked about the consequences of this strategy in conjunction with the sanctions that hindered the Iraqis' ability to make repairs. He observed, "People say, 'You didn't recognize that it was going to have an effect on water or sewage?' Well, what were we trying to do with sanctions—help out the Iraqi people? No. What we were doing with the attacks on infrastructure was to accelerate the effect of the sanctions." As one Air Force planner observed, "We wanted to let people know, 'Get rid of this guy and we'll be more than happy to assist in rebuilding. We're not going to tolerate Saddam Hussein or his regime. Fix that, and we'll fix your electricity.'"[5]

These deadly sanctions wreaked havoc on Iraqi society at many levels. For instance, Dr. Wolfgang Kluge, a member of an international medical delegation that visited Iraq in 1999, reported that previously eradicated diseases, such as malaria, tuberculosis, and cholera, had re-emerged. Due to the shortage of supplies and money, many people, from children to professionals, were forced to leave school or their professions to earn money in other ways, such as selling goods on the street. The severity of the sanctions also caused crime to increase.[6]

Even after it became clear that the devastating effects were falling mostly on the Iraqi civilian population and not on the Iraqi political leadership or military, the U.S. Administration under the first President Bush was unwilling to change the sanctions. In 1991, the President clearly stated the administration's objectives: "By making life uncomfortable for the Iraqi people, [sanctions] would eventually encourage them to remove President Saddam Hussein from power."[7]

Under the Clinton Administration, the United States continued to block attempts to modify the sanctions. Denis Halliday, who was appointed United Nations Humanitarian Coordinator in Baghdad, resigned in 1998 after criticizing the sanctions regime, saying, "I don't want to administer a program that satisfied the definition of genocide." Halliday's successor, Hans von Sponeck, also resigned in protest. Dr. Faris Abdul Abbas, of the Basra Maternity and Pediatrics Hospital, summed it up this way: "This is unacceptable in medicine, to have patients die because of a shortage of drugs and supplies that are readily available everywhere else. It is a crime against humanity."[8]

When she was the U.S. ambassador to the UN, President Clinton's Secretary of State, Madeleine Albright, was asked by *60 Minutes* correspondent Lesley Stahl, "We have heard that half a million children have died. I mean, that is more children than died in Hiroshima. And, you know, is the price worth it?" Ambassador Albright responded, "I think that is a very hard choice, but the price we think, the price is worth it."⁹

The bewildering aspect of the economic part of this campaign of terror against the Iraqi people was that they were in no position to make the changes demanded by the U.S. government. In fact, the sanctions destroyed the very structures of civil society that might have been able to organize opposition to the Hussein dictatorship. Instead, the punishment we inflicted upon the Iraqi people helped keep the dictator safe from his own people. As the sanctions caused more pain, Hussein's power also grew. The tragedy of this campaign of economic terrorism against the Iraqi people during the Clinton Administration is that long after it became obvious that the Iraqi people could not meet our demands, the campaign of terror continued for U.S. domestic political purposes—the Democratic Administration did not want to look weak on Iraq.

## Political Terrorism of the Strong

Another form of terrorism of the strong utilizes the institutional levers of political power. This form of terrorism is more often exercised by states against their own people. Certainly Saddam Hussein's reign of terror is a good example of how political institutional power can be used to terrorize a civilian population. In this past century alone a number of tyrants have utilized political terror to control their people. The Soviet Union's Josef Stalin, China's Mao Tze-tung, Cambodia's Pol Pot, Chile's Augusto Pinochet, Uganda's Idi Amin, North Korea's Kim Jong Il, and the Afrikaner Government of South Africa are just a few.

Like other forms of terrorism of the strong, political terrorism seeks to maintain or strengthen already existing power relationships. The levers of power used to intimidate, injure, humiliate, subjugate, and kill are often situated within a country's legislative and criminal justice systems; the system of law, courts, domestic and national security forces, and prisons give shape and form to political terrorism.

The immediate targets of political terrorism include opposition politicians, poets, writers, artists, student groups, human rights lawyers, union organizers, and any institution (including churches) that has the capacity to challenge the power of the state. Political terrorism aims to manage the expectations of the civilian population in order to get them to accept their lot in life. Those who employ political terrorism of the strong seek to maintain their grip on power.

In recent U.S. history, one example of political terrorism of the strong was the nexus of power in the South from the post-Reconstructionist period until the 1960s. It included most of the political establishment (formal and informal) of southern states (embodied in organizations like the White Citizens' Councils), along with paramilitary death squads like the Ku Klux Klan and the legal framework and cultural practices known as Jim Crow. The purpose of this nexus of legal, political, economic, and cultural power was to terrorize the black population into accepting second-class status.

More than a set of laws, Jim Crow was a system of etiquette and customs developed over time to maintain the inferior status of blacks and to perpetuate negative stereotypes of black people—especially with regard to gender and sexuality. For instance, in Georgia, no "colored" barber was allowed to serve a white woman or girl. In Alabama, no white female nurse could be required to serve in a hospital ward with "negro" men.[10] Violence and threats of violence enforced Jim Crow laws and system of etiquette. Blacks who violated either the written codes or the unwritten customs could be physically assaulted by whites at any time with almost no recourse.

Blacks had little protection under the law because whites controlled the entire criminal justice system, and because often the political and criminal justice leaders (judges, sheriffs, etc.) were themselves members of organizations like the White Citizens' Council or the Ku Klux Klan. The paramilitary death squads of the Ku Klux Klan became the ultimate enforcers of Jim Crow, and the most violent means of social control of the black population was the use of public lynchings. These mob actions were often brutal and sadistic. Between 1882 and 1968, there were 4,730 documented lynchings. While most victims were hung or shot, others were burned at the stake, beaten to death, castrated, and even dismembered.[11] These public lynchings had a profoundly terrifying effect on the black community.

Other communities of color have also been the targets of this kind of terrorism in the United States. American Indians have been the victims of genocidal wars and legal rulings that not only destroyed entire tribes, but also their cultures, communities, and beliefs. To terrorize a civilian population into abandoning its identity and forfeiting its land, political leaders used a combination of military and economic power that was legitimated by the use of political institutions.

Internationally, one practitioner of terrorism of the strong is President Robert Mugabe of Zimbabwe, who has a long record of human rights abuses against his own people. One recent campaign of repression clearly illustrates the concept of political terrorism. During "Operation *Murambatsvina*" ("Operation Clear the Filth"), launched in May 2005, the Mugabe government imposed forced evictions and mass displacement of nearly 6 percent of Zimbabwe's entire population. According to UN estimates, 700,000 people were forcibly evicted from their homes, made homeless, or lost their source of livelihood. About 18 percent of the population—2.4 million people—has been either directly or indirectly affected by "Operation *Murambatsvina*."[12] A September 2005 Human Rights Watch report, "Clear the Filth: Mass Evictions and Demolitions in Zimbabwe," documented how the government violated the human rights of its citizens by arbitrarily forcing them to destroy their property without due notice, process, or compensation, and by displacing thousands into rural areas without basic services such as health care, education, clean water, or means of economic support.

The humanitarian consequences of "Operation *Murambatsvina*" have been catastrophic. "The police are showing no mercy. . . . They were beating us with baton sticks and their boots if we didn't destroy our houses quickly enough," a young woman in Harare told Human Rights Watch. Speaking about the brutal methods of the police, she said, "It doesn't matter, women, children, and elderly people. They were all beaten up. What we want to know is why is God doing this to us?"[13]

Mugabe used many levers of state power to carry out this campaign of terror. The Minister of Local Government and Urban Housing, the Minister of Home Affairs, the Commissioner of Police, and other government officials organized the operation. Government officials justified the evictions by saying that they were merely enforcing municipal by-laws and getting rid of criminal activity. However, local human rights lawyers and local non-government organizations believe that the evictions were part of a campaign of retribution against those who voted for the opposition during recent elections.[14]

## TERRORISM OF THE WEAK

In general terms, those who engage in terrorism of the weak aim to change the status quo and to establish a new set of power relationships. Those who engage in terrorism of the weak often believe they are exploited, marginalized, and/or disenfranchised by the existing social, political, and economic order. While these terrorists attack "soft targets" with little regard for innocent civilians, their ultimate aim is to pressure those in power. (A "soft target" is nonmilitary or one not strongly defended by military or police power.)

Those who engage in terrorism of the weak do not have access to the economic, political, social, or military levers of power. Often, they are unable to directly confront the institutional power of those who rule. Therefore, they may employ asymmetrical tactics that avoid direct conflict with national or domestic security forces. They believe that by terrorizing civilians they can bring about the change they seek. Using such asymmetrical means, a small group of determined terrorists can devastate a country while leaving no clue as to where they came from or who ordered the attack. This kind of terrorism gives the weaker attacker the advantage of selectivity and surprise, forcing the more powerful defenders to try to protect against attacks on many fronts. Groups like al Qaeda in Iraq fall into this category.

If those who wage terrorism of the strong seek to escape culpability for the death of civilians by hiding behind the moral principle of intentionality, those who engage in terrorism of the weak often hide behind the moral principle of just cause to escape culpability for the death of civilians. These terrorists believe that because they are unjustly oppressed by those who control the levers of institutional power, they should not be held responsible for resorting to attacking "soft targets" that kill innocent civilians. They believe that because they are in a conflict of unequal power with their opponents, they cannot be expected to abide by the normal codes of moral conduct.

Worse yet, some who engage in terrorism of the weak reject the very idea of innocent civilians. Some believe that any member of society who in some way benefits from the current order or allows the current order to prosper, is a legitimate target—even noncombatants. Because there is no such thing as an innocent bystander for these terrorists, everyone is a potential enemy.

One example of this kind of moral rationalization was the campaign of terror waged against the Nicaraguan people and their government by the U.S.-backed counter-revolutionaries, also known as the Contras. During the war, the Contras targeted thousands of Nicaraguan teachers, health care workers, church catechists, and community activists, all considered collaborators with the Nicaraguan government. U.S. citizens with groups like Witness for Peace stood in solidarity with these Nicaraguans in an effort to protect them from terrorist attacks sponsored by their own government; this made them targets, too. In 1983, 23-year-old Ben Linder, a U.S. citizen and recent engineering graduate, went to the village of El Cuá in Nicaragua to help build a hydro-electric plant to bring electricity to the town. In 1987 the Contras ambushed and killed him. Linder's crime was to help improve the lives of the Nicaraguan people. This made him a legitimate target for the Contras. For the Contras, there were no innocent civilians; people were either with them or they were collaborators with the government. (This same moral calculus was often used by all sides during other Central American wars.)

While the forms of terrorism of the strong can be categorized according to the levers of institutional power they employ to terrorize civilians, the forms of terrorism of the weak can be categorized according to the institutions of power they target. For this discussion I will focus on three: economic terrorism, political terrorism, and cultural terrorism.

### Economic Terrorism of the Weak

Those who engage in economic terrorism of the weak target the institutional economic assets of the established order. This form of terrorism aims to damage the ability of those in power to accumulate wealth and/or manage their economy. This damage can be aimed directly at hard economic assets, like oil fields, railroads, factories, banks, or stock exchanges; or it can be directed at civilian consumers in order to disrupt or bankrupt a sector of the economy, like the airline, shipping, or food industries or public transportation systems. The terrorist attacks against Iraqi oil pipelines are an example of the first kind (directed at a hard target); the al Qaeda attacks of 9-11 (using passenger airliners) is an example of the second kind (directed at civilians).

### Political Terrorism of the Weak

Political terrorism of the weak attacks the political institutions of those in power as well as political leaders themselves.

This form of terrorism aims to damage the ability of those in power to govern and to sow confusion, fear, and doubt into the civilian population about the stability and effectiveness of its government. This damage can be directed against symbols of political power like parliament buildings, court houses, ministry buildings, or important civic monuments, as well as members of the political class. The terrorist attack on the Indian Parliament in December 2001 is an example of this kind of terrorism; it not only targeted an important government building, but also resulted in the death of political leaders. The assassination of Egyptian President Anwar Sadat in 1981 is an example of directly targeting a particular political leader.

## Cultural Terrorism of the Weak

Cultural terrorism of the weak can be difficult to distinguish from economic terrorism because so much of culture is linked to economics. (For instance, the New York City World Trade Center was both a cultural symbol of globalization and U.S. economic power as well as an important economic target.) However, the primary aim of those who engage in cultural terrorism is to resist and/or destroy dominating cultural, social, and/or religious institutions they believe are a threat to their own culture. Because culture is often communicated and carried by symbols, the targets of cultural terrorism are often chosen for their symbolic value.

One example of cultural terrorism can be found in the two-decade struggle of the Liberation Tigers of Tamil Eelam (LTTE), a separatist group that seeks self-determination in areas of Sri Lanka inhabited by ethnic Tamils. The Tamils are an ethnic minority group in southern India and Sri Lanka, set apart by their religion (most are Hindu) and language. In an act of cultural (religious) terrorism, a Tamil Tiger suicide truck bomb in 1998 damaged Sri Lanka's holiest Buddhist shrine, the sixteenth-century Temple of the Tooth. Thirteen people were killed including three suspected bombers.[15] In July of 2000, Tamil rebels attacked Valigamvehera Buddhist temple in northeast Sri Lanka, injuring a Buddhist priest and four civilians. For the Tamil Tigers, Buddhism is a cultural symbol of their oppression and marginalization. By attacking these cultural symbols, they hoped to drive out what they believe to be a "foreign" culture.

---

## TERRORISM OF THE WEAK
## BECOMING TERRORISM OF THE STRONG

There is one more factor to consider: often, terrorism of the weak becomes terrorism of the strong. In spite of their rhetoric, those who engage in terrorism of the weak are not actually interested in dismantling the current systems of power and domination; they want instead to replace those on top. As history often shows, exploited and marginalized groups who come to power through the use of terrorism of the weak eventually resort to terrorism of the strong to maintain their (new) power.

One of the more infamous historical examples of this dynamic was the terrorism employed in the early period of the French Revolution. The revolution began as a struggle to overthrow a cruel monarchy in the name of liberty, equality, and fraternity. But the road to victory detoured into a campaign of terror initially directed toward the clergy and nobility. Once the revolutionaries consolidated their power, the revolution quickly devolved into an eleven-month "Reign of Terror" (also known as "The Great Terror") that took the lives of 18,000-40,000 people when rival revolutionary factions turned on each other.

Much of this carnage was led by revolutionary idealist Maximilien Robespierre, leader of the Committee of Public Safety. This committee was set up by the National Convention, which effectively governed France at the height of the radical phase of the revolution. In a speech given in February 1794, Robespierre justified the use of terror, saying:

> If the spring of popular government in time of peace
> is virtue, the springs of popular government in revo-

lution are at once virtue and terror: virtue, without which terror is fatal; terror, without which virtue is powerless. Terror is nothing other than justice, prompt, severe, inflexible; it is therefore an emanation of virtue; it is not so much a special principle as it is a consequence of the general principle of democracy applied to our country's most urgent needs.[16]

Popular discontent with the brutal measures of the Committee of Public Safety finally turned the people against Robespierre. The members of the National Convention, fearing that a new purge being planned by the committee might target them, joined forces with Robespierre's enemies and overthrew him. Ironically, Robespierre became a victim of the same terror he helped to author. What started out as terrorism of the weak became terrorism of the strong, which then devolved into a self-destructive orgy.

A more contemporary example of the same dynamic was the rise to power of Charles Taylor, former President of Liberia. In 1989 Taylor launched a rebel attack against the military dictatorship of President Samuel K. Doe. President Doe's military regime was characterized by its utter disregard for human rights, including the widespread and systematic practice of torture, enforced disappearances, extrajudicial executions, imprisonment of opposition leaders, and restrictions on the freedom of expression.

Taylor's rebellion ignited a civil war that lasted six years and involved as many as eleven factions. Amnesty International reported that civilians suffered human rights abuses and death under virtually all of them, including Taylor's National Patriotic Front of Liberia (NPFL). According to Amnesty International, "Fighters have mutilated captives, using their victims' intestines to cordon off areas newly controlled by the victorious group. They have cut up human bodies and scattered them around villages."[17] As one Liberian refugee and former teacher testified:

At this moment I feel I have no words to speak of the calamities which the war has inflicted on me. The first tragedy was the untimely death of my dear wife. We had three children. She died in Buchanan in 1990. The second was the invasion of Greenville in October 1993. I had been confident that I was far from the battle front, but I was again engulfed by this senseless invasion . . . where civilians were easily slaughtered by both warring factions.[18]

In 1995, a peace agreement was signed, eventually leading to a presidential election in 1997 that Taylor won. Many observers argued that most Liberians voted for Taylor out of fear and in hopes of ending the violence. As one Taylor campaign slogan stated, "He killed my pa, he killed my ma. I'll vote for him."[19]

Unfortunately, once in power, Taylor turned his government into an illegal money-making machine that continued terrorizing the people of Liberia. The security forces and the police regularly carried out massacres, torture (including rape), ill-treatment, and forced recruitment of child soldiers. For instance, Amnesty International reported an attack on two churches where people had sought refuge but were instead killed. Other injured victims were dragged out of ambulances and killed, despite appeals by health personnel that they be allowed to receive urgent medical attention.[20]

As we can see, terrorism is a widespread phenomenon that wears many different faces and is employed for many different reasons. For people living in the United States, terrorism had been thought of as something that happened somewhere else. Our limited experience with terrorism had been confined to isolated attacks by people inspired by fringe hate groups or from mentally disturbed individuals. All of that changed on September 11, 2001.

# CHAPTER THREE

# Living in an Age
# of Fear and Terrorism

The terrorist attacks of September 11, 2001, left a deep psychological scar on our nation. In response to the attacks, President George W. Bush launched a "War on Terror." This war is waged not against a specific nation or group of people but against an emotional state of extreme fear. Therefore, the threat can come from anywhere at any time, and so we live in a time of color-coded terrorism alerts that can put us on the edge of panic at a moment's notice.

The culture of fear in the United States pre-dates the terrorist attacks of 9-11. Since the end of World War II, our national security policy has been based on the conviction that the nation was under siege, its survival threatened by international communism. The power of fear in shaping this conviction was so strong that our national security establishment was able to convince us—even after successfully defeating two global powers and emerging as the planet's most powerful nation—that we should fear the Soviet Union, a nation that lay in ruin and that lost over twenty million of its own people. That fear led us, over the course of the Cold War, into wars of intervention (in Korea, Vietnam, the Dominican Republic, and other places); to overthrowing democratically elected governments (in Iran, Iraq, Guatemala, Chile, and other places); to supporting repressive dictatorships (in Egypt, Saudi Arabia, Iran, Iraq, Nicaragua, South Africa, and many other countries); and to spend hundreds of billions of dollars on a dangerous conventional and nuclear arms race.

With the end of the Cold War and the collapse of the Soviet empire, the fear that fueled and maintained our national security institutions attached itself to shifting threats as events dictated. A number of bogeymen proved useful for a time (such as Libya's Muammar al-Gaddafi and Panama's Manuel Noriega). But with the terrorist attacks of 9-11, the national security establishment found a new threat that can engender a level of fear capable of fueling the conviction that our nation is once again engaged in a fight for survival. And, unlike previous post-Cold War threats, this threat is defined in such a way that it could last indefinitely.

Because the threats that engender this culture of fear are vague and often undefined, they can easily be used to manipulate us into counterproductive patterns of response and counter-response. Terrorism works on us primarily at a psychological level. To effectively meet this challenge, we need to understand how the psychology of terror works and how it predisposes us to respond to it. We need to be careful not to allow ourselves to be manipulated by the terrorists, nor by our own government's response to the terrorist threat. As people of faith, we have a great resource for dealing with the psychology of terror. The authors of the Bible were very familiar with the trauma of terror, and they believed that dealing with it was primarily a matter of faith. Their ancient wisdom is especially important to us as we face the challenge of living in an age of fear and terrorism.

---

## THE PSYCHOLOGY OF TERRORISM

Almost seven years have passed since the al Qaeda attacks on U.S. soil. Yet the fear level does not seem to have decreased. The power of terrorism is not just in the terrorist act itself, but in its effect on the people whom it is meant to influence. At its root, terrorism is not just about killing; it is about inflicting psychological trauma. The terrorist seeks to make civilians feel vulnerable, fearful, and uncertain about their future. Terrorists seek to make ordinary people feel that the political, social, and cultural institutions that had previously provided them with a sense of security may now be impotent. Often, people experiencing this kind of fear look to strong leaders who promise to restore their sense of security. Traumatized people are also more susceptible to simplistic answers and dualistic thinking that usually result in false choices.

In many respects, the "War on Terror" engenders a fear of the unknown. Today it may focus on al Qaeda; tomorrow it may focus elsewhere. Any world development that the administration can declare as a threat to the people of the United States can be rolled into the "War on Terror." This fear of the unknown has also become a central focus of our defense strategy. As the 2005 National Defense Strategy document describes it, "Uncertainty is the defining characteristic of today's strategic environment. We can identify trends but cannot predict specific events with precision. While we work to avoid being surprised, we must posture ourselves to handle unanticipated problems—we must plan with surprise in mind."[1]

Not only is this phantom an ever-changing enemy, it is, we are told, an irrational enemy with whom we cannot negotiate. President Bush stated it clearly in 2005:

> In fact, we are not facing a set of grievances that can be soothed and addressed. We're facing a radical ideology with unalterable objectives to enslave whole nations and intimidate the world. No act of ours invited the rage of killers and no concession, bribe or act of appeasement would change or limit their plans for murder. On the contrary, they target nations whose behavior they believe they can change through violence. . . . The terrorists are as brutal an enemy as we've ever faced, unconstrained by any notion of our common humanity or by the rules of warfare.[2]

When faced with a situation in which people feel powerless, afraid of an enemy portrayed as unknown and irrational, a terrorized community will look to any leader who manifests strength and conviction. People victimized by terrorism look for leaders who will act in ways that make them feel strong and confident again.

Fear of terrorist attacks can also serve as an effective way for political leaders to unify a nation. This fear, however, can easily become a tool of control. The more fearful people become, the more they are willing to cede their freedoms and rights to an authority figure who promises to protect them. This is nothing new. It has happened throughout our history, but too often it is only recognized after the fact.

The Bush Administration has used the fear of terrorism to get us to do many things that we would not otherwise do. For instance, the original PATRIOT Act, which had enormous consequences in its hundreds of pages, quickly passed through Congress, even though many members of Congress later admitted that they had not even read the bill. David Keene, chair of the American Conservative Union, writes that the Bush Administration "argues convincingly that roving wiretaps, reading people's e-mail, putting video cameras on every corner, and perusing their library habits will make it easier to catch terrorists before they act. . . . The problem is that once all this is in place, we will no longer be living in the same country we lived in prior to September 11."[3]

### Terrorism and "Our Way of Life"

But giving up these rights and freedoms is rather ironic, because we are also told that what terrorists threaten is "our way of life." Shortly after the 9-11 attacks, then-Secretary of Defense Donald Rumsfeld stated, "What this war is about is our way of life and our way of life is worth losing lives for." What exactly about this way of life requires that we sacrifice the lives of our young men and women in far-off countries like Iraq? In this context, "our way of life" means continuing access to an unequal share of the world's resources—an unequal share that must be protected by force. The truth about the cost of the U.S. way of life can be found in "Strategic Energy Policy Challenges for the 21st Century," a report submitted to Vice President Dick Cheney by the Baker Institute for Public Policy in April 2001. The "central dilemma" for the U.S. Administration, the report says, is that "the American people continue to demand plentiful and cheap energy without sacrifice or inconvenience." Thus, key to "our way of life" is economic prosperity: free trade, free markets, and free enterprise.[4]

The consequences go beyond fighting military wars. The 1992 Earth Summit is an example of the priority the United States puts on protecting this way of life and its economic prosperity. The first President George Bush reluctantly attended this conference, whose purpose was to negotiate and sign treaties to curb environmental damage caused by human activity. At the conference, Bush resisted the global call to set targets for cutting pollution by declaring that the "American way of life" was not negotiable. Robin Buckallew from the University of Northern Texas points out that in 2002, at the ten-year follow-up meeting to the Earth Summit, President Bush (the younger) sent Secretary of State Colin Powell in his place. Buckallew writes:

> White House press secretary Ari Fleischer was asked prior to the event whether the new president would be asking Americans to reduce consumption in order to reduce pollution. The answer was no. In fact, the comment made at that time was "The American way of life is a blessed one." It is to be protected at all costs. In fact, international policy makers were asked by the United States to endorse that goal. The rest of the world was being asked to sign on to the right of Americans to consume the resources of the world without consideration of the consequences for the rest of the world.[5]

The consequences are that our lifestyles have a price, not only in the lives of our young men and women that must be spent to "defend" it, but also in damage done to our world environment and the other inhabitants of the planet. Most troubling, for many in the United States (and politicians) unfettered consumption is placed on a par with civil liberties—and in some cases is portrayed as more important than civil liberties. More and more people think of their freedom primarily in terms of consumption; what they fear most is loss of consumer choice, not their civil liberties.

## Dualistic Thinking and Denial of Death

Once we let fear dominate our hearts and minds and do not consider all the consequences of our individual and collective choices, we are reduced to dualistic thinking. Things are right or wrong, good or evil, people are either with us or against us. Either we protect "our way of life" or we must give up everything. Policies based on fear present us only with stark choices, which are usually false. The danger inherent in these false choices is that in trying to protect what we think is essential, we may lose (or forget) what is of real value.

These false choices also keep us from understanding what is actually at the root of our fear. At its core, the psychology of terrorism exploits our collective denial of death. In his 1973 Pulitzer Prize winning book *The Denial of Death*, cultural anthropologist Ernest Becker argued that to avoid confronting the reality of our own mortality, we individually and collectively construct an illusion of invulnerability that allows us to go on with our lives without being paralyzed by the horrifying truth that death can come at any moment.[6] Many people numb themselves to their mortality and human frailty by engaging in an endless drive for consumer products and services that promise eternal youth, unlimited power, and a feeling of belonging that mask a deep sense of utter loneliness.

This terror of death and our need to avoid it gives terrorism its power. Becker calls this strategy of avoidance "vital lies"—lies that we tell ourselves in order to get on with our lives. Gene Weingarten points out, "We deceive ourselves into believing—not literally, but emotionally—that we are immortal. . . . That's where terrorism comes in. Terrorism penetrates that self-deception in a way that few things can."[7] A terrorist reminds us that our "lies" can be destroyed in an instant, and all of our systems of avoidance can be shattered. All the esteem and success we may garner, all the wealth and power we may acquire, cannot protect us from the reality of death. The terrorist destroys our carefully constructed illusions of security and invincibility. The terrorist asserts that he/she is in ultimate control and that our facades of order and systems of protection are merely sand castles in a rising tide.

## THE BIBLE AND TERRORISM

We certainly are not the first humans to face terror and uncertainty. To understand an alternate response to terrorism, Christians can look to what the Bible says. If we look at terrorism as acts of violence committed against others, it is clear from the testimony of the Christian Scriptures that Jesus rejects violence and calls upon his followers to do the same (Matthew 26:51-53). Beyond that, Jesus called his disciples to love their enemies and to pray for those who persecute them (Luke 6:27-31). As biblical scholar John McKenzie, SJ, summarized it, "If we cannot know from the Gospels Jesus' absolute rejection of violence and hatred in both his life and his teachings, than we cannot know anything about him. . . . If Jesus taught us anything, he taught us how to die, not how to kill."[8]

The testimony of the Jewish Scriptures regarding violent acts of terrorism is more ambiguous. The commandment against murder (Genesis 20:13) and the attempts to limit vengeance and vendetta justice by making the punishment fit the crime (Leviticus 24:19-20) show a general prohibition or limit on the use of violence. Justified violence in the Jewish Scriptures is often connected with the concept of Holy War. While violence (even the execution of noncombatants) is part of the Holy War tradition, it is clear from Scripture that it is God who fights on behalf of Israel, not Israel who fights on behalf of God (Exodus 17:8-13). God secures victory for the Israelites by God's own hand. The defeat of the enemy is not dependent upon the skill or the strength of the army, but on the faithfulness of the people to the covenant (Psalm 20). God is the author of life and only God can take life (Genesis 2:7, Psalm 104:29).

## The Bible and Psychological Terrorism

However, when we look at terrorism in the psychological sense—the power to terrorize others to compel a change in their behavior or beliefs—we find that the Bible contains some important insights. The *NIV Exhaustive Concordance of the Bible* lists seventy-four scripture passages containing Hebrew words that can be translated as "terror" and fifty-one scripture passages containing Hebrew words that can be translated as "terrified."[9] These passages address at least three distinct themes relating to the psychology of terror. The first theme is terror as an attribute of God; the second is the exhortation not to be terrorized by others; and the third is terror as a consequence of unfaithfulness to God. Let's examine each of these.

*Terror as an Attribute of God:* Bāhal *and* Phobeomai

One Hebrew word that can be translated as "terrified" is *bāhal*; it can also mean "dismayed," "tremble," or "make afraid." This word describes God as one who evokes terror. The Jewish Scriptures sometimes use it to speak about the awesome, overwhelming power of God in relation to humans, a terror of God that puts us in touch with our human frailty and mortality. The terror of God reminds humans that we are merely creatures and cultivates respect and faithfulness to God.

As the Psalmist declares, "You turn humans back to dust,

saying, 'Return, O children of humans.' For a thousand years in your sight are as yesterday . . . Truly we are consumed by your anger, and terrified (*bāhal*) by your indignation" (Psalm 90:3-4, 7). The book of Job is about every believer's struggle to understand the nature of suffering in light of the overwhelming power of a God who is beyond comprehending and who cannot be limited by any theology or ideology. "Therefore I am terrified (*bāhal*) before God; when I take thought, I fear God. Indeed, God has made my courage fail; the Almighty has terrified (*bāhal*)" (Job 23:15-16).

This sense of terror as overwhelming awe is also attributed to Jesus in the Gospels. The Greek word *phobeomai* can be translated as "terrified," "afraid," or "filled with awe." Two Gospel stories associate Jesus with the terror of God found in the Jewish Scriptures. First, in Matthew's account of Jesus walking on the water, we read, "When the disciples saw him walking on the water they were terrified (*phobeomai*). 'It is a ghost!' they said, and in their fear they began to cry out" (Matthew 14:26). The Greek word *phobeomai* is used in similar accounts from Mark (4:41) and John (6:19). The other story in which Jesus is associated with the terror of God is found in Matthew's story of the Transfiguration, "When they heard this, the disciples fell forward on the ground, terrified (*phobeomai*)" (Matthew 17:6). In both of these stories, the powerful manifestation of Jesus' divinity immediately evokes from his disciples a recognition of their creatureliness and their overwhelming awe of the power of God.

These scripture texts seem to indicate that terror (*bāhal* and *phobeomai*) is an attribute of God. The usage of these words also indicates that power and authority to strike terror belongs to God and God alone.

It was there Yahweh broke the flashing arrows,
the shield, the sword, the weapons of war.
The defeated warriors sleep in death;
the hands of the soldiers were powerless.
At your rebuke, horse and rider lay stunned.

You, and you alone, are to be feared.
Who shall stand when your anger is roused?
(Psalm 76:3, 5-7)

In the presence of God, all human pretenses to power evaporate in terror. In the presence of the divine, we are overwhelmed and our social constructs of invincibility and security shrink into insignificance. The terror of God reminds humans of our frailty and hence our need for God: "Take away their breath, and they die" (Psalm 104:29).

## Do Not Be Terrorized by Others: Āras and Hātat

However, when the community of believers found themselves in terror of other humans, God impressed upon them that their terror was misplaced and that the antidote was trust in God. This second Biblical theme related to the psychology of terror—the admonition not to live in fear of others—is exemplified in the Hebrew word *āras*, sometimes translated as "terrified," "given to panic," or "stand in awe." Jewish Scriptures contain many stories about how the psychology of terror grips the Hebrews because of their lack of faith. In a story from Deuteronomy about the Hebrew revolt at the report of giants living in the Promised Land, we read God's admonition, "But I say to you, 'Do not be terrified (*āras*) by them. Your God, who goes before you, will fight for you, just as God took your part before your very eyes in Egypt'" (Deuteronomy 1:29). Later in Deuteronomy, we find Moses speaking to the people as they finally gather the courage to cross over into the Promised Land. He encourages them, "It is your God who will cross before you; God will destroy these nations before you, that you may supplant them. . . . Be brave and steadfast; do not be afraid or terrified (*āras*) by them, for it is your God who marches with you; God will never fail or forsake you" (Deuteronomy 31:3, 6).

Another Hebrew word, *hātat*, can be translated as "filled with terror," "broken," "discouraged," or "stood in awe." The prophets sometimes use it to refer to the psychology of terror. Isaiah exhorts those who are faithful, who do justice and keep God's word, not to live in terror: "Hear me, you who know justice, you people who have my teaching at heart: Fear not the reproach of people, be not terrified (*hātat*) at their reviling" (Isaiah 51:7). When telling the story of his own call, Jeremiah recounts God's command: "Stand up and tell them all that I command you. Do not be terrified (*hātat*) by them, as though I would leave you crushed before them" (Jeremiah 1:17). Ezekiel had a similar encounter with God when he was called, "But as for you, mortal, do not be afraid of what they say or terrified (*hātat*) by them when they contradict you and reject you. . . ." (Ezekiel 2:6).

When the People of God are faithful to the covenant, when they answer God's call to speak out and work on behalf of justice, and when they smash every idol or false god in their lives, they have no reason to live in terror. The People of God will not make an idol of their consumer lifestyle; they will not sacrifice the lives of their sons and daughters out of fear of losing it. Because they fear only God, no human power or principality can terrify them. They understand that to succumb to feelings of terror from any power other than God is to become a slave to what they fear.

*Terror as a Consequence of Unfaithfulness to God:*
Pahad *and* Pahadl

But when the people fail to live by the covenant or when they engage in injustice or begin to worship idols, God allows them to be overwhelmed in terror of their enemies. The third theme in the Bible related to the psychology of terror deals with the consequences of breaking the covenant. Two Hebrew words that are sometimes used in this context are *pahad* and *pahadl*, which can be translated as "terror," "overwhelmed by dread," "live in terror," or "turn in fear."

One example of this usage is in Deuteronomy, where the author warns the people of the consequences of disobeying God's laws:

If you are not careful to observe every word of the law which is written in this book and to revere the glorious and awesome name of your God, God will smite you and your descendants . . . In the morning you will say, "Would that it were evening!" and in the evening you will say, "Would that it were morning!" for the terror (*pahadl*) that your heart must feel and the sight that your eyes must see (Deuteronomy 28:58, 67).

The prophet Isaiah speaks of the devastation of the world because of the Israelites' faithlessness: "Lo, God empties the land, lays it waste; God turns it upside down, scattering its inhabitants. . . . Terror (*pahadl*), pit and trap are upon you, inhabitants of the earth. The one who flees at the sound of terror (*pahadl*) will fall into the pit" (Isaiah 24:1, 17). Isaiah also takes special aim at idol makers, "Idol makers all amount to nothing and their precious works are of no avail. . . . they will all assemble and stand forth, to be brought down to terror (*pahad*) and infamy" (Isaiah 44:11).

Even though, for a time, God's people are abandoned to terror because of their unfaithfulness, God also promises forgiveness and an end to the scourge of terror. The prophet Jeremiah speaks of this: "Thus says God: 'A cry of dismay we hear; terror (*pahadl*) reigns, not peace. . . . How mighty is that day—none like it! A time for distress for Jacob, though he shall be saved from it'" (Jeremiah 30:4-5, 7).

*The Sin of Terrorism*

As we can see from this brief Biblical survey, the community of believers is called to live in awe-inspiring terror of God. In this terror of God, all self-constructed notions of security, power, and invulnerability are undone as we place our hope in God. From Scripture, we also learn that living in terror of any other power on earth is misplaced. When overwhelmed by feelings of terror, we are invited to deepen our trust in God's providential care. Finally, believers should be mindful that when we abandon our covenant with God—when we cut our life line to the Almighty—we are in danger of being overtaken by terror, whose source can come from anywhere at anytime: "The fool says in their hearts, 'There is no God.' They are corrupt, and their ways are evil. . . . There they are, overwhelmed with fear, in fear whose source is unknown!" (Psalm 53:1, 5)

This brief Biblical survey also adds to our theological understanding of the sin of terrorism. Not only are the violent acts of terrorism evil, but those who engage in the psychology of terrorism may be guilty of blasphemy as well. The traditional understanding of blasphemy is "abusive or contemptuous language directed toward God or sacred things."[10] But the *Catechism of the Catholic Church* includes another dimension of the sin of blasphemy: "It is also blasphemous to make use of God's name to cover up criminal practices, to reduce peoples to servitude, to torture persons or put them to death."[11] If terror is rightly considered an attribute of God, aren't those who use this power for criminal practices, for reducing people to servitude, for torture, or for putting people to death also guilty of blasphemy? When terrorists seek to exercise the same terrifying power as God, to command obedience and to control others for their own purposes, aren't they guilty of blasphemy?

In his book *War is a Force That Gives Us Meaning*, author and war correspondent Chris Hedges describes the seductive power of killing he witnessed in places like El Salvador and Bosnia. A characteristic of those who committed acts of terrorism during these conflicts was the almost narcotic feeling of power that killing gave them. In their former lives they might have been petty criminals, laborers, or peasants. But in the killing fields, they wielded the power of life and death. For those who carried out these atrocities, this power, over time, deadened their senses; execution of the innocent became god-play, a form of blasphemy.

> The seductiveness of violence, the fascination with the grotesque—the Bible calls it "the lust of the

eye"—the god-like empowerment over other human lives and the drug of war combines, like the ecstasy of erotic love, to let our senses command our bodies. Killing unleashes within us dark undercurrents that see us desecrate and whip ourselves into greater orgies of destruction.[12]

Could trepidation of blasphemous consequences be behind the comments made by atomic bomb creator Robert Oppenheimer after experiencing the terror of the first atomic blast in the desert of New Mexico? He said, "I remembered the line from the Hindu scripture, the *Bhagavad-Gita*: Vishnu is trying to persuade the Prince that he should do his duty and to impress him he takes on his multi-armed form and says, 'Now I am become Death, the destroyer of worlds.' I suppose we all thought that, one way or another."[13] His fears were soon realized when President Truman ordered the most deadly act of terrorism in modern history: the atomic bombings of Hiroshima (more than 90,000 immediate civilian deaths) and Nagasaki (more than 70,000 immediate civilian deaths).

## THE ROLE OF NARRATIVE IN TERRORISM

Terrorism, then, is not only the act of violence—it is also the psychological trauma the act sets in motion. This trauma can either be sustained or healed over time, depending on the stories that societies create to help them understand what has happened to them. Alfred Hitchcock, famed master of terror films, astutely pointed out, "There is no terror in the bang, only in the anticipation of it." In other words, it is not only the horror of the act itself but the account constructed around it that creates the terror. Hitchcock, the master storyteller, understood that to hold his audience in a state of terror, he had to construct a story that made the anticipation of the horrific act plausible in the minds of his audience. They needed to believe that the "bang" was coming, and they could do nothing about it; they needed to know that it might happen again without warning, and it could happen to them.

The perpetrators of terrorism seek to create this kind of story in the minds of those they target. More than a specific act of violence, they seek to plant the seeds of a narrative of terror in the hearts and minds of the civilian population. The power of terrorism is not only in the act of terror, but in the fear of future acts. Terrorism is primarily about psychology, not fire power. As Bill Moyers explains, "Terrorists plant time bombs in our heads, hoping to turn each and every imagination into a private hell governed by our fear of them."[14]

While terrorists seek to plant seeds of terror into the hearts and minds of a targeted community, the seed's growth depends upon the way a targeted community chooses to interpret the terrorist attacks or threats. In other words, the story the terrorists seek to create requires the willing participation of those who are attacked. For us in the United States, the narrative we create around the attacks of 9-11 determines whether the terror is sustained over time. Al Qaeda planted the seed, but ultimately the way we interpret the events of 9-11 will determine whether the seed of terror takes root in our hearts and minds.

To understand the nature of the terrorist threat directed at the United States, we need to understand the power of the narrative created around it and how we have participated in its creation. Then, to creatively and effectively respond to the threat of terrorism, we need to create an alternative narrative, one that does not feed into the cycle of attacks and counter-attacks, but helps us create a new dynamic capable of reducing the threat and giving hope for a better life to those who are marginalized and oppressed. This will be the aim of the next two parts of this book.

# PART II

## Creating an Alternative to the "War on Terror": Constructing a New 9-11 Narrative

According to a survey by the British newspaper *The Independent*, the first five years of the "War on Terror" killed a minimum of 62,006 people and created 4.5 million refugees. As of September 2006, the wars in Iraq and Afghanistan had cost the United States more than the sum needed to pay off the debts of every poor nation on earth.[1] It is time to ask what all this death, destruction, and huge expenditure of treasure have given us. Do we feel more secure? Are we less fearful about the future?

Frank Macchai, writing in *Pneuma: The Journal of the Society for Pentecostal Studies*, asks whether anti-terrorism technologies and changes in our society since the start of the "War on Terror" are making us feel safer. Reflecting on a TV show about anti-terrorism technologies, Macchai writes:

At the conclusion of the program, the interviewer
asked the questions that I am sure were on the minds
of many viewers, "Won't the terrorists find a way of
outsmarting this technology?" . . . In the process of
this escalation of terrorist and anti-terrorist technology, what kind of world will we create for our children? Will we end up in an existence so imprisoned
in security systems that paranoia becomes a way of
life? The irony here is that our technological success
over the terrorists may end up accomplishing their
goals against us. Isn't the terrorist campaign really
meant to make us our own worst enemies, to place us
in a perpetual state of fear and watchfulness?[2]

Can terrorism be defeated by technological innovations, or
do these new technologies just displace our fears from one sphere
of concern to another? Is there a way forward in addressing terrorism that can move us beyond the constant need to keep our
fellow citizens terrified? If we were to step back for a moment,
take a deep breath, and free our minds and hearts from the fears
that strangle our creativity, what might we be able to formulate as
an alternative to the "War on Terror"?

A first step in constructing this alternative might begin with
understanding the 9-11 narrative that created the "War on Terror"
and understanding the forces that drive it. Just as important, we
need to understand the al Qaeda 9-11 narrative, both the dynamics that give it such power within the Muslim/Arab world and
how our own actions may inadvertently validate it and contribute
to its appeal.

Narrative creation is not the same as public relations; we are
not talking about doing a better job of selling our story. Rather,
we are talking about being attentive to the way our stories shape
our choices. If we can better understand the role of narrative in
the conflict called the "War on Terror" and how it shapes our response to the threat of terrorism, we can begin to construct an
alternative 9-11 narrative that will do a better job of unifying our

nation, rebuilding our alliances, and appealing to people around the world. For this alternative 9-11 narrative to be authentic it must be more than empty slogans or rhetoric; it must have the power to shape our attitudes and determine our behavior. And if we are successful in constructing an authentic alternative narrative regarding the events and aftermath of 9-11, it will not only strengthen our alliances; it may also have the power to draw many Muslim/Arab communities away from the narrative constructed by al Qaeda and other terrorist groups.

# CHAPTER FOUR

# Narrative Creation and 9-11

From the time humans first communicated abstract concepts (like the notion of "yesterday"), they have been telling stories to help them make sense of their world and the events of their lives. It may even be impossible to understand the things that happen to us without creating stories around them: the more significant the event, the more important the need for creating a narrative.

For example, if you get into a traffic accident on your way home from work, you don't just announce to your family that you wrecked the car and leave it at that. What you do is tell a story about your experience. In fact, you began constructing your story about the accident within moments after the crash. Before getting home, you may have already compared your story with that of others who might have been involved in the accident. You may have solicited witnesses to tell their story of the event. Finally, the police may have required you to tell them your story. On your way home from the accident, you were still constructing and reconstructing the story in your mind, this time from a different point of view because your audience (your family) would have a different set of concerns. A year or two later, after the trauma associated with the crash had subsided, you may add new pieces to the story. It might become a cautionary tale on the importance of safe driving, or it might become a funny story of unfortunate circumstances, or it could become a testament to the horrors of insurance industry bureaucracy. In the end, the story you create to make sense of the crash ends up being more important than the crash itself.

The stories we create to understand and explain our lives are also important because they give us a framework for future decision-making; our past experiences (and the power we give them through stories) often dictate our future actions. What we learn from the past (the way we construct our personal narratives) predisposes us to respond to similar events in the future in a predictable way. Those who control our understanding of the past (construct our historical narratives) can also influence our future actions (set the parameters of our responses to similar events).

## CREATING 9-11 NARRATIVES

The horrific events of September 11, 2001, were much more traumatic than an automobile accident, but the same principles of narrative creation apply. In this chapter, we will look at how different narratives have been constructed around 9-11 and what this means to different constituencies. We will focus on two major players—the Bush Administration and al Qaeda—and see that while the stories they construct around these acts of terrorism are different, in many ways they mirror each other in their creation and purpose.

Each of us can probably remember where we were when we heard about the first plane crashing into the World Trade Center. I was in my car on the way to work, listening to National Public Radio. An announcement was read concerning a plane that had crashed into a building in the business district of Manhattan. I remember thinking that some small plane had probably lost control and crashed into a skyscraper. I wondered if the pilot had a heart attack or seizure. I asked myself why they would even let small planes fly around the tall buildings of Manhattan, and I remember thinking that somebody was going to catch hell for allowing this to happen. As you can see, within minutes of hearing about the first plane strike, I had already begun constructing a story around what was happening. Only when I got to work and was able to watch TV did I realize how woefully inadequate my telling had been.

As I watched the television coverage, I was amazed at how quickly the talking heads on TV news programs began constructing their own accounts to make meaning out of the events that were unfolding as they spoke. From out of nowhere, experts began appearing with important information that would help us "make sense" of what we were watching. The second plane attack caused our hearts to stop—"My God! How many planes are out there and when will the next one fall!"—and a new interpretation of the events began. Even as the second tower fell, we were beginning to collect little stories within the bigger story. There were heroic stories of sacrifice and compassion, stories of terror and desperation, stories of fear and abandonment. When the Pentagon attack was reported, this catalyzed an entirely new narrative: What other targets were going to be hit? When reports of another plane going down in a field in Pennsylvania surfaced, a new story line of heroism and sacrifice began to emerge.

These narratives we construct to tell the stories of our lives (individually and collectively) hold great power. They can ennoble us, giving us courage and strength; they can humble us, giving us perspective and compassion; and they can instruct us, giving us wisdom and understanding. Additionally, the terrifying nature of these terrorist attacks makes this process even more important; without a story to help us make sense of these attacks, we would have much more difficulty moving on with our lives. As I stated at the end of the last chapter, the threat emanating from the attacks of 9-11 comes not only from the acts of terror themselves, but from the narratives constructed to explain them.

This process involves many different participants, all with their own concerns and their own agendas. In this chapter, in addition to the creators of 9-11 narratives, I will look at two groups that participate as consumers in the ongoing process of constructing the 9-11 narrative. The two groups that create narratives are the Bush Administration and the al Qaeda terrorist network. Their narratives are aimed at two distinct audiences (consumers): first, the U.S. people (including politicians), along with U.S. allies in the "War on Terror"; and second, the Muslim/Arab world along with those not aligned with the United States. (As we will see in this chapter, the U.S. corporate media's role is not so much as independent actors but as tools to be manipulated.)

## The Role of "Facts" in Narrative Creation

Before we begin examining the creation and impact of these narratives, it is important to keep in mind the role of factual accuracy. Each creator believes that its narrative is based on facts. The Bush Administration and al Qaeda agree on the basic facts of the 9-11 attacks on the United States. Where they differ is in the interpretation of those facts; the mitigating circumstances which form the basis of the facts; the historical context in which to understand the facts; and the social, cultural, economic and political meanings of those facts.

In appealing to their intended audiences, the creators of these historical tellings use facts to support their story lines. Those facts that fit their narrative are highlighted; those facts that don't support their story line are ignored or downplayed. For this reason it is important to analyze these narratives as interpretive works; they are not the same as courtroom testimony. As such it would not be particularly helpful or constructive to argue the validity of either narrative based on the "facts."

The process of creating a narrative and having the intended audience accept it is not a matter of fact-checking as much as a matter of believability. What is important is what is believed, not what might be "true" by some objective measurement. The process of believing a narrative is complicated, involving many factors. For instance, acceptance depends on whether the source can be trusted, whether there is some cultural or social affinity with this source, and whether the narrative touches upon already accepted stories or beliefs that the intended audience holds deeply.

Further, if we take the process of narrative creation seriously as an important element in a strategy for combating terrorism, then we must be able to disengage ourselves enough from both narratives in order to contrast and compare them. In doing so, we may be helped by keeping in mind that the truth of something is often more than just the facts about it. An old Chinese proverb about the truth states that there are three truths: my truth, your truth, and THE truth. To better understand the threat we face, we need to be open enough to acknowledge the truth contained in each telling. And as our understanding increases, we will be able to more effectively utilize narrative creation in our efforts to address this threat.

## THE BUSH ADMINISTRATION'S NARRATIVE

In the aftermath of the terrorist attacks of 9-11, President Bush projected an image of strength and resolve that the country needed at that time. As mentioned in the previous chapter, when a civilian population is attacked by terrorists, it gravitates toward strong, decisive leadership that will help it overcome the trauma of helplessness and confusion. President Bush met that need for most people in the United States, and this put him in a unique position to be the primary creator of our national 9-11 narrative.

Taking full advantage of the opportunity given him, the President moved quickly to begin constructing a narrative of the 9-11 attacks, using the entire Executive Branch of government to make sure that the U.S. people, the terrorist attackers, and the rest of the world understood what the attacks meant. From the beginning, the Republican Party of President Bush has been the principal architect of the 9-11 narrative, but the Democratic Party has also played a supportive role in constructing it. While members of the Democratic Party have differed with the President and the Republican Party in terms of policy and strategy, the narrative created by the Bush Administration has, for the most part, been accepted without challenge by the Democratic Party. So, while I refer to this story as the Bush Administration narrative, I do not mean to suggest that it is solely a Republican Party narrative.

Almost from the beginning, President Bush and his Administration began constructing a narrative explaining the terrorist attacks of 9-11 within the context of a global struggle of epic proportions. This was the ultimate struggle between good and evil: "The war we fight today is more than a military conflict; it is the decisive ideological struggle of the 21st century." For the Bush Administration, the "War on Terror" is more than a slogan; it is "an inescapable calling of our generation" and the "challenge of our time."[1]

This narrative includes clear demarcations of good and evil that call for an unambiguous moral response. As President Bush put it, "There is no neutral ground in the fight between civilization and terror, because there is no neutral ground between good and evil, freedom and slavery, and life and death." The President's narrative has only two sides. On one side are "those who believe in values of freedom and moderation . . . [those who believe in] the right of all people to speak, and worship and live in liberty." On the other side are those who are "offended by our existence as free nations." They are the ones who want to overthrow moderate governments in the Middle East in order to "attack America" and "spread their hateful ideology." For this reason, President Bush demands that every nation make a fundamental choice about where it stands. As he reminded the world in 2006, "After 9/11, I stood in the well of the House of Representatives and declared that every nation, in every region, had a decision to make—either you were with us, or you stood with the terrorists."[2]

For those who may not fully understand how a group of fanatics living in Afghan caves could pose such an existential threat to a superpower like the United States, the President borrows from some of the great challenges of the nation's past. The President regularly seeks to link his "War on Terror" narrative to the epic struggles against the Nazis during World War II and the Communists during the Cold War. Speaking before a group of World War II veterans, the President declared, "As veterans, you have seen this kind of enemy before. They're successors to Fascists, to Nazis, to Communists, and other totalitarians of the 20th century." We are told that, like the Communists, Islamic radicalism "is elitist, led by a self-appointed vanguard that presumes to speak for the Muslim masses." Like the Communists, they teach that "innocent individuals can be sacrificed to serve a political vision." And like the Communists, this new enemy "is dismissive of free peoples, claiming that men and women who live in liberty are weak and decadent."[3]

In the narrative created by the Bush Administration, there is no rational or logical explanation for why the terrorists attacked us. In addition, those who died on 9-11 are portrayed as innocent victims, killed without warning and without cause. The Administration often uses the language of victimization. For President Bush, the central lesson of the tragedy of 9-11 is that our homeland is vulnerable to attack without warning by an irrational foe. The vulnerable people killed on 9-11 were innocent victims of a vicious crime and, more importantly, each of us is also a potential victim.

In the President's 9-11 narrative, not only are the terrorists hate-filled evil monsters (they have a mind-set that "rejoices in suicide, incites murder and celebrates every death we mourn"), but they are so irrational that it is impossible to talk with them. As President Bush tells us, "No act of ours invited the rage of the killers—and no concession, bribe, or act of appeasement would change or limit their plans for murder."[4]

In the Bush Administration's narrative, while the people who attacked us are irrational, they do have purpose. As Vice President Cheney tells us, their ultimate goal is to establish "a totalitarian empire that encompasses the region from Spain, across North Africa, through the Middle East and South Asia, all the way around to Indonesia." And if they accomplish that goal, they would not stop there. In the Administration's narrative, the terrorists come unglued at the thought of people exercising freedom. As President Bush reminds us, "They can't stand the thought that people get to decide the future of our country by voting. Freedom bothers them because their ideology is the opposite of liberty; it is the opposite of freedom." As Vice President Cheney explains, "They hate us, they hate our country, and they hate the liberties for which we stand. They want to destroy our way of life, so that freedom no longer has a home and a defender in this world."[5] These purposes stand in direct opposition to U.S. values and are another way the narrative sets clear demarcations.

The Bush Administration's narrative draws on past historical struggles, but it also focuses on the future. It tells the U.S. people that the terrorist attacks on 9-11 changed our world forever and that the past way of doing things can no longer provide the protection we seek. Because of this new reality, we must accept certain changes in the way we live. Our pre-9-11 notions of civil liberties, of international laws and treaties, and our understandings about the rule of law must be adapted to the new threats we face.

We are also told that dissenting against the President or questioning the narrative put forward by the Administration will be interpreted as weakness by our enemies. While limited debate of strategies and tactics might be allowed, any dissent from the "War on Terror" is fundamentally unpatriotic. Worse yet, it will give comfort and aid to the terrorists and endanger our troops. As President Bush warns us, "Any sign of weakness or retreat simply validates terrorist violence and invites more violence for all nations. The only certain way to protect our people is by early, united and decisive action."[6]

This narrative is not meant only for the U.S. people. President Bush's message to the Muslim/Arab world combines threat and treaty. On the one hand, he has made it clear that, in light of the attacks of 9-11, every country, particularly those that are Muslim, must decide to either be on our side or on al Qaeda's side. Those who do not choose rightly can expect to become a target of our wrath. Those who harbor terrorists (i.e., refuse to turn them over to us) and those who finance or support terrorists (as defined according to the narrative's own political and economic interests) in any way are subject to isolation or even military attack. However, those who do cooperate with the Administration and choose to be on our side in this struggle against terrorism have the promise of good relationship, financial support, and the protection of the U.S. military umbrella.

## Why Understanding the al Qaeda Narrative is Important

Some claim that trying to understand the al Qaeda narrative is a sign of appeasement or weakness. Some even claim that it is tantamount to treason to acknowledge a 9-11 narrative other than the one just described or to consider why some people hate the United States. Still others think that giving consideration to the al Qaeda narrative, to listen to the grievances of those who attacked us, is nothing more than "blaming America first."

Even President Bush admits that this struggle is primarily a battle of ideas, a conflict between competing ideologies and worldviews. By not trying to understand the source of anger and hatred toward us being fanned by the narrative of al Qaeda, we doom ourselves to fighting this threat blindfolded. By reducing the ideology and worldview of groups like al Qaeda to caricatures, we will only ensure that our response to their challenge will be misdirected. By refusing to understand the al Qaeda narrative, we will most assuredly and unwittingly continue to feed and nurture it.

However, attempting to understand this other telling is not easy. One of the biggest challenges in trying to understand the al Qaeda narrative of the 9-11 terrorist attacks is that most of what we know about their narrative comes to us through our own media. Often, statements made by Osama bin Laden and other al Qaeda leaders are edited for publication in our media with a particular purpose in mind. And even when it is possible to get a complete transcript of an al Qaeda statement, it is hard for non-Arabic speakers to know if the English translation accurately reflects what its authors intended. Even with these limitations, however, it is possible to sketch an outline of the al Qaeda narrative.

## AL QAEDA'S NARRATIVE

For the purposes of this analysis, I create a description of the al Qaeda narrative that parallels that of the Bush Administration in order to show their similarities. I do so to make the case that, contrary to what we have been told, al Qaeda is not an irrational force that cannot be understood. Explanations that members of al Qaeda and their followers are brainwashed by a perverted leader are an escapist simplification and will inevitably lead us to very wrong-headed responses. We cannot expect to develop an effective response to the terrorist threat if we do not take their narrative seriously.

Like the Bush Administration narrative of 9-11, al Qaeda's narrative sees the 9-11 attacks as an epic struggle played out on a global stage. Like President Bush, bin Laden and his followers believe that this struggle is the challenge of their generation. For al Qaeda, this epic global struggle is couched in the language of jihad (literally, "struggle"). This struggle is interpreted in different ways. BBC analyst Fiona Symon reminds us: "For some it means the struggle to defend one's faith and ideals against harmful outside influences. For others it has come to represent the duty of Muslims to fight to rid the Islamic world of western influence in the form of corrupt and despotic leaders and occupying armies."[7]

In the same way that the Bush Administration interprets this struggle as pitting good against evil, al Qaeda sees this ultimately as a moral struggle. A training manual found during a search of an al Qaeda member's home in Manchester, England, portrayed the

United States as merciless murderers with no conscience. "Martyrs were killed, women were widowed, children were orphaned, men were handcuffed, chaste women's heads were shaved, harlots' heads were crowned, atrocities were inflicted on the innocent, gifts were given to the wicked, virgins were raped. . ."[8]

In the al Qaeda narrative, the attacks of 9-11 were a way of giving the United States a taste of its own medicine, setting the attacks in a historical context. "What America is tasting now is something insignificant compared to what we have tasted for scores of years. Our nation (the Islamic world) has tasted this humiliation and this degradation for more than eighty years. Its sons are killed, its blood is shed, its sanctuaries are attacked, and no one hears and no one heeds." In his letter to the U.S. people, bin Laden says, "Why should fear, killing, destruction, displacement, orphaning and widowing continue to be our lot, while security, stability and happiness be your lot? This is unfair. It is time that we got even. You will be killed just as you kill, and will be bombed just as you bomb."[9]

By focusing the anger and frustration of their fellow Muslims on the policies and actions of the United States, the al Qaeda narrative provides this community a clear target for their anger, and it provides an unambiguous moral response to this evil. Al Qaeda calls on all Muslims to kill as many U.S. citizens as possible, seeing no difference between members of the military and noncombatants: "The ruling to kill the Americans and their allies—civilian and military—is an individual duty for every Muslim who can do it in any country in which it is possible to do it, in order to liberate the al-Aqsa Mosque and the holy mosque [Mecca] from their grip, and in order for their armies to move out of all the lands of Islam, defeated and unable to threaten any Muslim."[10]

Like the Bush narrative, the narrative of al Qaeda is also tied to a larger historical story. As the al Qaeda Training Manual states, "After the fall of our orthodox caliphates on March 3, 1924, and after expelling the colonialists, our Islamic nation was afflicted with apostate rulers who took over in the Moslem nation. These rulers turned out to be more infidel and criminal than the colonialists themselves. Moslems have endured all kinds of harm, oppression, and torture at their hands. . . ."[11]

In February 1998, al Qaeda issued a statement under the banner of "The World Islamic Front for Jihad Against the Jews and Crusaders" which also describes the historical context of their struggle:

> The Arabian Peninsula has never—since Allah made it flat, created its desert, and encircled it with seas—been stormed by any forces like the crusader armies spreading in it like locusts, eating its riches and wiping out its plantations. All of this is happening at a time in which nations are attacking Muslims like people fighting over a plate of food. . . . First, for over seven years the United States has been occupying the lands of Islam in the holiest of places, the Arabian Peninsula, plundering its riches, dictating to its rulers, humiliating its people, terrorizing its neighbors, and turning its bases in the Peninsula into a spearhead through which to fight the neighboring Muslim peoples.[12]

There are also similarities in the portrayals of current "enemies." Where President Bush sees bin Laden and his followers as irrational and beyond the reach of reason, al Qaeda sees the West as blind, deaf, and dumb to the suffering of those it considers as beneath them: "The West is incapable of recognizing the rights of others. It will not be able to respect others' beliefs or feelings. The West still believes in ethnic supremacy and looks down on other nations. They categorise human beings into white masters and colored slaves."[13]

Historical wrongs and the "evil" attributes of the enemy are not the only appeals used in the narratives. Just as the Bush Administration narrative of 9-11 is deeply steeped in the language of victimization, al Qaeda also uses the language of victimization in justifying its attack on the United States. In its narrative, the attacks of 9-11 were payback for crimes committed against it. Bin Laden claims that his idea for the 9-11 attacks came from watching the destruction of Lebanon by the Israeli army and the U.S. Navy bombardment of Beirut (1983-1984).

> As I was looking at those destroyed towers in Lebanon, I was struck by the idea of punishing the oppressor in the same manner and destroying towers in the U.S., to give it a taste of what we have tasted and to deter it from killing our children and women. That day I became convinced that iniquity and the premeditated murder of innocent children and women is an established American principle, and that terror is [the real meaning of] "freedom" and "democracy," while they call the resistance "terrorism" and "reaction."[14]

Like the Bush Administration, al Qaeda contrasts its goals to those of the enemy. President's Bush's narrative defines victory as eliminating terrorism from the face of the earth and establishing democratic nations throughout the Middle East. In al Qaeda's narrative, "the victory of Islam will never take place until a Muslim state is established in the manner of the Prophet in the heart of the Islamic world, specifically in the Levant, Egypt, and the neighboring states of the Peninsula and Iraq." In this narrative, victory will come in four stages:

> The first stage: Expel the Americans from Iraq. . . . The second stage: establish an Islamic authority or emirate, then develop it and support it until it achieves the level of a caliphate over as much territory as possible. . . . The third stage: extend the jihad wave to the secular countries neighboring Iraq. The fourth stage, it may coincide with what came before: the clash with Israel, because Israel was established only to challenge any new Islamic entity.[15]

(Al Qaeda is deeply anti-Semitic, stating that the nefarious acts of the Jewish state in the Middle East are behind its troubles: "if the Americans' aims behind these wars [the first Persian Gulf war in particular] are religious and economic, the aim is also to serve the Jews' petty state and divert attention from its occupation of Jerusalem and murder of Muslims there the aims behind these wars."[16])

A critical key to al Qaeda's "victory of Islam" is support from the "Muslim street" (disenfranchised and disillusioned Muslims in countries across the Middle East and around the world). Because al Qaeda's narrative is designed to appeal to these Muslims, any action on al Qaeda's part that might alienate this base of support could prove fatal to their strategic objectives. A letter from bin Laden's second-in-command, Ayman Muhammad Rabaie al-Zawahiri, to an al Qaeda leader in Iraq criticizes attacks against innocent Muslims as counter-productive to the larger goals of the struggle.

> This goal will not be accomplished by the mujahed movement while it is cut off from public support . . . In the absence of this popular support, the Islamic mujahed movement would be crushed in the shadows, far from the masses who are distracted or fearful, and the struggle between the Jihadist elite and the arrogant authorities would be confined to prison dungeons far from the public and the light of day.[17]

Like the Bush Administration's message to the Muslim/Arab world, al Qaeda's message to the U.S. people and its allies combines threat and treaty. On the one hand it says:

> As for us, we do not have anything to lose. The swimmer in the sea does not fear rain. You have occupied our land, defiled our honor, violated our dignity, shed our blood, ransacked our money, demolished our houses, rendered us homeless, and tampered with

our security. We will treat you in the same way. You
tried to deny us the decent life, but you cannot deny
us a decent death.

Along with this defiant posture, bin Laden also extended an
olive branch, "We do not object to a long-term truce with you on
the basis of fair conditions that we respect. We are a nation, for
which God has disallowed treachery and lying. . . . If you have a
genuine will to achieve security and peace, we have already an-
swered you."[18]

## THE TRAP OF MUTUALLY SUSTAINING NARRATIVES

By setting up the descriptions of the Bush Administration and
al Qaeda narratives as I have done, we see how, in some respects,
they are mirror images of each other. It is almost as if President
Bush and Osama Bin Laden used the same ghostwriters in constructing their narratives. Each sees the other as intrinsically evil;
each sees the other as guilty of horrific violence against innocent
people. And both the Bush Administration and al Qaeda like to
quote each other in attempts to validate their own narratives.

For example, the narrative created by the Bush Administration clearly asserts that the United States will never negotiate
with al Qaeda. Ironically, they support this position by quoting
from al Qaeda statements indicating they will never negotiate
with the United States. As President Bush says, "It is foolish to
think that you can negotiate with them. . . . This [al Qaeda] charter states that . . . 'We will not meet [the enemy] halfway. There
will be no room for dialogue with them.'"[19] We can see, in this one
example, how each side sets up mutually sustaining narratives
that become self-fulfilling prophecies.

The narratives of war created by the Bush Administration
and al Qaeda are both infused with the language of absolutes.
Neither leaves room for ambiguities or nuance. As Chris Hedges
writes in his book *War Is a Force that Gives Us Meaning*, "When

we allow mythic reality to rule, as it almost always does in war, then there is only one solution—force. In mythic war we fight absolutes. We must vanquish darkness. It is imperative and inevitable for civilization, for the free world, that good triumphs, just as Islamic militants see us as infidels whose existence corrupts the pure Islamic society they hope to build."[20]

And this is the problem for those of us in the United States: the Bush Administration has constructed a 9-11 narrative that has become a trap. It has created a mutually sustaining dynamic in which the two narratives feed off each other. Each is validated by the other. Instead of decreasing the threat of terrorism, the two narratives only perpetuate it. For al Qaeda, this is good news; they are the weaker party in this conflict and the longer they can keep the conflict going, the stronger they become. They don't need to defeat the United States to win; they just need to survive and recruit one generation after another into their mythical struggle against the Western Goliath. And, as we will see later, the Bush Administration's "War on Terror," which is derived from its 9-11 narrative, allows them to do just that.

## Waiting for Terror: Doing the Work of Al Qaeda

While in some respects the two 9-11 narratives mirror each other, there is one big difference: the way the Bush Administration and al Qaeda appeal to their base of support. Al Qaeda often addresses its base of support within the Muslim/Arab community by appealing to the historical wrongs committed against it and by appealing to the ongoing humiliation and oppression these communities suffer at the hands of the West (something the Bush Administration seeks to counter). The Bush Administration often chooses to appeal to the U.S. citizens and its allies in the "War on Terror" by promoting the fear of a possible future al Qaeda attack (something al Qaeda is all too willing to encourage). As Joseba Zulaika and William A. Douglass explain in their book *Terror and Taboo: The Follies, Fables, and Faces of Terrorism*, "The most typical mode of terrorism discourse in the United States has been, indeed, one of waiting for terror. . . . That which captivates every mind is something so meaningless that it may never happen, yet we are forced to compulsively talk about it while awaiting its arrival. . . . Terror consists of waiting in terror."[21]

In Chapter Three I pointed out that in launching terrorist attacks on the United States, al Qaeda sought to plant the seeds of a narrative of terror in the hearts and minds of the U.S. people, but their taking root would depend on whether we watered and nurtured those seeds. By appearing to be everywhere as a global power that can stand toe-to-toe with the United States, al Qaeda attempts to plant a seed of fear in our minds and hearts. Unfortunately, our own government nurtures the growth of this seed with statements by spokespersons like Vice President Cheney who warned us that "Scattered in more than 50 nations, the al Qaeda network and other terrorist groups constitute an enemy unlike any other that we have ever faced. . . . And as our intelligence shows, the terrorists continue plotting to kill on an ever-larger scale, including here in the United States." And, just in case we may not be terrified enough, he reminds us, "They are determined to commit indiscriminate murder against innocent, unsuspecting men, women and children."[22]

Al Qaeda wants to plant a seed of terror in the minds of the people of the United States by showing that it can strike fear into the hearts of the most powerful leaders in the world. So when asked by Katie Couric on the *CBS Evening News* about what scares him, President Bush nurtures this seed of terror by replying:

> Well—my biggest fear is somebody will come in and slip in this country and kill Americans. And I can't tell you how. Obviously there would be the spectacular. That would be the use of some kind of biological weapon or weapon of mass destruction. . . . And—you know, one way to look at it is we have to be right 100 percent of the time in order to protect this country, and they gotta be right once. And it's just a fact of life. We're facing an enemy, Katie, that just doesn't

care about innocent life. I mean, they really are evil people.[23]

To make the case that it poses an existential threat to the United States and to rally its supporters around the world, Al Qaeda takes great risks to produce and distribute audio and video recordings warning of terror attacks against the West and calling for global jihad throughout the world. Far too often these pronouncements become amplified by our own government. As the President once told the U.S. people, "We know what the terrorists intend to do because they've told us—and we need to take their words seriously. So today I'm going to describe—in the terrorists' own words, what they believe . . . what they hope to accomplish, and how they intend to accomplish it. . . . they are stalking us, seeking out our weakness and preparing to pounce in order to crush and destroy us."[24]

Another example of how we unwittingly do the work of Osama bin Laden was a Republican Party ad during the 2006 national elections. It showed images of Osama bin Laden and Ayman al-Zawahiri with a quote claiming that they might have acquired suitcase bombs. The quote is followed by an image of a huge explosion and the sound of a ticking clock. The ad ends with another quote (the same one used by President Johnson against Barry Goldwater in 1964): "These are the stakes." Clearly the Republican Party was trying to score political points against the Democrats by convincing people in the United States that they (the Republicans) could better protect them from al Qaeda. However, al Qaeda itself would be hard-pressed to produce a better propaganda tool to terrorize the U.S. people.

And not only is the Republican Party guilty of promoting the fear of an al Qaeda attack to score political points. For instance, in 2003 Senator Hillary Clinton tried to make a point about deficiencies in U.S. Homeland Security by catering to fear: "The truth is we are not prepared, we are not supporting our first responders, and our approach to securing our nation is haphazard at best. . . . After September 11th, the concept of war was forever changed. The battlefield is now anywhere at anytime, the front-lines are at our front doors." In scoring political points against the Bush Administration regarding chemical plant security, Senator Joseph Biden Jr. promoted fears of horrific proportions: "Many of the nation's largest chemical facilities are located in places where a toxic release could injure or kill tens of thousands of people." And in addressing budget priorities, Senator Robert C. Byrd also raised the specter of fear: "But today, our fight against terrorism has lost its focus. Our homeland security efforts are under funded. The Department of Homeland Security is a bureaucratic catastrophe. The White House has prioritized tax cuts over protecting our airliners and securing our ports."[25]

Since the terrorist attacks of 9-11, the U.S. populace has become the target of psychological terrorism from both al Qaeda and our own government leaders. The overall effect of this tag-team assault on the wellbeing of the people of the United States has been paralyzing to the point that any open debate calling into question the assumptions at the heart of the "War on Terror" is not only next to impossible, but also politically dangerous.

### The Corporate Media: Partners in Creating and Promoting a Narrative of Terror

To aid in promulgating its 9-11 narrative, the Bush Administration has also been able to use the powerful echo chamber of the corporate media. From the beginning, all of the major news outlets were more than willing partners with the Administration in terrorizing the people of the United States by keeping us paranoid about another impending terrorist attack. With people glued to their TV sets in anxious fear, twenty-four-hour news stations saw their ratings go up and commercial dollars roll in. After the attacks of 9-11, the corporate media took four full years to begin to raise serious questions challenging parts of the Bush Administration's narrative. Even now, its main story line continues to go unchallenged by any commercial network.

In addition to the echo chamber created by the media, a whole new industry in the United States has grown incredibly. The counter-terrorism industry, which before 9-11 was small and almost unheard of by the general public, started coming out of the woodwork. Suddenly, terrorism "experts" began appearing on news shows across the country. In describing the dynamic that this set in motion, Zbigniew Brzezinski (former National Security Advisory for the Carter Administration) wrote:

> Such fear-mongering, reinforced by security entrepreneurs, the mass media and the entertainment industry, generates its own momentum. The terror entrepreneurs, usually described as experts on terror, are necessarily engaged in competition to justify their existence. Hence their task is to convince the public that it faces new threats. That puts a premium on the presentation of credible scenarios of ever-more-horrifying acts of violence, sometimes even with blueprints for their implementation.[26]

As Brzezinski also pointed out, the entertainment industry has found ways of making money by terrorizing the U.S. public more effectively than al Qaeda ever could. TV shows like 24 that feature special operation squads and anti-terrorist commandos have become very popular. In response to the Administration's policy of using torture, the organization Human Rights First noted that incidents on TV depicting torture have increased from an average of four scenes a year prior to 9-11 to over 100 a year. In almost every instance where torture is depicted, the torture works. In a panel discussion about torture, Supreme Court Justice Antonin Scalia sought to justify torture by appealing to the fictional character Jack Bauer from the TV show 24, "He saved hundreds of thousands of lives. . . . Are you going to convict Jack Bauer?"[27]

In addition, Hollywood (that supposed bastion of liberalism) has made millions of dollars capitalizing on the fear of a future terrorist attack. Not only does Hollywood produce thrillers about last-minute heroics stopping terrorist attacks, but its movies also tap into an even deeper level of fear: total annihilation. Movies about earth-ending catastrophic threats are also big box office winners. While it is true that theater can provide some healthy cathartic release of built-up tension and fear, it is also fair to ask if our entertainment industry has crossed the line, no longer just providing relief from fear, but acting to increase the level of fear.

## RESPONDING TO THESE NARRATIVES

Just as you might create a story to deal with the fear caused by a car accident on the way home from work, the U.S. government and al Qaeda, the two major players of the 9-11 attacks, have been working hard to create narratives around the attacks. In many ways, these stories are similar: both are couched in the language of an epic moral struggle tied to heroic struggles of the past; both make appeals to wrongs committed by the other who is portrayed as immoral, irrational, and intent on doing harm. Because they mirror each other, they interact in a way that sustains and feeds off the other, creating a perpetual cycle of strikes and counter-strikes. While both appeal to each other's base of support with both threat and treaty, the Bush Administration's narrative (with the cooperation of our corporate media) seems to amplify the psychological effect of al Qaeda's narrative by intensifying the fear and insecurity of the American people. By stepping back and looking at these historical creations, we have taken a first step to moving outside of them and creating an alternative narrative. But it is not enough. Now, to break out of it, we must examine why this narrative of fear has been created.

# CHAPTER FIVE

# Moving Beyond the Politics of Fear to Challenge the al Qaeda Narrative

In the last chapter, we saw how the entertainment industry, the corporate news media, and even terrorism entrepreneurs might benefit from stoking the level of terror in our nation. But the more important question is, why would the Bush Administration engage in the politics of fear? Why would the Bush Administration promote a 9-11 narrative that does the work of al Qaeda by keeping the U.S. people at the edge of terror over the possibility of a future terrorist attack? And most importantly, how can we move beyond the politics of fear in order to meet the challenges of terrorism?

Many of the reasons for promoting a narrative of fear fall under three broad objectives. First, promoting terror serves important strategic foreign and domestic policy goals of this administration. Second, promoting a narrative of fear serves the vested interests of specific sectors of the economy. And third, promoting terror serves as an important tool in strengthening national unity, purpose, and identity. Additionally, in this chapter, we also examine how the "War on Terror" has enhanced the appeal of the al Qaeda narrative in many communities throughout the Arab/Muslim world and what we can do to change this dynamic.

## Sustaining Terror for Strategic Purposes

One reason for keeping the U.S. people terrorized is to compel them to accept an aggressive, expansionist, and unilateralist approach to foreign policy; the threat of terrorism is thus used for strategic political purposes. This manipulation by fear plays out politically in several ways: as a way of implementing a specific doctrine or approach to U.S. foreign policy, as a way of expanding the power of the Executive Branch of the U.S. government, and as a way of overcoming historical and moral objections of the U.S. people to certain policy decisions and directions.

Prior to the terrorist attacks of 9-11 and the election of the Bush-Cheney Administration, a group of foreign policy advocates known as the neoconservatives was waiting to put their theories of global power politics into practice. These neoconservatives (neocons) believe in an assertive U.S. foreign policy with the expressed goal of transplanting U.S. values and democracy throughout the world, using military power when necessary—especially in the Middle East.

During the Reagan Administration, they were skeptical of détente with the Soviet Union. Since then, they have had a general disdain for negotiating with any who might be hostile to U.S. global aims. They also oppose any significant role for the United Nations except as a surrogate of U.S. foreign policy. When the Soviet empire was being dismantled and many in the United States were looking to redirect money invested in the Cold War into the many social issues facing our nation and world, the neocons were calling for maintaining a strong military capable of advancing their vision of the U.S. global agenda. Beginning in 1986, neocon Irving Kristol argued that the United States should establish a foreign policy of "global unilateralism." In 1990, neoconservative columnist Charles Krauthammer called for the United States to establish a "unipolar world" where it would rule as the "unchallenged superpower." So that it could fulfill its destiny, he called on the United States to adopt a foreign policy that "unashamedly

[laid] down the rules of world order and . . . [should be] prepared to enforce them."[1]

The main vehicle for developing and promoting this neoconservative thought and policy was the Project for the New American Century (PNAC), a think tank founded in 1997 by William Kristol and Robert Kagan. Its "Statement of Principles" argued that the United States should assume the role of global leader and be prepared to "challenge regimes hostile to our interests and values." Krauthammer most clearly stated PNAC's philosophy by writing, "America is no mere international citizen. It is the dominant power in the world, more dominant than any since Rome. Accordingly, America is in a position to . . . create new realities . . . by unapologetic and implacable demonstrations of will."[2] No fringe group, PNAC's early members included Elliot Abrams, John Bolton, Richard Perle, James Woolsey, and, most importantly, Dick Cheney, Scooter Libby, Donald Rumsfeld, and Paul Wolfowitz.

PNAC has long focused on areas that are currently major theaters for the "War on Terror." Three months before President Bush took office, the PNAC published a document entitled "Rebuilding America's Defenses" that called for a new military strategy of preserving and extending U.S. global domination. One area of the world that drew PNAC's special attention was the Middle East, and one person in that region was a special focus: Saddam Hussein. In a 1998 letter to President Clinton, members of PNAC (including Perle, Rumsfeld, and Wolfowitz) urged the United States to undertake military action to eliminate "the possibility that Iraq will be able to use or threaten to use weapons of mass destruction." That same year, Kagan and Kristol wrote an op-ed piece for *The New York Times* entitled "Bombing Iraq Isn't Enough," calling for "finishing the task left undone in 1991."[3]

But while these plans and directions had been articulated for many years, the neocons had not been able to implement them. The biggest obstacle for the PNAC in implementing these dreams of transforming the United States into the new Roman Empire was the U.S. citizenry. Most people in the United States could see that Iraq, crippled by years of devastating economic sanctions and constant military air strikes, was no threat to the United States—even though they may have despised Saddam Hussein. In addition, most were not interested in transforming their democracy into a global empire. This did not mean that they were disengaged from the world; they just did not want any part of the grand imperial plans of the PNAC.

The terrorist attacks of 9-11 changed all that. With the creation of the "War on Terror," the Bush Administration and its PNAC members could fulfill their dreams of expanding U.S. global military hegemony, advancing an aggressive, unilateralist foreign policy and reshaping the Middle East—beginning with Iraq. And they did it by terrorizing the U.S. people, keeping them scared enough to overcome any hesitations they might have about exerting U.S. military power throughout the Middle East. Shortly after the 9-11 attacks, in an interview in *The New York Times*, Secretary of Defense Donald Rumsfeld remarked that 9-11 had created "the kind of opportunities that World War II offered, to refashion the world." The White House's "National Security Strategy" of September 2002 stated that "The events of September 11, 2001, fundamentally changed the context for relations between the United States and other main centers for global power, and opened vast new opportunities."[4]

Until the attacks of 9-11, the neocons could not find a way to convince the U.S. people to wage another war against Iraq. As neocon Kenneth Adelman was quoted as saying, "At the beginning of the administration people were talking about Iraq but it wasn't doable . . . That changed with September 11th." As Richard Clarke (former chief counter-terrorism adviser for the Bush Administration) pointed out, the President's PNAC foreign policy advisors wanted to go after Iraq, and they used the tragedy of 9-11 as an excuse to test their theories about reshaping the Middle East.[5]

In addition to the war in Iraq and an opportunity to advance unilateralist foreign policy doctrines, the Bush-Cheney Administration has other reasons to want to keep U.S. citizens in a constant state of terror. As stated before, when a terrorized population feels vulnerable to future terrorist attacks, they will look to a strong and decisive leader who can give them a sense of security. The attacks of 9-11 provided the Bush Administration with a unique opportunity to put into practice its long-held theory of unitary executive power. This theory argues for strict limits on the power of Congress to interfere with the President's power to control the Executive Branch of government. Proponents of the unitary executive argue that the Constitution creates a "hierarchical, unified executive department under the direct control of the president."[6] In a 2002 interview, Vice President Cheney lamented what he referred to as "an erosion of the powers and abilities" of the President to do his job because of "unwise" compromises made over the last thirty-five years.[7] With the creation of a 9-11 narrative designed to keep the country at the edge of terror, the Vice President was now in a position to roll back the reforms of those years in order to create an all-powerful Presidency, one with little or no constraints or checks on its power.

The Bush Administration has interpreted the theory of unitary executive power more expansively than any other administration, and it often uses the fear of a future terrorist attack to fend off critics and win the approval of the U.S. people. For instance, the Administration has argued that the use of military force is not reviewable by Congress or the courts. Normally the U.S. people would not stand for this kind of presidential arrogance. However, if people feel that they may become the victims of a terrorist attack at any moment, they are more willing to give the president such powers.

Since taking office, the Vice President has led efforts by the Administration to increase the power of the presidency. The attacks of 9-11 gave the Administration the opportunity, but they realized early on that to maintain the support of the U.S. people for such an audacious grab of executive power, they would have to keep the U.S. people terrorized. Writing in the *Journal for Crime, Conflict and Media Culture*, Professor David Altheide shows how the Administration justified its grab for power by promulgating the fear of becoming a victim of terrorism:

> Terrorism and especially the attacks of 9-11, enabled political actors to expand the definition of the situation of all Americans as "victims." Moreover, all those fighting to protect actual and potential victims should be permitted to do their work, unimpeded by any concerns about civil liberties or adding context and complexity to the simple analysis that was offered: evil people were attacking good people and evil had to be destroyed.[8]

Fear has also been used to quash any moral objections to this expansion of powers or specific actions. Normally, U.S. citizens would be appalled by the use of torture or the notion of secret prisons. But by keeping people terrorized by the threat of a future attack, even the morally abhorrent becomes justifiable, legalized, and condoned at the highest levels of government. The White House memo justifying torture of terrorism suspects and holding terrorism suspects without access to courts arose from the President's claim of unitary executive powers. For instance, the White House torture memo written by Vice President Cheney's lawyer David Addington says, "In light of the president's complete authority over the conduct of war, without a clear statement otherwise, criminal statutes are not read as infringing on the president's ultimate authority in these areas." The memo also claimed that prohibitions on torture "must be construed as inapplicable to interrogations undertaken pursuant to his commander-in-chief authority. . . . Congress may no more regulate the president's ability to detain and interrogate enemy combatants than it may regulate his ability to direct troop movements on the battlefield."[9]

In the past, fear has been used to convince us to abandon our national values and moral principles. But courageous leadership in times of national crisis should appeal to the best in us, not the worst. General Charles Krulak (who commanded the

Marine Corps from 1995-1999) and General Joseph Hoar (commander-in-chief of the U.S. Central Command from 1991-1994) wrote about the public's fear of another terrorist attack and the failure of leadership at the highest level of government when it condoned torture:

> Fear can be a strong motivator. It led Franklin Roosevelt to intern tens of thousands of innocent U.S. citizens during World War II; it led to Joseph McCarthy's witch hunt, which ruined the lives of hundreds of Americans. And it led the United States to adopt a policy at the highest levels that condoned and even authorized torture of prisoners in our custody. . . . We have served in combat; we understand the reality of fear and the havoc it can wreak if left unchecked or fostered. Fear breeds panic, and it can lead people and nations to act in ways inconsistent with their character. The American people are understandably fearful about another attack like the one we sustained on Sept. 11, 2001. But it is the duty of the commander in chief to lead the country away from the grip of fear, not into its grasp.[10]

## SUSTAINING TERROR
## FOR VESTED ECONOMIC INTERESTS

Fear of terrorism has been used to justify a unilateralist foreign policy in service to the imperial ambitions of the neoconservatives and to increase Executive Branch power. But these political objectives also serve specific economic interests. Keeping U.S. citizens in a state of terror has enabled various sectors of the U.S. economy to reap large profits. Two of these sectors are the oil industry and the military-industrial complex.

The intersection of foreign policy and economic interests has a long history in the United States. This is particularly true of the oil industry. In the George W. Bush Administration this played out at a level never before seen. Shortly after President Bush took office, meeting the growing U.S. demand for oil was never far from his mind. Both President Bush and Vice President Cheney have long and personal relationships with the oil industry. They brought those relationships with them when they took office: eight cabinet secretaries and the national security advisor were directly recruited from the oil industry, along with thirty-two others in the secretaries of Defense, State, Energy, Agriculture, Interior, and the Office of Management and Budget.[11]

These connections have had a great impact on U.S. policy decisions and the "War on Terror," especially the war in Iraq. A short time after coming into office, Vice President Cheney was chosen to chair the National Energy Policy Development Group, also known as the Energy Task Force. In spite of repeated efforts by Congress and others to find out about the membership and purpose of this task force, very little is known. We do know that the task force included government agencies and energy industry executives and lobbyists. Speculating on the work of the task force, Richard Behan, professor of natural resource policy at the University of Montana, noted:

> One brute fact had to be apparent to the Task Force: in the Caspian Basin and beneath the Iraqi deserts there are 125 billion barrels of proven oil reserves and the potential for 433 billion barrels more. Anyone controlling that much oil could break OPEC's stranglehold overnight. By early March, 2001, the Task Force was poring over maps of the Iraqi oilfields, pipelines, tanker terminals, and oil exploration blocks.[12]

(The group Judicial Watch forced these documents into public view several years ago under the Freedom of Information Act.[13]) Almost a full year before the Bush Administration's "War on Terror" established a new front by invading Iraq, the State Department produced a policy-development initiative called "The Future of Iraq Project" whose final report stated that Iraq "should be opened to international oil companies as quickly as possible after the war."[14]

By keeping the U.S. people in a state of terror about future attacks and conjuring images of mushroom clouds over U.S. cities, the Administration overcame the objections of the U.S. people and launched a war of aggression against Iraq. By manipulating evidence, cherry-picking intelligence, and attacking anyone who offered alternative interpretations of the evidence (ones that were contrary to its own narrative), the Administration sought to accomplish two long-time goals of the oil industry: breaking the stranglehold of OPEC on oil supplies and getting access to the huge reserves of oil in Iraq. (Even though the Administration's war of aggression against Iraq has bogged down in a costly quagmire for the U.S. taxpayers, the resulting chaos in Middle East oil markets and the growing demand for oil in countries such as China and India have nonetheless produced huge windfall profits for the U.S. oil industry.)

This manipulation of evidence was not limited to a few isolated instances, but was part of a concerted, coordinated campaign of deceit. A year after the war in Iraq began, the Minority Staff of the Special Investigations Division of the House Committee on Government Reform prepared a detailed account of the selective use of intelligence and the manipulation of facts by the Bush Administration. That report concluded:

These five officials [President Bush, Vice President Cheney, Secretary Rumsfeld, Secretary Powell, and National Security Advisor Rice] repeatedly made misleading statements about the threat posed by Iraq. In 125 separate appearances, they made 11 misleading statements about the urgency of Iraq's threat, 81 misleading statements about Iraq's nuclear activities, 84 misleading statements about Iraq's chemical and

biological capabilities, and 61 misleading statements
about Iraq's relationship with al Qaeda.[15]

The campaign of lies and deceptions manufactured by the
Bush Administration was critical in achieving the economic objectives of the oil interests in the United States. The Administration knew that U.S. citizens would never send their sons and
daughters into harm's way in order to control the flow of oil from
the Middle East. So instead, they played upon our fears by claiming that if we did not go to war in Iraq, the terrorists would come
here and kill us. When the 9-11 narrative of fear was evoked to
rally the U.S. people to support a war of aggression against Iraq,
many of our young idealistic sons and daughters gladly offered
to make the sacrifice. By convincing the U.S. citizenry that the
leader of Iraq was involved with the terrorist attacks against us
(even though no Iraqis were among the hijackers), a war of aggression can be justified as an act of retaliation. Our soldiers so
strongly believed the power of the Bush Administration's narrative about Saddam Hussein's involvement in the terrorist attacks
of 9-11 that even after the President had to publicly admit that it
was not true, a recent poll found that 85 percent of soldiers still
believe we invaded Iraq mainly "to retaliate for Saddam's role in
the 9-11 attacks."[16]

The oil industry is not the only sector of the economy that has
profited by keeping U.S. citizens in a state of terror. The power of
the military industry in our political system is legendary. Using
its political influence to convince our nation of foreign threats
fueled high military spending throughout the Cold War.

President Eisenhower presided over this country when the
Cold War was in its early stages. But, unlike President Bush,
Eisenhower sought to be candid with the people about the challenges we faced, while setting a tone of calm determination and
prudent, measured responses. He warned at that time, "Crises
there will continue to be. In meeting them, whether foreign or
domestic, great or small, there is a recurring temptation to feel
that some spectacular and costly action could become the mi-

raculous solution to all current difficulties."[17]

Eisenhower knew that the threats of the time needed to be faced, but he also warned about the unwarranted influence of the military-industrial complex. As he said:

> This conjunction of an immense military establish-ment and a large arms industry is new in the Ameri-can experience. The total influence—economic, po-litical, and even spiritual—is felt in every city, every state house, and every office of the Federal govern-ment. . . . In the councils of government, we must guard against the acquisition of unwarranted influ-ence, whether sought or unsought, by the military-industrial complex. The potential for the disastrous rise of misplaced power exists and will persist.[18]

Unfortunately, Eisenhower's warnings have long been for-gotten, and for those in the military industry, the "War on Ter-ror" comes as a god-send. Not since the Cold War has this sector of the economy seen its future grow so brightly. Because the "War on Terror" is, by its very definition, perpetual war, it provides a never-ending rationale for continued increases in military spend-ing. As long as a weapon-system can be connected in some way to the fight against terror, it can find support in Congress. And if people are kept in a state of terror, they will raise few questions or offer little opposition to this spending. And by keeping U.S. military members in the field for years on end, politicians don't dare question military funding for fear of being accused of not supporting the troops.

While war profiteering has been part of every war in history, the level of profiteering in Iraq, the central front in this "War on Terror," is unique in its scope and audacity. Among the most egre-gious profiteers is Halliburton, the company formerly headed by Vice President Cheney. As Representative Henry Waxman stated in his fact sheet on Halliburton at the end of 2004, the value of Halliburton's Iraq contracts had crossed the $10 billion threshold;

government auditors had issued at least nine reports criticizing Halliburton's Iraq work; and there were multiple criminal investigations into overcharging and kickbacks involving Halliburton's contracts.[19] Waxman pointed out that one audit found that Halliburton had overcharged the Defense Department by $61 million to import gasoline into Iraq from Kuwait.

Testifying before Congress, documentary filmmaker Robert Greenwald relayed personal stories from soldiers and Halliburton employees in Iraq regarding the company's practices and their wastefulness and unnecessary charges. While making his film, Greenwald met Shane Ratliff, a truck driver from Ruby, South Carolina. Greenwald testified, "When Shane started telling me that empty trucks were being driven across dangerous stretches of desert, I assumed he was mistaken. Why would they do that? Then he explained that Halliburton got paid for the number of trips they took, regardless of whether they were carrying anything."

In another example, Greenwald related his conversations with another Halliburton worker, James Logsdon, about burn pits in Iraq:

> Burn pits are large dumps near military stations where they would burn equipment, trucks, trash, etc. If they ordered the wrong item, they'd throw it in the burn pit. If a tire blew on a piece of equipment, they'd throw the whole thing into the burn pit. The burn pits had so much equipment; they even gave them a nickname—Home Depot. . . . I naively asked, how big are they . . . He laughed, and referred to one that he had seen that was 15 football fields large, and burned around the clock! It infuriated him to have to burn stuff rather then give it to the Iraqis or to the military. Yet Halliburton was being rewarded each time they billed the government for a new truck or new piece of equipment. With a cost-plus contract, the contractors receive a percentage of the money they spend.

As Greenwald told the House Subcommittee, "Cost-plus and no-bid contracts are hopelessly undermining our efforts and costing the taxpayers billions. They do not operate within a free-market system and have no competition, but instead create a Stalinist system of rewarding cronies."²⁰ Why would Congress approve no-bid, cost-plus contracts to corporate war profiteers like Halliburton that are tailor-made to encourage looting the U.S. Treasury? The Administration and Halliburton lobbyists and friends in Congress have worked hard to make the case that because our very survival is at stake in the "War on Terror," no cost is too great and no time can be wasted on debating the merit of decisive action. The powerful 9-11 narrative created by the Bush Administration puts every decision related to the "War on Terror" in stark terms and dire consequences. Questioning the means or wisdom of the supreme effort is not just unpatriotic; it is heretical. As a result, the checks and balances created by our nation's founders have not been exercised by Congress or the Courts.

While companies like Halliburton have garnered plenty of headlines, other lesser-known companies have also reaped huge financial gains as a result of the "War on Terror." One of the most influential firms that has made huge profits is the Washington-based private equity firm, The Carlyle Group. President Bush's father works for Carlyle; so do former Reagan Defense Secretary Frank Carlucci and former Secretary of State James Baker III. Its star-studded management roster also includes former Joint Chiefs of Staff General John Shalikashvili and former British Prime Minister John Major. The group has $12.5 billion in investments and showed a return of more than 34 percent over the last ten years.

Mark Fineman reported in 2002 that in a single day, Carlyle earned $237 million selling shares in United Defense Industries, the Army's fifth-largest contractor. The decision to take the company public occurred only after the attacks of 9-11, when Congress had vastly increased support for defense spending.²¹ United Defense Industries benefited because of its cornerstone system: the Crusader Advanced Field Artillery System, a huge, high-tech, high-speed cannon originally priced at $20 billion. Because it did not fit the vision of military planners, its future was in serious trouble. But the terrorist attacks of 9-11 changed that. With tens of billions of dollars in new defense spending, United Defense modified the Crusader, making it lighter and more appealing to the Army. On September 26, 2002, the Army signed a $665 million modified contract with United Defense to complete the Crusader's development phase through April 2003.

Carlyle's lobbyists and promoters in Washington argued that the new artillery system was essential to prosecuting the "War on Terror" and that spending $665 million in 2002-2003 to develop this new system was in the nation's best interests. But at the same time that Carlyle's lobbyists and promoters were toasting their victory on Capital Hill in the name of the "War on Terror," U.S. soldiers were being sent into Iraq, with what turned out to be inadequate protection or supplies. In his testimony to Congress, Greenwald quoted Sgt. Phillip Slocum, "In previous experiences I went off to war with extra everything, and then some. This time however, Uncle Sam sent me off with one pair of desert boots, two uniforms, and body armor that didn't fit."[22] The powerful 9-11 narrative of fear created by the Bush Administration made it easy for vested special interests like Carlyle to redirect millions of dollars to developing previously unwanted weapon systems— even to the detriment of the real needs of U.S. soldiers placed in harm's way.

And the money train flows on. For Fiscal Year 2008, the Bush Administration asked Congress to approve a defense budget of $481 billion, an historic high, even when adjusted for inflation. Furthermore, the President asked for an additional $165 billion for the wars in Afghanistan and Iraq. This brings the grand total for defense spending to $646 billion. However, heads of the military services are already in line to make the case to Congress that it needs more. As Peter Spiegel of the *Los Angeles Times* points out, with this request for the wars in Iraq and Afghanistan, the cost of these wars will bring war spending above the total cost of the war in Vietnam.[23] Much of this spending will end up in the pockets of military industries and their lobbyists.

Chances are that most members of Congress will not challenge or review most of the proposed spending. Nor will it be challenged too much by the public. When the people are kept in a state of terror, they will do (or agree to) anything to stay safe. And so industries (like the oil and military companies) will be further enriched.

The 9-11 narrative of fear that gave birth to the "War on Terror" has the power to radically alter our national spending priorities. And because the "War on Terror" is designed to tap into our deepest fears without providing any practical means of re-establishing our pre-9-11 sense of security, we can be manipulated into spending hundreds of billions pursuing an illusion. While this might benefit the bottom line of some sectors of the economy, it has a devastating effect on the ability of our nation to address its real needs. Commenting on this dynamic, social activist and religious leader Reverend Jim Wallis wrote:

> September 11th shattered the American sense of invulnerability. But instead of accepting the vulnerability that most of the rest of the world already lives with, and even learning from it, we seem to want something nobody can give us—to erase vulnerability. We want it to just go away. If the government says wars can do that, many people will say fine. If they say suspending civil liberties can do that, many will say fine. If they claim spending more and more of our tax dollars on the military and homeland security—at the expense of everything else—many will say fine.[24]

---

## SUSTAINING TERROR FOR NATIONAL PURPOSE

While the 9-11 narrative enabled the Bush Administration to achieve some political and foreign policy objectives and served the interests of various sectors of the economy, the "War on Terror" also provided a way to create a renewed sense of national unity. This was done by tying the 9-11 narrative to other wars in our nation's history and by appealing to the concept of victimhood.

President Bush consciously used the metaphor of war as the central dynamic of his narrative story line. The Administration often tells us that the attacks of 9-11 constitute our generation's Pearl Harbor; making this kind of historical connection links the narrative of 9-11 to the larger national narrative. Framing his 9-11 narrative in the language of war helped the President to unite the nation and to give it a sense of higher purpose in responding to the terrorist threat.

The language of war (especially when coupled with historical ties) is a powerful force for national unity and purpose. For a nation rocked back on its heels after the 9-11 attacks, confused and stunned by what had happened, the call to war provided clarity and focus. As Hedges makes clear in *War Is a Force That Gives Us Meaning*:

> War makes the world understandable, a black and white tableau of them and us. It suspends thought, especially self-critical thought. All bow before the supreme effort. We are one. Most of us willingly accept war as long as we can fold it into a belief system that paints the ensuing suffering as necessary for a higher good, for human beings seek not only happiness but also meaning. And tragically war is sometimes the most powerful way in society to achieve meaning.[25]

In creating a war narrative, one important element is the concept of "first victims." The undeserved suffering of the first victims provides the rationale and sanctification for all the maiming, killing, and destruction that follows; they become the unifying cause for war. Elias Canetti, the 1981 winner of the Nobel Prize in Literature, wrote about crowd behavior as it relates to mob violence and other human behavior. Hedges quotes Canetti about the importance of the first victim in war:

It is the first death which infects everyone with the feeling of being threatened. It is impossible to over-rate the part played by the first dead man in the kindling of war. Rulers who want to unleash war know very well that they must procure or invent a first victim. It need not be anyone of particular importance, and can even be someone quite unknown. Nothing matters except his death; and it must be believed that the enemy is responsible for this.[26]

The narrative of terror created by the Bush Administration links us with the first victims (in this case, those who died on 9/11) by reminding us that we too could become victims. In this way, we share an intimate bond, even though most of us do not know any of them. In some small way we share in the same terror as those who died on 9-11 because, as the President constantly tells us, we could be the next victim. As in the past when our nation was united behind slogans like "Remember the Alamo!" and "Remember Pearl Harbor!" now we are rallied by the call "Remember 9-11!"

The sacred memory of these first victims is tied inextricably to the Bush "War on Terror" narrative. They can never be separated from it, and those that try to do so are targeted. As Hedges explains, "The cause, sanctified by the dead, cannot be questioned without dishonoring those who gave up their lives. We become enmeshed in the imposed language. When any contradiction is raised or there is a sense that the cause is not just in an absolute sense, the doubts are attacked as apostasy."[27]

When some of the families of those who died in the terrorist attacks of 9-11 raised serious questions about the Bush Administration's "War on Terror," even they were dismissed by most and discredited and vilified by others. In one instance, conservative columnist Ann Coulter attacked a group of New Jersey widows whose husbands perished in the World Trade Center because they dissented from the Bush narrative. Calling them "self-obsessed women," Coulter claimed these women were only trying to get lawsuit money and media attention. She went on to write, "I've never seen people enjoying their husbands' deaths so much."[28] Dissent thus becomes impossible or very difficult, because the dissenter is framed out of the narrative that unites the nation.

The Bush Administration created a sense of national unity built upon the fear that we are all potential victims (like the first victims) because of the possibility of a future terrorist attack. And by tying the memory of the victims of 9-11 to his "War on Terror" narrative, President Bush created a sense of national purpose. But the problem is that the President's "War on Terror" (like all wars) reduces the world to an oversimplified cut-and-dried morality, limits us to either/or thinking, and stunts our creativity by marginalizing alternative points of view. War produces unity, but it is the unity of totalitarianism. It is only a small step from calling for national unity to demanding blind, unquestioned obedience. When people who are kept in a state of terror become convinced that war will keep them safe, they are more willing to suspend good judgment and give their leaders the benefit of the doubt. And when fear overrules good judgment, a nation can easily become trapped in a cycle of revenge and reprisal against an enemy that, over time, becomes less a reflection of reality and more a projection of its own phobias.

---

## THE U.S. ROLE IN STRENGTHENING THE APPEAL OF THE AL QAEDA NARRATIVE

The U.S. 9-11 narrative furthers the political and economic interests of those in power and creates a national unity and purpose for the citizenry. Understanding these interests and purposes can help us to create another 9-11 narrative (which we will look at in the next chapter). We also saw in the last chapter how the U.S. narrative and the al Qaeda narrative are similar and sustain each other. To understand how to break out of this trap of mutually sustaining 9-11 narratives that perpetuates a cycle of revenge and retaliation, we need to better understand the dynamics that drive the al Qaeda narrative. And we need to look at how the United States plays into this dynamic, as well as its real-world effect.

Like the Bush Administration's narrative, the narrative created by al Qaeda seeks legitimacy by rooting itself in a larger historical account that has strong appeal in many communities in the Arab/Muslim world. We need to understand this appeal if we are to counter it. Some of the best work in understanding how our actions can strengthen or weaken the appeal of al Qaeda's narrative is being done by John Paul Lederach, who teaches International Conflict Resolution at the Kroc Peace Institute at Notre Dame University. Lederach believes the most important question is: how do people reach such a level of anger, hatred, and frustration? Anger of this sort (generational, identity-based anger) is constructed over time through a combination of historical events, a deep sense of threat to identity, and direct experiences of sustained marginalization or oppression. In other words, this anger is the product of a story that has been constructed over a long period of time within many Muslim/Arab communities. And the reason that al Qaeda's 9-11 narrative is so persuasive in this community is because it fits into this larger, long-term narrative.

This is very important for us to understand because our response to the ongoing threat of terrorism has everything to do with whether we continue adding new chapters to this old narrative, resulting in future cycles of revenge and violence, or we act in ways that radically change the story line. We need to act outside of the expectations their story creates about us. Lederach points out:

> We should be careful to heed one and only one strategic plan: Don't do what the terrorists expect. What they expect is the lashing out of the giant against the weak, the many against the few. Whether our military actions reinforce the anger can be judged only from the responses of the people so many call our enemies, and then only in the context of our overall response

over time. But unless we are careful we will end up reinforcing the myth they carefully seek to sustain: that they are under threat, fighting an irrational and mad system that has never taken them seriously and wishes to destroy them and their people.[29]

Thus, in the long run, dismantling the validity of the al Qaeda narrative in those Muslim/Arab communities that have embraced it is more important than killing terrorists. New leaders and recruits can always be found, but once their narrative has been discredited among their base of support and disconnected from a long history of struggle, they are finished.

Unfortunately, the Bush Administration has, so far, played directly into the hands of Osama bin Laden and al Qaeda. From the beginning, the Administration was determined to transform what was a crime against humanity committed on 9-11 into a global conflict that would determine the fate of the world. David Kilcullen, an Australian army counter-insurgency officer and senior advisor on counter-terrorism for the U.S. State Department stated it this way: "It is not the people al Qaeda might kill that is the threat. Our reaction is what can cause the damage. It's always al Qaeda plus our response that creates the existential danger."[30] Our response had the effect of transforming a group of criminals on the fringe of Islam into a power equal in stature to the entire Western world.

Bin Laden's strategy has been to bait the United States into over-reacting. Saudi exile and political reformer Saad al-Faquih explains how easy it has been: "The American mentality is a cowboy mentality—if you confront them . . . they will react in an extreme manner. In other words, America with all its resources and establishments will shrink to a cowboy when irritated successfully. They will elevate you, and this will satisfy the Muslim longing for a leader who can successfully challenge the West."[31]

The response and over-reaction arising out of the Bush Administration's 9-11 narrative has also conferred upon al Qaeda a legitimacy it had long sought. By raising up the specter of al Qaeda as an existential threat to the West, the President also raises the stature of Osama bin Laden in the Muslim/Arab world. To many, bin Laden has come to symbolize resistance to the destruction of Arab culture and Muslim values and faith. In many Arab/Muslim communities he has been able to hijack the dominant historical account of Arab resistance to Western domination. Even though the vast majority of Arabs and Muslims around the world condemned the criminal actions of al Qaeda, they identify with this compelling struggle. Al Qaeda becomes the heroic "David" battling the foreign "Goliath."

The Bush Administration launching a preemptive attack on Iraq provided further confirmation to the Muslim/Arab world that bin Laden's narrative was valid. In addition, the Bush Administration's foreign policy of abandoning any semblance of evenhandedness in the Palestinian/Israeli conflict, along with the detention and torture of Muslim captives in its "War on Terror," has made even moderate Arabs and Muslims give bin Laden's 9-11 narrative a serious hearing.[32] And the Administration's domestic policy of deporting as many Arab and South Asian immigrants as possible, and criminalizing any Muslim in the United States who practices charity toward the victims of Israeli/U.S. policies in the Middle East, has turned bin Laden and his lieutenant al-Zawahiri into prophetic defenders of Islam.

Yet the continued power of al Qaeda's narrative depends on al Qaeda's most important asset: the ongoing goodwill and support of the Muslim/Arab world. Al Qaeda does not operate in a vacuum; it needs communities where it can take refuge. These communities don't need to be directly involved in acts of terrorism nor even support terrorism. They just need to be alienated and disenfranchised enough from their own political leaders and/or angry enough at U.S. foreign policy to turn a blind eye to what may be going on in their own neighborhoods.

A successful strategy of discrediting the al Qaeda narrative would address the larger Muslim/Arab account in a way that takes seriously its legitimate grievances with the West. As David Clark (a former Labor Party government advisor in the United

Kingdom) points out, "We must start by acknowledging that their long history of engagement with the west is one that has left many Arabs feeling humiliated and used."[33]

The way the Bush Administration framed its response to the 9-11 terrorist attacks may have served some of its political and economic interests, but it also set into motion a series of foreign policy actions (especially the war in Iraq) that has inadvertently strengthened the appeal of the al Qaeda narrative. The overall result of these actions has been to increase the number of terrorist attacks since 9-11.[34]

Yet some claim that because we have not experienced a terrorist attack on U.S. soil since 9-11, our "War on Terror" has been successful. If this is true, if our measure of "success" is the safety of our own people, what does that say to our allies around the world? Is this global war only about protecting the U.S. homeland? How long do we think the rest of the world is going to be willing to sacrifice themselves for our safety? If the "War on Terror" is only about making the United States safe from terrorism, then our 9-11 narrative will lose its appeal around the world. We will find ourselves alone in this struggle.

Some claim that we are fighting terrorists in Iraq so as to not have to fight them here at home. But by what metaphysical process are the tens of thousands of our fellow citizen soldiers killed and wounded in Iraq not part of our homeland? Each soldier killed or wounded in Iraq breaks a heart in the United States. The bullets might be fired in Baghdad, but the wounds are inflicted in Boise, Baltimore, and Birmingham. While civilians in the United States stay safe, military families suffer the toll.

And while it is true that because, as President Bush likes to say, Iraq is the "front line" in the "War on Terror," we civilians in the United States are at lower risk of becoming collateral damage, hundreds of thousands of Iraqi people have been unwillingly drafted into the role of innocent victims in this war. In her book, *Baghdad Burning II: More Girl Blog from Iraq,* a 26-year old Iraqi blogger going by the pseudonym Riverbend offers a litany of grief over what has been happening to her homeland since the start of the war. Reflecting on the statement made by U.S. General John Vines, "We either deal with terrorism and this extremism abroad or we deal with it when it comes to us," Riverbend writes, "Don't Americans realize that 'abroad' is a country full of people—men, women and children who are dying hourly? 'Abroad' is home for millions of us. It's the place we hope to raise our children—your field of war and terror. The war was brought to us here, and now we have to watch the country disintegrate before our very eyes."[35] While such horrors may not fit into the U.S. story, they certainly fit into the narrative of groups such as al Qaeda.

And what is the net result of this "front line" strategy? According to a 2006 National Intelligence Estimate prepared by all U.S. intelligence agencies, the war in Iraq has helped to fuel Islamic radicalism around the world. Titled "Trends in Global Terrorism: Implications for the United States," the report says that the Iraq war has made the overall terrorism problem worse.[36] Part of the reason is that al Qaeda's narrative grows stronger by the day. Every time the United States acts in ways that validate al Qaeda's worldview, new recruits become available and more Muslim/Arab communities become safe havens for them to grow.

## UNDERSTANDING THE NATURE OF THE CONFLICT AND DOING THE UNEXPECTED

In the next chapter of this book, we will delve into creating an alternative 9-11 narrative as a way of addressing the challenge of terrorism. But before we can do that, we need to understand the true nature of this conflict. It is not a contest between competing armies, nor will it be determined by whomever has the greater firepower. Primarily, this clash is between two competing narratives. As long as our actions continue to legitimize and validate al Qaeda's narrative, we will never be able to break out of this cycle of violence. As Lederach points out:

The way to break such a process is not through a frame of reference of who will win or who is stronger. In fact the inverse is true. Whoever loses, whether tactical battles or the "war" itself, finds intrinsic in the loss the seeds that give birth to the justification for renewed battle. The way to break such a cycle of justified violence is to step outside of it. The most significant impact that we could make on their ability to sustain their view of us as evil is to change their perception of who we are by choosing to strategically respond in unexpected ways. . . . Military action to destroy terror, particularly as it affects vulnerable civilian populations will be like hitting a fully mature dandelion with a golf club. We will participate in making sure the myth of why we are evil is sustained and we will assure yet another generation of recruits.[37]

As we are discovering through a painful and costly experience in Iraq and Afghanistan, military power is not the best way to combat the threat of terrorism. The problem is that armies are built around the conquest of real estate. Military power is about taking and holding ground. It is best suited to fighting other armies, and it measures success in terms of battles won and territories conquered. Yet in the struggle to end terrorism, none of these is of much value.

President Bush wants to stop terrorism by waging a war, but terrorists are not interested in conquering our military. They do not have armies that wear uniforms. They prefer to infiltrate countries, not conquer their lands. Terrorists measure success not in terms of winning battles, but in terms of provoking their enemies into acting in ways that confirm their worldview and aid in the recruitment of followers.

On an action level, the best way to deal with these organized criminal enterprises is with good police and intelligence work. Unfortunately, since 2001 the Administration has allocated huge amounts of money to the Defense Department for the "War on

Terror" while only allocating a fraction of that amount for the kind of police work necessary to find and stop terrorist cells. Terrorism can never be totally eliminated, just as murder, robbery, and other crimes cannot be completely eliminated. But good international law enforcement and intelligence gathering can keep terrorism in check in the same way that they have kept other organized crime syndicates in check.

There is, however, a distinct difference between good police work and acting like a police state. The needless and counter-productive governmental assault on Arab and South Asian immigrants in this country in the wake of the terrorist attacks of 9-11 has been one of the largest blunders in the "War on Terror." Instead of using proper police investigative procedures, the Bush Administration decided to round up thousands of Muslim immigrants, hold them without due process or legal protections, and deport thousands for minor immigration irregularities or infractions. This had the effect of driving a wedge of distrust and fear between these communities and the U.S. government. Instead of seeing Arab and South Asian immigrant communities as assets in the efforts to end terrorism, the Administration treated them as potential enemy combatants. It is hard to calculate the magnitude of this reckless and counter-productive strategy.

These actions have also been compounded by a lack of any real attempts to understand Arab/Muslim cultures—or languages. The Iraq Study Group found that only six of the nearly 1,000 people employed at the U.S. embassy in Iraq spoke the local language. Our FBI and CIA lack enough Arabic speakers to translate important intercepts between suspected terrorists. And even more distressing, al Qaeda has used our policies of intimidation and oppression against Muslims in the United States as proof that we are waging a war against Islam—further validating their narrative.

In almost every successful instance of stopping al Qaeda or al Qaeda-inspired terrorist attacks or uncovering their terrorist cell groups around the world, members of the local Muslim community have played a crucial role. It is safe to say that if it were not for the cooperation of members of the Muslim community, most of the foiled terrorist plots associated with al Qaeda in this country and around the world would not have been intercepted. In spite of this, our government is still determined to wage an unrelenting campaign of intimidation and harassment against our Muslim neighbors.

Rather than isolating people or pitting groups against each other, tactics of inclusion could have created a very different type of security. As former National Security Advisor Zbigniew Brzezinski lamented:

> The events of 9-11 could have resulted in a truly global solidarity against extremism and terrorism. A global alliance of moderates, including Muslim ones, engaged in a deliberate campaign both to extricate the specific terrorist networks and to terminate the political conflicts that spawn terrorism would have been more productive than a demagogically proclaimed and largely solitary U.S. "war on terror" against "Islamo-fascism." Only a confident, determined and reasonable America can promote genuine international security which then leaves no political space for terrorism.[38]

How differently might things have turned out, if, instead of seeing our Muslim neighbors as a threat, our government saw them as allies in the struggle to end terrorism. Imagine the world-wide impact if, after learning of the 9-11 terrorists' identities, President Bush would have publicly convened Muslim leaders from across the United States at the White House to jointly craft a response to the terrorist threat. What if our government presented to the world a response to al Qaeda's attack that included members of all religions and cultures, especially Muslims?

What if, in response to the attacks of 9-11, the President and Congress established legislation to create a privately funded United States Center for Islamic Studies that would invite Muslim scholars from across the United States and from around the world to study and discuss different interpretations of Islam? Let the theologians and propagandists from al Qaeda and the Taliban come and debate their vision of Islam with Muslim leaders from around the world. If, as President Bush says, this is a struggle of ideas, then let us bring these dark forces into the light to see if their ideas can withstand the scrutiny of open debate.

What if legislation creating a Center for Islamic Studies had the further mandate of educating U.S. citizens about the Islamic faith and its many cultural expressions? It could provide speakers and resources to schools and congregations around the country to teach about Muslim beliefs and practices. It could host and foster interreligious dialogues and develop crisis response teams that would be available locally to deal with conflicts or misunderstandings between Muslim communities and other groups.

Imagine what a difference it would have made if the United States could have harnessed the energy, creativity, and expertise of its U.S. Muslim neighbors to serve as U.S. ambassadors of goodwill to Muslim communities around the world. They could tell the story of how Islam and Western culture can coexist. They could give personal testimony about how most people in the United States are open to Muslims, and they could make the case that al Qaeda and other fanatic fringe terrorist groups do not represent the best of Islam. I know Muslim neighbors who might even have been willing to risk their lives in pursuit of this kind of agenda.

Imagine how different things might be if, in addition to everything listed above, Muslims were asked to work hand-in-hand with local and state governments to address social, economic, and cultural issues within Muslim communities and to help identify any potential threats. What if, instead of deporting as many people as possible for immigration infractions, the government offered them a path to citizenship that included serving as a resource in the struggle to end terrorism? What if, instead of imprisoning them for trying to fulfill their religious duty to provide charity to fellow Muslims around the world, we worked with them to ensure that monies donated are used for the intended charitable purposes?

These are just a few examples of doing the unexpected in the struggle to end terrorism and of attempting to address the actual nature of the conflict. Each of these steps carries risk, but no more so than all of the risks taken thus far in the President's "War on Terror." The biggest difference is that each of the steps above has the potential of striking a decisive blow against al Qaeda and the terrorists in the arena that matters most to them—the appeal of their narrative. Osama bin Laden would have a much more difficult time framing this struggle as the Christian West against the Muslim world. In the end, I believe the appeal of al Qaeda's narrative would lose its power.

It is hard to say whether it might be too late to employ this drastically different set of policies and strategies. So much damage has already been done. However, I think it is still worth a try. Most Muslims still harbor an enormous amount of love and respect for this country—in spite of being treated so badly.

Of course, these changes alone are not enough to turn the tide in the struggle to end terrorism. In addition to developing a strategy to discredit and invalidate al Qaeda's 9-11 narrative, we need to articulate a new U.S. 9-11 narrative that has the power to not only unite our own base of support in this country and around the world, but has the power to attract Muslim/Arab communities around the world away from al Qaeda.

# CHAPTER SIX

# Principles at the Foundation
# of an Alternative 9-11 Narrative

What would be the basis for a counter-terrorism strategy that was not held hostage to fear? What kind of 9-11 narrative would give us the moral grounding, sense of purpose, and courage of conviction to enable us to decrease the threat of every form of terrorism in the world? For a new U.S. 9-11 narrative to have the power to unite our nation and allies, it must be grounded in our most treasured values and principles. For this new story to appeal to members of the Muslim/Arab world on which al Qaeda and its narrative depend, it must be based on those values and principles that make our nation great, not those that make us feared. If we can do this, we will have a better chance of directly challenging the validity of the al Qaeda narrative.

Because of its vast and overwhelming military and economic power, the United States must do everything it can to maintain the moral high ground in this struggle over competing narratives. But maintaining the moral high ground is not the same as claiming the moral high ground. As a superpower, we have the capability to impose our will on others, but that does not confer upon us any moral superiority. Might does not make right. Any appeals based on moral authority will prove empty and counterproductive if not backed up by concrete actions that demonstrate that we know the difference between might and right. As long as we continue to act in ways that confirm al Qaeda's narrative of its mythical epic struggle against the evil West, we will lose, no matter how many terrorists we kill and no matter how many terrorist plots we foil. Sir Richard Dearlove of Britain's secret intelligence agency MI-6 talks about the importance of maintaining the high moral ground in the struggle against terrorism:

> The United States is so powerful militarily that by its very nature it represents a threat to every other nation on earth. The only country that could theoretically destroy every single other country is the United States. The only way we can say that the U.S. is not a threat is by looking at intent, and that depends on moral authority. If you're not sure that the United States is going to do the right thing, you can't trust it with that power, so you begin thinking, how can I balance it off and find other alliances to protect myself?[1]

A number of important moral principles—representing the best of our U.S. tradition—are crucial to any 9-11 narrative capable of uniting our country, rallying our allies, and appealing to those communities that terrorist groups depend upon. Our revolutionary forebearers made the principle of equality under the law the linchpin of their drive for independence from the British Crown. Although we still fall short in living out this principle, the ideal we struggle to attain is foundational to our national character. Democratic self-determination is a principle often associated with the United States, but too often it is trivialized to the point of losing any real meaning. This principle is crucial to an alternative 9-11 narrative precisely because it needs to be rehabilitated and rescued from those who have debased it for geopolitical and economic gain. While the principle of the common good has always been part of our national tradition, it has lately fallen victim to an excessive emphasis on individualism. Yet the common good is not only crucial in our efforts to address the root causes of terrorism, it is essential to reviving our nation's social and political lives. Finally, the civic principle of tolerance and the value of diversity are the glue that hold our pluralistic nation together. If we hope to build a truly global community of peace with justice, we will need to make this principle and value an important part of our alternative narrative.

## EQUALITY UNDER THE LAW

Equality under the law is based upon the convictions that every person should be subject to the same laws and regulations and that no indidivual or class of individuals should have special legal privileges. To be credible in our relationships with the rest of the world, this principle is especially important to uphold. The United States is at its best when we champion this principle in all of our international relations.

This was especially true at the end of World War II when the United States, along with its allies, recognized the need to establish a regime of international law that would be binding upon all nations and all national leaders. Many of those laws grew out of the experience of the trials against Nazi and Japanese leaders for crimes against humanity. Justice Robert Jackson, Chief Counsel for the United States at the Nuremberg Trials, spoke prophetically at the sentencing of Nazi war criminals:

> If certain acts of violation of treaties are crimes, they are crimes whether the United States does them or whether Germany does them, and we are not prepared to lay down a rule of criminal conduct against others which we would not be willing to have invoked against us. . . . We must never forget that the record on which we judge these defendants is the record on which history will judge us tomorrow. To pass these defendants a poisoned chalice is to put it to our own lips as well.[2]

Today, we can see the importance of his words and their application to the "War on Terror." Without a strong commitment to apply the principle of equality under the law in all of our efforts to combat terrorism, we risk being viewed as hypocritical and our conduct interpreted as evidence of a double standard. This will, in turn, further legitimate the al Qaeda narrative and further diminish our own standing in the world.

Eighty-eight year old Henry King, a Nuremburg prosecutor who now teaches law at Case Western Reserve University in Ohio, spoke about the Bush Administration's contempt for the principle of equality under the law in the way it has treated detainees in legal proceedings conducted at Guantánamo. He believes these trials betray the principles of fairness that made the Nazi war crime trials the standard in the application of international law.

> I think Robert Jackson would turn over in his grave if he knew what was going on at Guantanamo. It violates the Nuremburg principles, what they're doing, as well as the spirit of the Geneva Conventions of 1949. The concept of a fair trial is part of our tradition, our heritage; that's what made Nuremberg so immortal—fairness, a presumption of innocence, adequate defense counsel, opportunities to see the documents they're being tried with.

King was also dismayed that the rules at Guantánamo left open the possibility of using evidence obtained through torture. "To torture people and then you can bring evidence you obtained into court? Hearsay evidence is allowed? Some evidence is available to the prosecution and not to the defendants? This is a type of 'justice' that Jackson didn't dream of."[3]

The consequences of not adhering to equality under the law not only undermine the appeal of our 9-11 narrative in many Arab/Muslim communities around the world, they also have deadly consequences for individuals—and for our own humanity. Ann Wright, who spent twenty years as a U.S. Army Reserve colonel and sixteen years as a U.S. diplomat, resigned in March 2003 in opposition to the war in Iraq. She has written about three Guantánamo prisoners who took their own lives on June 10, 2006, rather than continue the uncertainty of detention without trial. Only twenty-one years old when he committed suicide, Yasser al-Zahrani had been detained by the Bush Administration for over four years. No one had told him that he was to have been released in three days. In desperation and feeling no hope for the future, he committed suicide on the same day as two other prisoners. Prior to these three, there had been forty-one suicide attempts among twenty-nine prisoners. Taking up the prophetic warning of Justice Jackson at Nuremburg, Colonel Wright wrote:

> One of the greatest costs to our humanity is when one who has been falsely imprisoned takes his own life in desperation. . . .
>
> The Bush administration pushed the military to sacrifice its own time-honored and time-tested regulations. The president then did an end run around the Supreme Court and pressured Congress to capitulate to change by US domestic law our country's interpretation of the Geneva Conventions. . . .
>
> For the citizens of the United States to stand by and let these abuses continue would mean our own moral and ethical suicide.[4]

While vigorous police action to find terrorists and bring them to justice is crucial to the effort to end terrorism, this must be matched with an unshakable commitment to the important U.S. principle of equal justice under the law. Part of our U.S. story is that whether you are the president of the United States or a homeless person, you and everyone else are accountable to the same law.

But President Bush's 9-11 narrative tells us that, given the terrifying threat of another attack that could come at any time and from any place, we need to set aside this fundamental principle at the heart of our larger national story. We are told that because of the 9-11 attacks, we must also abandon the U.S. story of how the principle of equality under the law, over the course of our history, moved from being a right only given to white male landowners to one extended to more and more people. The Bush Administration wants us to forget our 230-year struggle for greater inclusion. They want us to celebrate Martin Luther King Jr. Day, but forget about the appeal he made to the conscience of the U.S. populace when he reminded the nation of the unfinished business of fulfilling the promises enshrined in our founding documents. Dr. King had more than a dream when he spoke from the Lincoln Memorial that day. He came with a demand that all people in this nation be included in the promise of equality under the law:

> In a sense we've come to our nation's capital to cash a check. When the architects of our republic wrote the magnificent words of the Constitution and the Declaration of Independence, they were signing a promissory note to which every American was to fall heir. This note was a promise that all men, yes, black men as well as white men, would be guaranteed the "unalienable Rights" of "Life, Liberty and the pursuit of Happiness." It is obvious today that America has defaulted on this promissory note, insofar as her citizens of color are concerned. Instead of honoring this sacred obligation, America has given the Negro people a bad check, a check which has come back marked "insufficient funds." But we refuse to believe that the bank of justice is bankrupt. We refuse to believe that there are insufficient funds in the great vaults of opportunity of this nation. And so, we've come to cash this check, a check that will give us upon demand the riches of freedom and the security of justice.[5]

As Dr. King knew, part of this U.S. story also included those moments in our history—often acknowledged only after the fact—when we lost our way because we allowed those in power to cloud our minds and hearts with fear (e.g., the internment of Japanese Americans in World War II and the Senator McCarthy anti-Communist witch hunt in the 1950s). And now once again, at this moment of truth in our nation's history, those in power tell us that expedience should trump principle.

But if we hope to effectively discredit the al Qaeda narrative, we must expand our understanding of this U.S. principle to include not only the non-citizens living in our nation, but every member of the human family—especially those called enemy by our government. When the framers of the Declaration of Independence penned those famous words, "We hold these truths to be self-evident, that all men are created equal, that they are endowed by their Creator with certain inalienable rights," they did not qualify that claim by saying that only subjects of the British Crown were endowed with inalienable rights; they did not claim that only residents of the thirteen colonies were endowed with inalienable rights. They claimed that everyone, by virtue of being human, was endowed with these rights. And even though our founders only apportioned these rights to white male landowners, the audacious claims in the Declaration of Independence continue to inspire generations in the struggle to expand and protect the inalienable rights of everyone. But every time we act to limit our recognition of these rights to only "qualifying" human beings, we betray the aims of those framers who were engaged in constructing a new kind of narrative, founded on recognizing every person's freedom and rights.

Some people claim that the ruthless terrorists and their supporters who attacked us do not deserve the protection of the law. As syndicated columnist Ann Coulter wrote shortly after 9-11, "This is no time to be precise about locating the exact individuals directly involved in this particular terrorist attack. Those responsible include anyone anywhere who smiles in response. We should invade their countries, kill their leaders, and convert them to Christianity."[6] Most in the United States would not condone this kind of radical hatred, but unfortunately, too many of us are willing to deny the humanity of those who engage in terrorism as well as those who give credence to the al Qaeda narrative.

And this is how the cycle of violence and the dynamic of mutually sustaining narratives are set in motion. When our government threatens Muslim/Arab communities, when it refuses to grant them the same rights and freedoms we demand for ourselves, when media pundits and religious extremists in our country demonize other religions or cultures, al Qaeda's narrative is validated. As a result, our government's actions and attitudes reinforce the hatred and suspicion of us preached by al Qaeda. Many in this country, in turn, interpret their anger and mistrust of us as proof that they are all terrorist sympathizers and undeserving of any rights or respect.

Breaking the power of al Qaeda's narrative will require us to act in ways that show that we respect the Muslim faith. It will require that we be strong enough not to threaten punishment in order to persuade others to cooperate with us in eliminating all forms of terrorism. It will require that we act in ways that demonstrate our conviction that they too have "inalienable rights." But, we cannot expect Muslim/Arab communities to respect our words about equality under the law if our own government continues to place itself above international laws, treaties, and courts. When we abandon our own tradition of law, when we jettison international laws and treaties in our fight against terrorism, we undermine the very legitimacy of our struggle. Michael Green, a professor of political science at Hofstra University, cautions about the cost of abandoning the principle of equality under the law that is at the foundation of our U.S. narrative. Responding to the continuing revelations of legally questionable activities of this Administration, Green writes, "Torture, wiretaps, planted news stories, secret prisons, one unmasked war justification after another—each week brings fresh outrages. This country faces some very real threats, but must we give up everything that makes America America in order to live safely within our borders?"[7]

To the credit of many in this country, even at the height of anti-Muslim, anti-Arab hysteria after the 9-11 attacks, many ordinary citizens were unwilling to give up the values at the heart of our national commitment to equality. They acted to protect their Muslim neighbors and guard their mosques and worked in their local communities to foster interreligious understanding and tolerance. Even as the Bush Administration was whipping up fear of another terrorist attack to support its "War on Terror," others understood that the principle of equality under the law should not be written out of our U.S. story.

For example, in the aftermath of 9-11, the Blue Triangle Network was formed to stand with communities and individuals targeted by the government because of their religious and political beliefs or ethnic backgrounds. The group takes its name from the Nazi practice of designating color-coded markings for the "inmates" in their deadly concentration camps. The blue triangle was used to identify "emigrants," foreigners, and stateless people. By taking the blue triangle as their symbol, its members demonstrate their solidarity with targeted immigrant communities.

The Blue Triangle Network's mission is to speak out against racial profiling and to defend the civil liberties of Muslims, Arabs, South Asians, and others. They shine the light of public scrutiny on the un-American actions of our own government when it engages in roundups of immigrants, indefinite detentions, secret charges, secret evidence, and secret military tribunals. In the finest of U.S. traditions, the Blue Triangle Network insists that people should not be singled out for government harassment based upon where they were born, the language that they speak, the color of their skin, or the religion that they practice. Shortly after the media reported the torture of detainees in Iraq and Afghanistan, the Network released a statement about the conditions facing immigrants inside the United States. They pointed out that thousands of Muslims, Arabs, and South Asians in the United States had experienced the same kind of humiliation and pain as torture victims in Iraq and Afghanistan. Speaking about the consequences of these actions, the Network stated:

Many thousands of Muslim, Arab and South Asian individuals in the U.S. have experienced the same kinds of humiliation and pain that captures the attention of the world in these abuses. The report by the Inspector General of the Justice Department is clear that the same violations of human rights and decency were commonplace for those detained in the U.S., on no more pretext than their religion, national origin or political beliefs, under the cloak of "homeland security".[8]

For our alternative 9-11 narrative to be effective in countering that of al Qaeda, our commitment to the principle of equality under the law must not be based upon any individual's background or beliefs. It also should not depend upon reciprocal treatment. It should not be conditioned on how others might treat us. It is a U.S. principle that speaks to who we say we are, not to what we might believe about our "enemies." Our 9-11 narrative needs to be based on the conviction that terrorism will end when all nations, great and small, adhere to and are accountable to the same laws and courts. The same rules that we use to judge the behavior of Osama bin Laden must also apply to all U.S. political and military leaders. In a passionate plea to a United States he sees as captive to its own fears, Duke University professor Ariel Dorfman wrote:

> Can't the United States see that when we allow someone to be tortured by our agents, it is not only the victim and the perpetrator who are corrupted, not only the "intelligence" that is contaminated, but also everyone who looked away and said they did not know, everyone who consented tacitly to that outrage so they could sleep a little safer at night . . . Are we so morally sick, so deaf and dumb and blind, that we do not understand this? Are we so fearful, so in love with our own security and steeped in our own pain, that

we are really willing to let people be tortured in the name of America?[9]

As long as the Bush Administration's 9-11 narrative calls for a U.S. foreign policy based on the principle that might makes right, that torture is acceptable under certain circumstances, and that the rule of law can be set aside when inconvenient, then those we exclude will strike back as best they can. As long as the strong can lord it over the weak, terrorism will be the choice of the disenfranchised. Unless we are willing to take our place in the community of nations—as an equal not as its overlord—we can always expect to be the target of those who are oppressed.

## DEMOCRATIC SELF-DETERMINATION

Another founding U.S. principle we can bring to the struggle against terrorism is a commitment to democratic self-determination. The central theme in the story of our nation's birth is the conviction that all people have a right to participate in the process of government and have a right to select leaders who represent their views and values. Any 9-11 narrative capable of discrediting the al Qaeda narrative would need to make democratic self-determination, along with protecting civil and human rights, the guiding principle of its foreign policy.

However, the history of U.S. commitment to democratic self-determination (at home and abroad) is at times murky. Instead of demonstrating a consistent and unequivocal commitment to self-determination for all the people of the world, our government too often prefers to employ political spin and rhetoric about democracy that is designed to further geopolitical and economic aims mostly benefiting the rich and powerful.[10] Even though President Bush and past presidents have offered lip service and a good deal of political rhetoric in support of the principle of democratic self-determination, many of the world's poorest people see the United States acting in ways that instead support (their own) undemocratic governments.

This is especially true in the Arab world. None of the so-called moderate Arab governments that the United States supports financially and militarily are democracies. Many believe that U.S. foreign policy is designed to maximize corporate profits, not democracy and human rights and a commitment to self-determination. The clearest example is the U.S. relationship with Saudi Arabia. In 1945, President Franklin Roosevelt met with King Abdel-Aziz ibn Saud and formalized a deal that the United States would protect the autocratic and undemocratic Saudi monarchy in exchange for unlimited access to their oil. Michael Klare, author of *Resource Wars* and *Blood and Oil: The Dangers and Consequences of America's Growing Petroleum Dependency*, writes that to keep the Saudi royal family in power, the United States helped establish and train the Saudi secret police, which used their power to crush any dissent or calls for democratic self-determination. Klare points out that this protection was formally expanded to include all other oil-producing despots in the region with the 1980 "Carter Doctrine" (after the Iranian revolution deposed the Iranian monarchy). That doctrine explicitly stated that the United States would use military means to ensure its access to Middle East oil.[11] Another example of U.S. intention in the region was the response of our military when looters rampaged throughout Iraq after the fall of Baghdad, destroying much of the civilian infrastructure. In the midst of the chaos, U.S. soldiers were instructed to only protect the Ministry of Oil. What did these actions demonstrate to the Iraqi people about U.S. priorities?

How can the Muslim/Arab world take our words about democracy seriously when the United States supports undemocratically elected world leaders such as Pakistan's military dictator Pervez Musharraf? Musharraf seized power in 1999 through a bloodless coup. Although the United States initially treated him as a pariah, Musharraf turned this around after the terrorist attacks of September 11 by cutting support for the Taliban in Afghanistan and joining the anti-terror "coalition of the willing." Over the years, the United States has called Musharraf an important ally in the fight against terrorism. Along with Musharraf, another "ally in the effort" to spread democracy throughout the Middle East is the dictator of Egypt, Hosni Mubarak. During the May 2005 referendum allowing more than one person to run for president of Egypt, Mubarak henchmen attacked members of the opposition during peaceful demonstrations in the center of Cairo while the police looked on and did nothing.[12]

The insincerity of the Bush Administration's commitment to democracy is demonstrated in the way it applies a double standard to the principle of democratic self-determination. On the one hand, the Administration claims the mantle of champion of democracy in the Middle East, insisting that promoting democracy is the best way to stop terrorism. But when democracy does not produce the results that the Bush Administration wants, it has no problem exerting undemocratic means to achieve "regime change."

In an internationally verified fair election, the Hamas political party won elections to govern in Palestine. The United States responded by cutting off funding to the Palestinian government and supporting the Israeli government's illegitimate confiscation of tax revenues belonging to the Palestinians. The Administration claims its policy toward Hamas is based on Hamas' refusal to recognize the state of Israel and to renounce the use of violence. However, the United States had no problem supporting and funding the Israeli government when it was led by the Likud Party, which does not recognize the right of Palestinians to their own state and has never renounced the use of violence against the Palestinians. As recently as 2002, the Central Committee of the Likud Party, led by former Prime Minister Benjamin Netanyahu, voted to rule out the establishment of a Palestinian state. If the President intended to win the hearts and minds of Arab communities in the Middle East by his rhetorical commitment to democracy, what are those communities learning from his actions?

In another instance, on the one hand, the Bush Administration praised as a healthy sign of democracy large street demonstrations in Lebanon that called for the resignation of the pro-Syrian government after the assassination of a former prime minister. The Bush Administration called it the "Cedar Revolution." And yet less than a year later, when the Lebanese people took to the streets—in even greater numbers—to call for the resignation of the pro-U.S. government for failing to protect over one thousand Lebanese civilians killed by an Israeli invasion, the Bush Administration called it a threat to democracy.

The people of the Middle East, like those of the United States, are not stupid. They can see through the hypocrisy and double standards of the Bush Administration. The cynical attempt to pass itself off as a champion of democracy in this region only fuels the anger and resentment that the rhetoric is meant to reduce. Investigative journalist Robert Parry writes about the failure of the Bush Administration's attempts to overcome anti-Americanism in the Middle East by promoting democracy—by force if necessary. The problem is that the President is hated so intensely that whenever the people get the chance to vote, they either vote along sectarian lines (as in Iraq) or for candidates who stand up against the United States. Parry concludes that if our undemocratic allies in the Middle East were allowed to vote, "the likelihood is that the elected governments would join the 'coalition of the hostile' against the United States."[13]

When the rhetoric of our narrative does not match our behavior, it can be doubly destructive to the goal of appealing to the Muslim/Arab communities that we seek to draw away from al Qaeda and other terrorist organizations. Hypocrisy and double standards are the most devastating means of discrediting our own 9-11 narrative and validating al Qaeda's. Terrorism will end when we allow other people the right to self-determination: to create their own forms of democracy (regardless of whether they fit with U.S. goals and beliefs) and to not have a particular form of government or economic model imposed upon them. Unless all the people of the world are free to create their own futures, the explanations of groups like al Qaeda will have an endless supply of politically disenfranchised recruits who will find them appealing.

## THE COMMON GOOD

Another important U.S. principle that must be included in our alternative to the "War on Terror" is that government should work for the common good, not just for those who are rich and/or powerful. The common good refers to those social conditions that allow all people to develop to their fullest human potentials. More than a social condition, the common good is also a social ethic based on the understanding that each person's destiny is inextricably tied to the destiny of everyone else. This ethic was most eloquently stated by Dr. Martin Luther King Jr. when he declared that "injustice anywhere is a threat to justice everywhere."[14]

The idea of the common good was enshrined at the founding of our nation in those immortal words, "We the People." At our best, this affirmation of our common destiny as one people has been a guiding principle of our democratic republic. It has been tested by crises like the Civil War, to determine if our nation would continue to exist half slave and half free. It was tested through the Great Depression and the New Deal, to determine if our nation would devolve into a plutocracy of privilege for the few or continue to persist as a genuine democracy of equal opportunity for all. It was also tested by the many civil rights movements, to determine if we would protect the rights of only some people or guarantee the rights of all.

The crisis of the common good that we now face in this age of globalization is realizing that the common good of any particular nation cannot be realized apart from the needs of the entire human family. For members of Protestants for the Common Good, this context of mutuality stretches from the smallest social unit, the family, to the entire global community. As they point out in their Principles Statement, "No person may be left behind, because the greater participation of each is the greater enrichment of all and, thereby, the greater fulfillment of God's purpose."[15] If our alternative 9-11 narrative is to have the power to inspire our allies and to win over communities who mistrust us, it must be rooted in this more expansive understanding of the common good.

As the late Pope John Paul II pointed out, because of the increasingly interdependent and global world we live in, the common good of humanity has to be worked out on the international level. He pointed out that the basis of what he called the "universal common good" is found in the promotion and preservation of human rights and the just distribution of the earth's resources and wealth. For the Pope, the common good was the basis of peace. And the question of peace cannot be separated from the question of human dignity and human rights.[16]

Our alternative 9-11 narrative should be based on recognizing that terrorism will end when we create international economic mechanisms to distribute the wealth and resources of this world in a way that ensures that all people live in dignity. As long as a wealthy elite in the United States and around the world controls most of the world's wealth and consumes most of the world's resources at the expense of those who are destitute, terrorism will continue to be an outlet for the frustration and anger of the alienated, disenfranchised, and dispossessed.

Governmental and non-governmental agencies around the world recognize that this is true. When answering written questions from members of Congress in 2002, the CIA noted that while the United States was striking major blows against al Qaeda, "Several troublesome global trends—especially the growing demographic youth bulge in developing nations whose economic systems and political ideologies are under enormous stress—will fuel the rise of more disaffected groups willing to use violence to address their perceived grievances." Even the World Bank recognizes that poverty is a breeding ground for terrorism, as weak and corrupt governments serving only the rich and powerful result in a steady supply of recruits for terrorists who capitalize on the discontent. A 2006 World Bank report identifies "fragile" countries whose "deepening poverty puts them at risk from terrorism." This list jumped from seventeen countries in 2003 to twenty-six in 2006.[17]

The dangerous dynamic set in motion by poverty, corrupt governments, and wealth concentrated in the hands of the few is well described by David Cortright, co-founder of the Center on Global Counter-Terrorism Cooperation:

> These deeply-held grievances generate widespread political frustration and bitterness in many Arab and Muslim countries, including among people who condemn terrorism and al Qaeda's brutal methods. As these conditions fester and worsen, support rises for the groups that resist them. Finding solutions to these dilemmas can help to undercut support for jihadism. The strategy against terrorism requires undermining the social base of extremism by driving a wedge between militants and their potential sympathizers. The goal should be to separate militants from their support base by resolving the political injustices that terrorists exploit.[18]

Resolving these injustices means moving beyond the narrow parameters of responding to the terrorist threat with military power and violence. In 2002, the late Pope John Paul II stressed this, recognizing that retaliatory violence and force were only reactionary responses to terrorism that failed to address the root causes, making the threat greater and the cycle of violence deeper. To respond to terrorism, he said, it is necessary

> to undertake new and creative political, diplomatic and economic initiatives aimed at relieving the scandalous situations of gross injustice, oppression and marginalization which continue to oppress countless members of the human family. . . . History, in fact, shows that the recruitment of terrorists is more easily achieved in areas where human rights are trampled upon and where injustice is a part of daily life.[19]

As Prime Minster of Great Britain, Tony Blair also warned against the complacency of the West toward the degrading poverty and hopelessness experienced by the majority of the world's people. Calling us to embrace the principle of the common good that included the welfare of all people, he said:

> One illusion has been shattered on 11th September: that we can have the good life of the West, irrespective of the state of the rest of the world. The war against terrorism . . . needs to be a series of political actions designed to remove the conditions under which such acts of evil can flourish and be tolerated. . . . The dragon's teeth are planted in the fertile soil of wrongs unrighted, of disputes left to fester for years or even decades, of failed states, of poverty and deprivation.[20]

President Bush has made modest attempts at increasing aid to impoverished countries, especially in Africa. But to live up to the principle of the common good, we need more than the charity of the rich nations towards the poor of the world. The principle of the common good calls for restructuring global economic institutions in ways that redistribute economic power and resources and allow all people in the world to actively participate in the economic decisions that affect their lives. If the right of each person to meaningful partcipation in the economic life of her or his community were part of our 9-11 narrative to the world, we would offer something to our Muslim and Arab brothers and sisters that al Qaeda never could.

## TOLERANCE AND CELEBRATION OF DIVERSITY

Added to these core U.S. values is one more principle that can play a crucial role in our alternative 9-11 narrative and that would create a powerful means of separating al Qaeda and other terrorist groups from their support bases. Fundamental to our U.S. character is our tolerance of people from different cultures, faiths, and ethnic backgrounds. Although our history is filled with examples when we have failed to live up to this ideal, at our best we understand that, in a nation and a world as diverse as ours, tolerance and respect go hand-in-hand with peace and unity.

For those of us who are part of the dominant culture, it can be very difficult to comprehend how those who do not share our culture might see it as a threat. In her book *The Battle for God*, Karen Armstrong writes about the long, painful, and often violent accommodation that took place between the emerging new economic, social, political, and intellectual models that shook the foundations of Western Europe in the sixteenth and seventeenth centuries and the culturally conservative elements within Christianity and Judaism. The indigenous revolution that swept across Europe had a uniquely European outcome. Even though it had its share of violent backlash (especially religiously motivated violence), over time European communities worked out their own ways of accommodating with the modern secular world. (Although, as stated before, the cultural wars in the United States indicate that this is still a work in progress.)

But while Christianity and Judaism had the luxury of over 300 years to accommodate and negotiate their place in the modernity that sprang from the Age of Reason and the Enlightenment, Islam in the Arab world had modernity and secular culture forced down its throat. Worse yet, the economic, social, political, and intellectual fruits of the Enlightenment came on the back of colonialism and were cynically used by the superpowers to wage their Cold War by proxy. As Karen Armstrong put it in an interview with Bill Moyers, some Muslims have experienced secularism not as a liberating process, but as a deadly assault. For example, the shahs of Iran once ordered that their soldiers go out and rip off women's veils with their bayonets to make their societies look modern. In another example from 1935, the Shah Reza Pahlevi gave his soldiers orders to shoot at unarmed demonstrators who were protesting against the Shah's demand that everyone wear western dress. Hundreds of Iranians died that day.[21]

Some Muslims feel they are battling forces that threaten their most sacred values and identity. The pro-U.S. Shah of Iran is not the only example of Arab Muslims being "assaulted" with Western notions of "liberation" and "enlightenment." As Armstrong reminds us, in Egypt the pro-Soviet President Gamal Abdel Nasser was hell-bent on secularizing Egypt on a Western (socialist) model that called for the separation of mosque and politics. In his relentless campaign to make Egypt Western, he imprisoned thousands of members of the Muslim Brotherhood, most of whom did nothing more than attend meetings or pass out leaflets. But while in prison, they developed a fundamentalist ideology in response to this forced secularization. In the prisons of Egypt, disenchanted people like al-Zawahiri (bin Laden's second-in-command) adopted and later promoted new more radical schools of thought. When Mustafa Kemal Ataturk, founder of present-day Turkey, "modernized" that Muslim nation, he closed down the religious schools (*madrassas*) and forced all men and women into Western dress. Law forbade public displays of religion. Resentment and anger over this forced Westernization still reverberate across that country.

In creating our alternative 9-11 narrative, we need to be careful not to convey the impression of cultural superiority or to claim that our ways of doing things are the only or correct ones. Our efforts to combat terrorism will be more effective if we understand that terrorism will end when all cultures are respected and the (currently) dominant white Western culture is not forced on others. It is important to realize that, in our relentless efforts to open foreign markets for our goods and to satisfy our insatiable appetite for resources, we often insist that all people become like us, adopting our social, cultural, economic, and political systems. But many Muslims (among others) see our culture and way of life as decadent and believe that their own culture and religious values are under attack. As long as we continue to act in ways that destroy and disrespect other people's cultures, and hence their identities, al Qaeda's narrative will be validated and we can expect terrorist attacks against us to continue.

Because terrorism arises from many different communities around the world, we will need a different strategy to engage each of them in ways that respect their cultures. For instance, there is much we can do on the cultural front to combat terrorism arising from the Arab/Muslim world. Most importantly, we can assist, under the direction of people in the region, in building civil societies that reflect the values, culture, and self-determination of the people there. (Civil society is the network of voluntary associations that provide the soil and nutrients for developing culture—the arts, science, education, medicine, intellectual thought, and theology.) This allows people who have experienced modernity as a component of colonial exploitation to develop their own accommodations with modernity.

Many sectors within civil societies across the Muslim world are fully engaged in this work. They are working to define and develop uniquely Muslim expressions of democracy. They are exploring and articulating the foundations of pluralism and civil rights within Islam. Everywhere there are Muslim artists, writers, intellectuals, and activists who are working hard to accommodate modernity with Islam. In doing so, they are rejecting some of the Western formulations of these principles; in other cases, they are articulating new and deeper understandings of so-called Western values and political culture.

Every time we nurture, support, or promote a poet, artist, writer, reformer, scientist, or educator in the Muslim world, we help create a civil society that has the power to offer the alternative of life and hope to those who feel assaulted and marginalized. In contrast, every bullet or rocket we fire in that region and every military boot we impose on the ground only strengthens the hands of radical extremists by pushing more and more disenfranchised people into their world of paranoia and hate.

While promoting civil societies as expressed by the people in the region is a productive mechanism for creating an alternative 9-11 narrative, our government at times seems intent on thwarting any attempt to build relationships between Muslim civil society and our own. Since passage of the USA PATRIOT Act, a number of Muslim academics have been denied U.S. visas or had them revoked. The most outrageous case is that of Professor Tariq Ramadan, one of the foremost scholars of Islam in the world today. After being invited to teach at the University of Notre Dame, a last-minute visa revocation kept him from coming to the United States. The Department of Homeland Security spokesperson cited Section 411 of the PATRIOT Act, which excludes foreigners who "endorse or espouse terrorist activity." But Ramadan has consistently condemned terrorist acts, though he has been critical of many U.S. policies toward the Muslim world.

Are we so intellectually insecure, so afraid of ideas that might challenge our stereotypes and prejudices, that we deny entry into this country to anyone who does not confirm what we already hold to be true? What message does our treatment of Professor Ramadan send to the Muslim world? What message does this send to those sectors of Muslim civil society that want to engage with the West?

Because the economic and political interests of the West in the Middle East have always been a higher priority than honoring the will and aspirations of the people, the al Qaeda narrative has been able to capture the Islamic imagination by calling for re-establishing the Caliphate (the supreme leader of the Muslim community, successor to the Prophet Mohammed). The vast majority of Muslims in the Middle East are not interested in establishing a new religious political order in the region. But the call for re-establishing the Caliphate does capture people's religious imagination and articulates the desire for what has been called a second flowering of Islam.

The first flowering of Islam—the golden age of Islam—occurred over one thousand years ago. Following the establishment of Islam in the seventh century and its spread throughout North Africa and the Middle East, Baghdad quickly became a major cultural center. In the early ninth century, the Abbasid caliphs established the "House of Wisdom," an academy of science that studied and translated scholarly Greek and Sanskrit manuscripts, which led to a new era of scientific and mathematical creativity lasting until the fourteenth century.

During this flowering, in the eleventh century, lived one of the most famous Arabic mathematicians, Umar Al-Khayammi, known to the West as "Omar Khayyam." Also a poet, scientist, and philosopher, his writings were very influential in developing European intellectual life. In fact, the translation of Arabic texts into Latin by Jewish scholars living in Spain was largely responsible for Europe rising from the Dark Ages, which eventually led to the Age of Reason and the Enlightenment.

Just as Arab Islam helped give birth to so much of what we now consider part of modern Western intellectual culture, we in the West can play a constructive role in encouraging a second flowering of Islam—a new golden age of Islamic culture. We must do so, not from a position of superiority or pity, but from a deep and genuine desire to be enriched by what Islam has to offer. Some might see the emergence of a new golden age of Islam as a threat to the West, but this would be short-sighted and tragic. We should do all we can to promote the best of Islam, to engage its scholars and artists, its musicians, poets, and theologians in an ongoing dialogue about the essential questions of our common existence.

Encouraging and participating in this dialogue will need to be at the heart of our alternative narrative because the 9-11 narrative offered by the Bush Administration is based primarily on threats and ultimatums: "you are either with us or with the terrorists." The way to dispel the darkness of the ideology of hate and paranoia put forward by al Qaeda's 9-11 narrative is not by deepening the darkness, as Vice President Cheney suggested to the nation shortly after 9-11. At that time he warned, "A lot of what needs to be done here will have to be done quietly, without any discussion, using sources and methods that are available to our intelligence agencies." From now on, according to the Vice President, "our government would have to operate on the dark side."[22]

We need to reject this approach; it is not what the United

States is about. The only way to dispel the deceptions and lies of terrorism is with openness, humility, and a willingness to put the search for truth ahead of ideologies and vested interests. We are at our best when we speak our truth with honesty, humility, and a willingness to learn from others. Through dialogue, debate, and the exchange of ideas, a common culture of understanding, respect, and tolerance can be built between Muslim communities throughout the world and the other faith communities in the West. The more we break down walls, refuse to hate, find ways to cultivate and celebrate authentic cultural identities, and learn to reverence the humanity in each person, the more we can drive out the terrorist ideologies of hate.

Supporting Muslim civil societies by following their lead in bringing about a new flowering of Islam will allow Muslim communities from around the world to more freely determine their own destiny in a way that preserves their dignity and is authentic and loyal to the tenets of Islam. In the light of this choice, the nihilistic ideology of terrorism expressed in the al Qaeda narrative will flee back into the shadows of society where radical extremists of other faiths are consigned. An Islam that is free to choose its own way of accommodating modernity and free to find its own expressions of economics, politics, and the arts will not feel threatened by the West, and the narratives of the Osama bin Ladens of the world will have no appeal.

## THE RISKS

Does adopting these principles in reshaping our 9-11 narrative and in guiding our policies and strategies hold the potential for losses, defeats, setbacks, great sacrifices, and costs? Without a doubt. Are there risks in taking this alternative approach to combating terrorism? Absolutely. Like any struggle against a violent and determined foe, this alternative approach poses great risks and costs. But isn't that also true of our current "War on Terror"? The difference between this alternative approach and the current "War on Terror" is that while we may suffer great losses, we will not lose ourselves. We might be called upon to make great sacrifices, but we will not sacrifice our ideals and principles. Terrorists might destroy our bodies, level our buildings, and poison our lands, but they will not be able to destroy our souls, level our democratic traditions, or poison the hearts and minds of our young people. Only we have the power to do these things.

# On That Day

## an alternative 9-11 narrative in free verse

*Narrative creation is a process that can take place over a long period of time. Even after it takes shape, it can still be reshaped and reinterpreted. A dynamic, living narrative cannot be fully contained in a single form of communication, like a White Paper, a policy document, or even a historical chronology. Authentic narrative also includes the arts, like music, painting, and poetry. In this vein, I offer this alternative 9-11 narrative in free verse.*

On September 11, 2001, we were attacked
 by men intent on terrorizing us.
On that day of horror the world was attacked
 by men intent on terrorizing the world.

On that day those who died in the World Trade Center
 were not only part of our community,
 they were part of our world community.
On that day they were from countries near and far;
 they were immigrant janitors and foreign bankers;
 they were young with dreams of raising families;
 they were old with dreams of spoiling grandchildren.

On that day when we were attacked
by men intent on terrorizing us,
our sons and daughters ran into buildings as they collapsed around them;
they carried the injured down flights of stairs only to return for more;
they pulled the injured from the rubble and bound up their wounds.

On that day when we were attacked
by men intent on terrorizing us,
our men and women in uniform and their civilian co-workers
went to work with the desire to serve and protect our nation,
not knowing that on that day their calling would cost them their lives.

On that day when we were attacked
by men intent on terrorizing us,
some of our fellow citizens sacrificed their lives
in order to bring down the terrorists' plot to use their plane
as a weapon of mass destruction.
        (Before they died they called their loved ones
        and then gave up their lives.)

On that day when we were attacked
by men intent on terrorizing us,
we too called our loved ones to make sure they were alright;
we hugged our children a little tighter;
we lowered our flags, we lit our candles; we held each other's hands.

On that day when we were attacked
by men intent on terrorizing us,
we stopped to appreciate how precious and precarious life can be;
we made a commitment to make each day count a little more;
to give of ourselves a little more
to look out for each other a little more
to be a little more of what we were called to be.

**On that day when we were attacked
by men intent on terrorizing us—they failed.**

Because on that day we learned that our Muslim neighbors
love this country as much as we do,
and were horrified that these men of terror
had not only hijacked those planes
but had hijacked their faith as well.

On that day we experienced what too many people
around the world experience;
feeling vulnerable to unspeakable violence;
feeling violated by forces beyond their control;
feeling rage at the callous actions of others
who think of human lives as nothing more than collateral
in some game of power politics.

On that day we realized that to end the scourge of terrorism
we needed the help of every person around the world;
to make our global laws stronger in the service of justice;
to make our global community stronger to ensure that no one
has to feel vulnerable, or violated by forces beyond their control.

On that day we realized that we were
strong enough not to give into the temptation to seek a pound of flesh;
smart enough to understand that all Muslims are not a threat
and many are allies;
patient enough to do the hard work of finding the guilty
and bringing them to justice;
wise enough to realize that those who were not against us,
were actually for us.

On that day we understood that to defeat this threat
we must be careful not to abandon those principles
that make us who we are.

On that day we understood that the greater threat
was not what these men might do to us,
but what we might do to ourselves out of fear and ignorance.

On that day we determined to work with every nation
to make democracy more than a slogan;
> by nurturing the seeds of freedom in every land
> and letting those seeds grow at their own pace in their own way
> and bear fruit of their own indigenous flavor.

On that day we committed ourselves to work with every nation
to make sure that all children have all they need to grow
> to their fullest potential;
> by doing all we can to provide a life of dignity to every person;
> by giving them a real stake in the economic life of their communities
> and by putting the needs of people before the desire for profit.

On that day we determined that our rich diversity was a gift not a threat,
a tribute to the amazing creative capabilities of the human family;
> not a problem to be solved
> but a force to be appreciated, understood and cherished
> by supporting the work of artists, writers, poets and musicians
> and by encouraging the exchange of ideas and beliefs.

**On that day when we were attacked
by men intent on terrorizing us—they failed.**

# PART III

## Re-Visioning Peace in our U.S. Narrative: Understanding the Things that Make for Peace

In the previous section of this book, I dealt with the importance of narrative in creating an alternative to the "War on Terror." I compared and contrasted the Bush Administration's 9-11 narrative with that of al Qaeda in order to understand how they mirror each other and create a mutually sustaining dynamic that fuels continuing cycles of violence. As an antidote to this dynamic, I suggested ways of creating an alternative 9-11 narrative founded on U.S. civic and moral principles that can both unite our allies and appeal to the Muslim/Arab communities that al Qaeda depends on to survive.

As important as all of this is, it is still not enough. The Bush Administration's "War on Terror" narrative is appealing because it has been linked to and has its underpinnings in a larger U.S.

narrative, a story rooted in a particular vision of peace. To counter the appeal of this dominant narrative, we first need to understand this vision of peace—a vision popular in our culture and public discourse. Then we need to be able to re-vision our U.S. narrative based on a different vision of peace, one that will have greater appeal to our fellow citizens because it more fully represents the best of who we are.

Part III of this book begins with a chapter examining the vision of peace at the heart of the dominant U.S. story and looks at the ways this vision predisposes us to make choices—especially in our efforts to combat terrorism and create a more peaceful world. How is peace understood in the dominant U.S. narrative, and how does that understanding influence our choices? How is security understood? How does the vision of peace at the heart of this dominant narrative frame the challenges of terrorism in ways that are self-defeating and counterproductive?

The vision of peace at the heart of the dominant U.S. narrative is not all that different from that of most other powerful nations throughout history. Whether it be the vision of *Pax Romana, Pax Americana,* or the vision of a Communist or Socialist workers' paradise or whether it be the dream of Christendom or the Caliphate, humankind has spent an enormous amount of blood and treasure trying to create a world of peace. Regardless of the political or religious ideologies that provided the rationale for these various attempts to establish peace and security, at a fundamental level they all hold in common the conviction that the path to peace is through enforced order. That order might be seen as "God's will" or "the triumph of the working class" or what is necessary for the "optimal functioning of a free market," but fundamentally it is about imposing order as a means of achieving peace. Chapter Seven argues that *Peace as Enforced Order* is at the heart of the dominant U.S. narrative.

While it is true that every powerful nation operates primarily out of a vision of *Peace as Enforced Order,* it is also true that most nations contain a latent potential for another path to peace. Chapter Eight offers a different vision of peace: one that is rooted in an alternative national narrative that can better equip us to deal with the threat of terrorism. This vision can be called *Peace as the Enterprise of Justice*. For some nations, this alternative vision is always in play with the more dominant vision of *Peace as Enforced Order*. In other nations, *Peace as the Enterprise of Justice* exists only as part of the founding myth, a utopian dream or final state of evolution.

Chapter Eight argues that *Peace as the Enterprise of Justice* is an equally important, if largely unknown, part of our U.S. narrative. It shows how important parts of this alternative vision of peace within our U.S. story have been hidden from us, co-opted, or forgotten. Can this alternative vision of peace help us to re-vision our national story in a way that is even more authentic and true to what we believe about ourselves? Can we create an alternative that will enable us to act in ways that truly match our civic values and moral virtues? Can a U.S. narrative based on *Peace as the Enterprise of Justice* serve us better in combating all forms of terrorism than one based on *Peace as Enforced Order*?

Chapter Nine builds on our alternative U.S. narrative by setting out important challenges to address as part of an effective counter-terrorism strategy. Can an alternative based on *Peace as the Enterprise of Justice* provide us in the United States with the vision and energy we need to combat the racism, militarism, poverty, and environmental degradation that contribute to the rise of terrorism around the world? Can we find within our own re-visioned national narrative the resources to sustain us in this struggle? Can we identify within this re-visioned national narrative the heroes and sheroes we need to inspire us?

# CHAPTER SEVEN

# Peace as Enforced Order: At the Heart of the Dominant U.S. Narrative

*Peace as Enforced Order* is based on the conviction that peace is the absence of open conflict. It is structured around strategies of reducing conflict by maintaining a degree of certainty in human interactions (whether economic, political, or social). *Peace as Enforced Order* allows for some changes in the social order, but only within proscribed parameters that ensure that the fundamental dynamics of institutional and systemic power and privilege remain unchallenged.

This vision of *Peace as Enforced Order* is not particular to the United States; it can be found within the stories of many nations that seek to establish this kind of peace within their own borders and in nations powerful enough to try to establish this kind of peace internationally. We must also remember that *Peace as Enforced Order* is a major narrative construct for those who engage in terrorism, both terrorism of the strong (those who want to maintain their control and power) and terrorism of the weak (those who want to replace the ones in control). *Peace as Enforced Order* is familiar territory for terrorists. They are comfortable fighting in this arena; their tactics are designed to have optimal effect when the conflict with those they wish to depose is defined in these terms.

In this chapter, we look at the fundamental principle of scarcity and the virtue of acquisition that drive the need for control and make conflict inevitable for those who embrace *Peace as Enforced Order*. The need for control, rudimentary to this vision, dictates that we all understand our places within the social and economic order. It is the role of the dominant narrative to provide the rationale and justification for this order. Making sure that we stay in our places requires social, political, and even religious mechanisms of control, including the use of police and military force if necessary. But, as we shall see, maintaining a national narrative based on a vision of *Peace as Enforced Order* requires a number of often-hidden trade-offs and internal contradictions. And, in times of crisis, a national narrative wedded to a vision of *Peace as Enforced Order* can ultimately become self-destructive.

## THE PRINCIPLE OF SCARCITY

Scarcity is the fundamental principle guiding the strategic thinking of those who seek *Peace as Enforced Order*. The principle of scarcity holds that all those things that make for the "good life" are in limited supply. Because of this, there will always be competition and conflict for these goods. Organizing our lives (or the life of a nation) around the principle of scarcity means viewing the world through a zero-sum framework. If someone's power is growing, then someone else's power must be diminishing. If someone is gaining, then someone else must be losing. Implied in the principle of scarcity is that there is not enough to go around.

This principle has been a core assumption behind much of our nation's foreign policy from its beginning. One of the clearest articulations of this principle was written in 1948, shortly after World War II, when our modern national security state was forming. George Kennan (who worked at the U.S. State Department at that time) wrote, "We have about 50% of the world's wealth, but only 6.5% of its population . . . In this situation, we cannot fail to be the object of envy and resentment. Our real task in the coming period is to devise a pattern of relationships which will permit us to maintain this position of disparity without positive detriment to our national security." In a more contemporary restatement of this foreign policy principle, in the 1980s Army General Maxwell Taylor stated, "As the leading 'have' power, we may expect to have to fight to protect our national valuables against envious 'have nots.'"[1]

The principle of scarcity dictates that because competition and conflict are inevitable to secure access to limited resources, only those who are strong enough to impose their will on others will survive. This competition and conflict have been central to U.S. military strategy for a long time. One of its more recent articulations can be found in "Rebuilding America's Defenses: Strategic Forces and Resources for a New Century." This 2000 PNAC (Project for the New American Century) publication outlined what was to become the blueprint for the Bush Administration's national security policy. Arguing that securing global hegemony should be the main goal of U.S. foreign policy, it stated:

> At present the United States faces no global rival. America's grand strategy should aim to preserve and extend this advantageous position as far into the future as possible. There are, however, potentially powerful states dissatisfied with the current situation and eager to change it, if they can. . . . Up to now, they have been deterred from doing so by the capability and global presence of American military power.[2]

Since the beginning of the Bush-Cheney Administration (and some would argue earlier), official U.S. policy has been to keep any nation or bloc of nations (including the United Nations) from exercising global power on the scale of our nation. Along with our allies (in the role of junior partners), we have claimed to ourselves the right to create a new world order that ensures our global military and economic domination and thus keeps resources flowing to the United States at a relatively low cost to ourselves.

## THE VIRTUE OF ACQUISITION

If we believe that we live in a world of scarcity, then acquiring and/or controlling as much of the world's resources as possible inevitably becomes the most important task. Therefore, acquisition is the highest virtue in a narrative based on *Peace as Enforced Order*. The more you have, the more powerful you are. As Kennan pointed out, the United States has long had more than its share of resources. And fear over losing that control and access has been the engine fueling national security planning since the United States became a superpower.

Any number of strategic resources could illustrate this point, but the first that comes to mind is oil. Employing military means to guarantee the flow of oil has been an important focus of U.S. foreign policy since World War II, second only to containment of the Soviet Union. As stated in the previous chapter, the Carter Doctrine declared that securing the flow of Gulf oil was of vital interest to the United States and that the United States would use any means necessary, including military force, to protect that access.

Oil is a limited resource. If gaining access to and controlling its limited supplies is the goal of the United States and other countries, conflict is bound to result. If the principle of scarcity informs our worldview and if acquisition is a defining virtue of our national story, then assuring access and controlling the flow of oil will be at the forefront of U.S. military planning. Michael T. Klare, a professor in the Peace and World Security Studies Department at Hampshire College, has written about how national leaders around the world have recently accelerated attempts to control major sources of oil and natural gas. Iraq is not the only place where the U.S. military is deployed for this purpose. Klare points out that U.S. troops all over the world risk their lives on a daily basis to protect pipelines and refineries or to supervise local military forces assigned to this mission. In addition, U.S. sailors are deployed around the world to protect sea lanes critical to oil transportation. As Klare concluded, "the American military is increasingly being converted into a global oil-protection service."[3]

In addition, as we will see later, this dynamic necessitates acquiring and controlling human resources in the form of cheap labor. In the competition for limited resources and in service to the virtue of acquisition, a national narrative wedded to *Peace as Enforced Order* will often justify treating some humans as nothing more than tools of production.

And when acquisition becomes the most important national priority, over time it subverts all other civic virtues and moral principles. A national narrative that speaks of acquisition as a virtue often confuses unlimited growth with progress and strength. A national narrative that speaks of acquisition as a virtue offers an ideal of "the good life" that is ultimately unattainable because one can never get enough to satisfy. It breeds anxiety and frustration that need to be constantly medicated (either by drugs—legal and illegal—or by addictive consumerism.)

Of course, the dynamics that drive *Peace as Enforced Order* are not new in human history. They are as old as the Bible.

## BIBLICAL MODEL

The fear-based principle of scarcity which gives rise to the virtue of acquisition and necessitates adopting a national story based on *Peace as Enforced Order* is illustrated quite well through Biblical stories of the Egyptian Pharaohs. Scripture scholar Walter Brueggemann explains that the Pharaohs of the books of Genesis and Exodus are portrayed as rulers of a powerful empire who are intent on holding on to their power by enforcing order upon all those under their rule.

Yet while they are on top of the world, they are fearful rulers. In chapter 47 of Genesis, we are introduced to a Pharaoh who is haunted by dreams. It takes an insightful young Joseph to decipher the Pharaoh's malaise. As Brueggemann points out, "Pharaoh dreams that there will be a famine in the land. . . . For the first time in the Bible, someone says, 'There's not enough. Let's get everything.'[4] Because he fears scarcity, he sets out to control as much as he can. Pharaoh creates structures to monopolize the food supply. When famine comes, he will call the shots.

The fearful Pharaoh, haunted by dreams of scarcity, is followed in Exodus by the Pharaoh whose fear of scarcity drives him to enslave the Hebrews because they were growing more numerous than the Egyptians (Exodus 1:9-10). And, to ensure that the Egyptians had all they needed, the Pharaoh gave the Hebrew slaves the task of building Pithom and Raamses to store Egypt's surplus wealth.

Do these dynamics sound familiar? In the United States, we too build versions of Pithom and Raamses to store our surplus wealth. One of the fastest growing industries in the United States has been the self-storage and portable storage container business. Even though homes have grown gargantuan in the last few decades, people find it necessary to rent space to store their surplus wealth. Many of today's three-car garages occupy 900 square feet, just about the average size of an entire home in the 1950s. And yet, the number of people who indicated to pollsters that they were "very happy" peaked in 1957, even through we now consume twice as much as we did in the 1950s.[5]

Accumulating surplus wealth while keeping people who were poor in their places was a major preoccupation of the ruling class of ancient Israel. It was during those times that God would send prophets to challenge the existing order. Bruggemann has written about how the prophets of the Jewish Scriptures struggled against what he calls the royal consciousness. Royal consciousness represented the ethos of Israel's ruling elites. The overriding message of those in power was "that there can be no future that either calls the present into question or promises a way out of it."[6] By blocking any possibility of anything genuinely new, those in power control the people by managing their expectations. Some limited forms of change can be tolerated as a strategy to thwart serious institutional and systemic change, but the fundamental arrangements of power and privilege are always kept in place.

## WHO NEEDS TO BE CONTROLLED AND WHY

Who needs to be controlled, and why is it important that their expectations be limited? If the dominant narrative is based upon a struggle over limited goods and resources, and if acquiring as much of these goods and resources as possible is the highest virtue, then a rationale for social control must be an essential element of a nation's historical account. In fact, the primary function of the dominant U.S. narrative is to not only provide justification for this struggle over goods and resources, but to construct a rationale that explains why those who do not have enough should either blame themselves or accept their circumstances.

U.S. political and military strategists have recognized that future threats have their roots in the economic disparity between those who are rich and those who are poor. And because so many of the natural resources needed to sustain our way of life are located in parts of the world where many of the poorest people live, our military capabilities must be global in reach and preeminent in power. Our foreign policy must be directed toward ensuring uninhibited access to the world's resources and unhindered access to the world's markets.

A worldview dominated by the principle of scarcity often produces economic and social policies that exacerbate the divisions between the rich and the poor. A United Nations Development Report recently stated, "Global inequalities in income and living standards have reached grotesque proportions."[7] According to a 2006 report from the World Institute for Development Economics Research, the richest 2 percent of adults in the world own more than half of all household wealth, while the poorer half of the world's population owns barely 1 percent of global wealth. A national narrative that extols acquisition as a virtue in a world it believes functions on the principle of scarcity is not troubled by these inequities; they are seen as part of the natural order in a zero-sum world. For those who are captivated by the vision of *Peace as Enforced Order*, the billions of people in the world who are poor are viewed primarily as charity cases; relief aid is viewed as important in a strategy of global security. Outside of charity, these billions of people are considered disposable to the dominant narrative; they are easily replaced as tools of production, and they are nonexistent to the market because they have no money to spend. And the real strategic challenge is to keep people who are poor under control and/or to get them to accept their fates.

Within the United States, economic inequalities are almost as bad. One in every four children in this country is born into poverty, and more than forty-five million people have no health care insurance. The richest 13,000 households earn nearly as much income as the bottom twenty million, and the top 1 percent owns more wealth than the bottom 90 percent.[8]

## Enforced Order: Knowing Your Place and Staying in It

The challenge both in the United States and around the world is essentially the same: getting those who are disenfranchised and economically powerless to accept their fates and to convince those who are not poor that the current systems and institutions of the status quo are beyond their capacity to change. A national narrative wedded to a vision of *Peace as Enforced Order* must provide its citizens with a compelling rationale for why some are very rich while so many others struggle to get by. (At the same time, it must provide a compelling reason for why billions of people throughout the world live in abject poverty, while its citizens are comparatively well-off.)

One way this narrative convinces us to accept our places in the social and economic order is by holding out the hope of limited social advancement. We are told that we cannot change the rules of the game, but if we work hard, we might just make it up one more rung of the ladder. The dynamic driving this story line is similar to lottery promotions. Even though the chances of winning are minuscule, people keep spending their hard-earned money on tickets because a few lucky people do get rich. As long as the lottery promoters tell the story of how the lottery changed the lives of those few winners, people will convince themselves that they could be next and will continue to buy more tickets.

Another way our dominant national narrative convinces us to accept our places is through the socialization process itself. Each of us finds a place in the world through a process of socialization that tells us who we are in relation to others. Over time, we learn our places in our families, our communities, and eventually in the larger society. Although the rules that determine our place are not written anywhere, in time we come to know them. Our place in the social hierarchy is largely determined by our race, class, and gender. Part of the function of the dominant narrative is to provide a rationale for why this order is necessary and good.

One major purpose of social hierarchies is to determine the distribution of power and privilege in a society and to determine the consequences for challenging this status quo. In his book *War on the Poor*, Jack Nelson-Pallmeyer quotes a lay church-worker from El Salvador whose experience of working to improve his life taught him a lesson about knowing his place: "Our crime is to be poor and ask for bread. Here the laws only favor the rich. However, the great majority of people are poor. . . . And so we demonstrate. But to speak of justice is to be called a communist, to ask for bread is subversive."[9]

Learning our place in the social hierarchy begins when we are children. In his account of the lives of inner-city children in the book *Amazing Grace*, author Jonathan Kozol relates a conversation with an adolescent from a Harlem youth center who understood her place: "It's not like being in jail; it's more like being 'hidden'. It is as if you have been put in a garage where, if they don't have room for something but aren't sure if they should throw it out, they put it there where they don't need to think of it again. . . . If people in New York woke up one day and learned that we were gone . . . I think they'd be relieved."[10]

Many social, cultural, and even religious forces keep people in their places; they serve as the first level of enforcement. In *Amazing Grace*, Kozol gives a good example of this dynamic in a conversation he had with a young woman named Maria:

My mother can't speak English, so I go with her to welfare. I always feel like crying when I see the way she's treated. "Fill this application! Hurry up! Sit down! It's not your turn!" This is not the way that people should be treated. It's not even the way you talk to dogs because you wouldn't bark at dogs. I hear this lady say to another lady, to a social worker, or a supervisor, "Why are they here if they don't speak the language? Why don't they go back where they're from?" But it isn't only language, because no one talks that way to a rich lady who does not speak English. Go downtown. You'll see what I mean. Sometimes these women come from Italy or Argentina or from Spain. They go in the stores in their beautiful clothes. They're treated like celebrities. It isn't the language. It's skin color and it's being poor.[11]

## Economic and Social Mechanisms of Control

The Salvadoran churchworker, the teenager in Harlem, and Maria are among those who have been socialized into accepting their places. Even though they have "learned their place" from the social cues they receive from the larger community, they and others who are poor and marginalized, often people of color, also experience social control through economic and social mechanisms.

In the United States, this is done through a system of economic apartheid. We no longer have a system of legal apartheid, laws that keep people separated by race. In its place, we have constructed a system of economic apartheid that, while claiming to be colorblind, in practice accomplishes the same results as the system of legal apartheid. The Supreme Court ruling in *Brown v Board of Education* may have legally ended school segregation, but white flight and economic disinvestment in the inner cities, along with school funding systems that favor children from wealthy communities, have created schools just as segregated (in the North as well as the South) and unequal as in the days of Jim Crow. (Additionally, recent rulings by the U.S. Supreme Court disallowing school districts from using race as a factor in assigning students to schools have dismantled one of the most effective means of enforcing *Brown v Board of Education*.) We no longer have housing associations with written covenants barring people of color, but the practice of "steering" by real estate agents, discrimination in mortgage availability or rates, and the disappearance of mixed-income neighborhoods have produced the same results. And as the 2005 American Community Survey from the Census Bureau shows, racial disparities in income, education, and home ownership persist, and by some measurements are growing.[12]

Often, economic mechanisms of control are combined with social mechanisms. A national story that seeks to convince its citizens that the principle of *economic opportunity* is more important than the principle that a nation should provide for the *economic well-being* of all its citizens is only possible if social myths support it. Steven Biko, the South African freedom fighter, once said that the most powerful weapon in the hands of the oppressor was the mind of the oppressed. If poor people can be taught to internalize certain beliefs about themselves, even if those beliefs serve the interests of those in power rather than the people themselves, keeping them in their places is easier.

One way of enforcing control over people who are poor is promulgating myths regarding the causes of poverty. One of these myths is a belief that those who are poor and marginalized are in their situation because of their own moral failings. Although seldom mentioned in polite conversation, there is a widely held belief across every race and class line that those who are poor are somehow less moral, less hard-working, and less intelligent than others. (This is not to deny that people often find themselves in financial crisis because of poor personal choices. However, it is woefully inadequate to assume that bad personal choices, by themselves, are the cause of poverty and marginalization. Most rich people who make bad personal choices or act immorally do not end up living in poverty.)

For the working poor on the edge of financial solvency, this myth delivers a double blow. No matter how hard they work, if they find themselves out of a job or unable to sustain their families or maintain a home, they not only suffer degrading destitution, they may also internalize the message that they are somehow morally flawed and/or lacking in character. This internalized oppression keeps people trapped in victimhood and keeps them from asking questions about the way the system works, questions that might make those in power nervous. More importantly, it keeps them from imagining a different future and keeps them from joining together with others to work for systemic change.

This myth of poverty also allows those who are rich and powerful to exercise a strategy of charity that does not question the institutions or systems that create poverty, but in fact protects the status quo. If poverty results from individuals making poor choices, then solutions are limited to individual intervention to "help the less fortunate." In this way, those who exercise power can set the terms of their "charity" by sorting out the "deserving poor" from the "undeserving poor." In the end, charity without institutional and systemic change serves as an enabling mechanism that keeps the system intact.

## The Ultimate Enforcers of *Peace as Enforced Order*

If people forget their places or if social, cultural, economic, or religious forces fail to keep them in their places, the police (at home) and the military (abroad) serve as the ultimate enforcers of peace. One of the most important roles played by our dominant national narrative—wedded to a vision of *Peace as Enforced Order*—is providing us with a rationale for why our prisons are filled with so many poor people of color. At the same time, it must provide us with a rationale for why we need military bases all over the world and why we must support some of the world's most oppressive governments. A national narrative that can appeal to the fear-based principle of scarcity is often all that is needed to overcome most people's qualms. Any threat to our ability to sustain a lifestyle based on unlimited acquisition can often silence nagging doubts.

Most of the time, the deterrent effects of the police and military are enough to keep people in their places—especially those who are poor and marginalized. But when deterrence fails, these ultimate enforcers of the established order can be brought into play.

## Around the World:
## The Military and the Military-Industrial Complex

We can see how *Peace as Enforced Order* plays out by looking at the way the U.S. military is used in Central and South America. Over the past forty years, the United States has poured billions of dollars in military aid into countries in that region, even though very few of these countries faced or face a military threats from any of their neighbors. During the Cold War, the rationale of our dominant narrative was rooted in the principle of scarcity (if Communists came to power, we could lose access to important resources) or an appeal to the virtue of acquisition (if Communists came to power, they could threaten "our way of life").

After the Soviet Empire collapsed, selling the threat of communism in this region was hard to maintain. Now we speak about "leftist governments" that threaten our access to resources and our way of life. Regardless of the dominant narrative's rationale, the real reason for all this military aid was to control the populations of these countries in order to maintain a social and economic order benefiting those at the top and maintaining the position of U.S. economic interests, keeping resources flowing north.

This military aid may be designated for fighting the drug trade or rebel forces, but in countries like Colombia, it does more than this, as the military and police also maintain the economic and social power structure that protect both the ruling class of that country and U.S. investments and profits. Recent investigations show how right-wing paramilitary groups work hand-in-hand with the Colombian military and other national security forces to maintain order. For instance, in 2007, Salvatore Mancuso, the former Commander of the right-wing United Self-Defense Forces of Colombia (AUC), testified that high-ranking Colombian military officers routinely aided paramilitary groups in training and logistics.[13]

Any social group (like unions or peace organizations) that tries to challenge the power relationships in Colombia can become a target of the security forces. For example, in February of 2005, Alejandro Pérez, a member of the Peace Community of San José de Apartadó was killed by a member of a paramilitary group under the command of the Army's 17th Brigade.[14] Members of the Peace Community not only called for an end to the civil war in Colombia, they also called for social and economic justice for those who are poor.

The murder of Alejandro Pérez was not an isolated incident. In Colombia, as elsewhere, when the economic interests of the powerful are threatened, violence can become widespread. The repression not only targets civic organizations like the Peace Community of San José de Apartadó, it often spreads to other sectors of the civil society like churches and unions. An April 2004 report from a fact-finding delegation to Colombia headed by New York City Council Member Hiram Monserrate looked at the situation of organized labor in that country, especially those unions working for U.S.-based corporations. The delegation contended:

> To date, there have been a total of 179 major human rights violations of Coca-Cola's workers, including nine murders. Family members of union activists have been abducted and tortured. Sinaltrainal Union members have been fired for attending union meetings. The company has pressured workers to resign their union membership and contractual rights, and fired workers who refused to do so.[15]

Today, union leaders continue to routinely receive death threats and attempts on their lives.

Sinaltrainal accuses Coca-Cola and two of its bottlers of failing to protect workers and using right-wing paramilitaries of the AUC to murder and terrorize them. Shortly after announcing plant closings in 2004, armed men kidnapped the 15-year-old son of labor leader Limberto Carranza in Barranquilla as he rode his bicycle home from school. The kidnappers beat and tortured him and stated that his father was on a list of people whom they planned to murder. During the boy's ordeal, his father received a telephone call in which an individual said, "Unionist son-of-a-bitch, we are going to kill you . . . and if we can't kill you, we will kill your family."[16]

This violence also affects the wider community. According to a United Nations report released on March 15, 2007, Colombian security forces killed civilians in several states during the previous year and falsely labeled many as leftist rebels slain in combat.[17] Often those who work to change the status quo in Colombia's social order are labeled rebels and then assassinated or driven into exile.

To the economic and political elites of Colombia, even drug traffickers are less of a threat than those who try to redistribute political and economic power in the country. (The traffickers are only interested in making money and protecting their market share, not in changing the social order.) As bad as the drug trade has been for Colombia, for those who wield power in that country, the bigger threat is any social movement, organization, or group that would threaten the current social and economic order.

A military's ability to play this role in countries allied to the United States, such as Colombia, is possible because of the weapons and training we provide. Our military industries provide the weapons to many countries around the world, and our armed forces provide the advisors and trainers that sustain and protect the distribution of power and privilege at the expense of the majority of the people. To these ends, the United States has become the world's largest exporter of weapons. A report compiled by the nonpartisan Congressional Research Service found that in 2005 the United States provided nearly half of the weapons sold to militaries in the developing world, the highest level in eight years. According to the annual assessment, in 2005 the United States supplied $8.1 billion worth of weapons to developing countries—45.8 percent of the world's total and far more than second-ranked Russia (15 percent) and Britain (a little over 13 percent).[18] While in some cases these arms sales might be justified for protection from external threats, for the most part they are destined to be used to keep order within these countries. Because arms sometimes flow to all sides in a conflict, those who deal in the arms trade (both legal and illegal) make higher profits from the increase in mayhem and destruction.

## At Home: The Criminal Justice System

In the United States, the police play a crucial role in enforcing the law and protecting citizens from harm—often at great risk to themselves. But the police in this country also often play the same role of maintaining the social and economic order that U.S.-backed military establishments around the world do. In the same way the military-industrial complex plays an important role in the business of protecting the global social and economic order, the criminal justice system and the prison-industrial complex play important roles in the business of protecting the social and economic order within the United States. And keeping people in their place here at home is also lucrative business. Together with the cost of the entire criminal justice system, law enforcement is one of the largest budget items in state and local governments.

When it plays out in the criminal justice system, every form of social and economic control used to keep people in their places is magnified a hundred fold. The racism that exists in society as a whole can become lethal when expressed through the criminal justice system. The stereotypes that exist about those who are poor in society exact a terrible price when expressed through the criminal justice system. It is not that the majority of men and women employed in the criminal justice system are any more racist or judgmental toward those who are poor than anyone else; but because they are assigned the added task of social control, their racism is sometimes expressed in brutal and demeaning ways. They have been given the thankless task of being the "thin blue line" protecting a society that would rather not be confronted with the effects of its racism or economic apartheid.

Probably no event in recent history more clearly illustrates the role of the police in keeping people in their place than the 1991 police beating of Rodney King, the subsequent acquittal of the police officers by a Simi Valley jury, and the South Central Los Angeles uprising that followed. The mostly white, middle-class people of Simi Valley and others in the dominant culture viewed the beating of Rodney King "from above." Sympathetic to the police, they viewed the black man as a "dangerous animal" and thus saw the acquittal as good and the uprising as bad. On the other hand, those who revolted in the streets saw the police beating as another example of a system designed to enforce their societal inferior status; the uprising expressed their anger over this system of oppression designed to keep them in their place.[19] And the King beating is by no means an isolated example, which explains that while white parents teach their children that the police are their friends, many parents of color teach their children how to survive an encounter with the police.

Encounters with the police in this nation increasingly lead to incarceration, a very overt form of control. In their pastoral statement "Responsibility, Rehabilitation and Restoration: A Catholic Perspective on Crime and Criminal Justice," the U.S. Catholic Bishops pointed out that the United States has an imprisonment rate that is six to twelve times higher than other Western countries. By the end of 2006, a record 7.2 million people—one in every thirty-one U.S. adults—were behind bars, on probation, or on parole. And these numbers continue to grow. At the start of 2007, more than one in every one hundred adults in the United States were behind bars (in jail or prison)—more than 2.3 million people. The United States incarcerates more people than any country in the world, even those that are more populous.[20]

Far too often, incarceration and other involvement with the criminal justice system target those who need to be "kept in their place"—especially blacks and Latinos. This disturbing reality is often hidden by a dominant narrative that portrays poor people of color as threats to "our way of life" (defined by the principle of scarcity and the virtue of acquisition).

The rhetoric and policies associated with the "War on Drugs" has also greatly assisted this historical telling. In their statement on the criminal justice system, the U.S. Catholic Bishops cut through the rhetoric of the "War on Drugs" to the reality of poor communities of color under siege. For instance, they link these large incarceration rates with anti-drug policies such as the "three strikes and you're out" and "zero-tolerance" for drug offenders. Writing in the *Chicago Tribune*, Darnell Little notes that twenty-five years after President Reagan declared a "War on Drugs," many criminologists say drugs are now cheaper and more potent. But what the war did do was help to more than quadruple the size of the nation's prison population from 1980 to 2005, with urban blacks and Latinos hardest hit. Little went on to write that according to federal data, "blacks make up just 13 percent of the nation's illicit drug users, but they are 32 percent of those arrested for drug violations and 53 percent of those incarcerated in state prisons for drug crimes. In Illinois, studies show that more than 70 percent of the state's illicit drug users are white, while 14 percent are black. But 65 percent of arrests for drug offenses are of African-Americans."[21]

In fact, prisons are one of the largest growth industries in this country. And in more recent years, there has been tremendous growth in privately run prisons. This growth is furthered by another "war": the war on undocumented immigrants. The Bush Administration's get tough policy on undocumented immigrants and its increase in enforcement spending has benefited many companies that build and run private prisons around the country. The Bush Administration estimated that by the fall of 2007 about 27,500 immigrants would be in detention each night, an increase of 6,700 over the 2006 custody numbers. At an average cost of $95 a night, that adds up to an estimated total annual cost of nearly $1 billion. Wall Street has taken notice of the potential growth in the industry. The stock of Corrections Corporation of America climbed to $53.77 from $42.50, an increase of about 27 percent, from February (when President Bush proposed adding to spending on immigrant detention) to July of 2006.[22]

---

## TRADE-OFFS AND INTERNAL CONTRADICTIONS

*Peace as Enforced Order* can provide stability, but it can also mask deep divisions and crushing injustices. While it can, to some degree, provide predictability in social, economic, and political relationships, it can also make it harder to understand or adapt to the pressure for change from below. *Peace as Enforced Order* can reduce open conflict, but it can also create conflicts that are harder to identify and even harder to resolve.

In the dominant U.S. narrative, *Peace as Enforced Order* is guided by a fear-based worldview that makes us an easy target for terrorists. As stated at the beginning of this chapter, *Peace as Enforced Order* is familiar ground for terrorists. They know how to fight a nation that operates out of this vision of peace because it is the same as theirs. A nation given over to this vision of peace can easily be provoked into responding in-kind to terrorist attacks. This, in turn, sets up a cycle of attack and counter-attack that plays to the advantage of the terrorists. A nation given over to *Peace as Enforced Order* can also become one-dimensional in responding to threats. If the world is understood as a zero-sum game (where one's gain is only possible because of another's loss), then dualistic thinking is portrayed as strength while acknowledging nuances is a sign of weakness.

Because it assumes that every other nation or people is a competitor that must be controlled or defeated, a nation that organizes itself around a vision of *Peace as Enforced Order* must expend an enormous amount of energy and resources to maintain and protect what is prizes above all else: order. Thus, the dominant U.S. narrative based on *Peace as Enforced Order* is a "fortress America" that spends more of its wealth projecting its military power around the world than it does on diplomacy and development aid. While it may give lip service to higher ideals and principles at times when its security seems secure, its true nature is revealed in times of crisis or when it feels vulnerable.

The dominant U.S. narrative, wedded to *Peace as Enforced Order*, must always be searching for an enemy on which to focus its obsessive fear of vulnerability and need for security. Knowing the planet does not have enough resources to duplicate the lifestyle of its own people for the rest of the world, it tries to convince itself that those who are poor are envious of all that its members have achieved through hard work and moral superiority, while at the same time constantly looking over their shoulders for fear that others might threaten their place in the social order. It also creates a civilian population that sees enemies everywhere (in their Arab and South Asian neighbors or in the undocumented Mexican worker who cuts their lawns and cleans their office buildings).

Based on fear and a need for enemies, any national narrative completely given over to *Peace as Enforced Order* cannot operate as a true democracy. It can have all the trappings of a democracy—elections, a multi-party system, an independent judiciary, and a free press—but when threatened, all of these facades collapse like a house of cards. During these times of crisis, the only true imperative takes precedence—maintaining control and preserving power and privilege.

Of course, this is not totally true for the United States, because we are not totally given over to the vision of *Peace as Enforced Order*. Another force is at work in the United States that sees peace as something quite different; and it is part of a very different kind of U.S. narrative. In the next chapter, we will examine this alternative.

# CHAPTER EIGHT

# Peace as the Enterprise of Justice: At the Heart of an Alternative U.S. Narrative

If the fear of loss—based on a worldview of scarcity and un-remitting competition for control of resources by the few in power—drives *Peace as Enforced Order*, how do we construct and promote an alternative understanding of peace that does not hold us hostage to this fear? If nations committed to *Peace as Enforced Order* can be manipulated by terrorists who exploit this fear, doesn't combating terrorism need to include changing our understanding of how to establish peace?

We can do this by constructing an alternative narrative of *Peace as an Enterprise of Justice*. In the Roman Catholic tradition, the understanding of peace is articulated in the *Pastoral Constitution of the Church in the Modern World*, which states that peace is not merely the absence of war, but "an enterprise of justice."[1] This vision is grounded in the Christian understanding of peace as both a gift of God and a human work, constructed on the central human values of truth, justice, freedom, and love. In the Christian faith, peace is viewed in positive terms; *Peace as Enforced Order* sees peace in negative terms—the absence of conflict.

Pope Paul VI laid out a marker by which all notions of this positive view of peace are measured. Speaking to the UN General Assembly in 1972, he asked the world's leaders to recognize that all over the globe, people who were poor were crying out for justice. At that time, he made this passionate plea: "Why do we waste time in giving peace any other foundation than Justice? . . . Peace resounds as an invitation to practice Justice: 'Justice will bring about Peace' (Is. 32:17). We repeat this today in a more incisive and dynamic formula: 'If you want Peace, work for Justice.'" Nearly thirty years later, in the rubble of South Central Los Angeles after the uprising sparked by the acquittal of the police officers who beat Rodney King, a group of local pastors echoed Pope Paul VI's warning that when we ignore justice, we undermine peace: "Indeed, as long as violence remains the language by which the dominant culture maintains its power, the unheard will be forced to use violence to reach us with their demands for justice."[2]

In Christian thought, justice is understood in two ways. Commutative justice calls for fundamental fairness in all agreements and exchanges between individuals or private social groups. Distributive justice requires evaluating the allocation of income, wealth, and power in society in light of its effects on persons whose basic material needs are unmet. If persons are to be recognized as members of the human community, then the community has an obligation to help fulfill these basic needs.[3]

The central dynamic of *Peace as an Enterprise of Justice* is primarily about distributive justice: ensuring that all the world's people have enough to live in dignity and have access to the resources necessary to develop to their full human potentials. In the absence of this kind of justice, terrorists will find a fertile breeding ground for their extremist and violent ideologies in the frustrated hopes of people who are poor. Around the world, terrorists are counting on us to respond to their attacks from a position of *Peace as Enforced Order*. When we make establishing order a priority over addressing the root causes of why some people do not have access to the resources they need to live in dignity (distributive justice), we risk driving people who cry for justice into the arms of the terrorists. Our challenge is to not give the terrorists what they want. As Benjamin Barber writes of terrorists in his book *Jihad vs. McWorld*, "Their message is: 'Your sons want to live, ours are ready to die.' Our response must be this: 'We will create a world in which the seductions of death hold no allure because the bounties of life are accessible to everyone.'"⁴

While a nation committed to *Peace as Enforced Order* is likely to interpret the cry for justice from those who are poor as a threat, a nation committed to *Peace as an Enterprise of Justice* is likely to interpret this cry for justice as an invitation to solidarity. To move our nation away from the dominant national narrative based on *Peace as Enforced Order* to embracing an alternative based on *Peace as an Enterprise of Justice*, we need to demonstrate to our fellow citizens that the principle of scarcity that drives the vision of *Peace as Enforced Order* is not central to our national story. Instead, we will need to articulate an alternative that demonstrates that the principle of abundance is more central to who we are and what we strive to be. In the same way, to move our nation away from the dominant narrative that sees acquisition as a national virtue, we will need to articulate an alternative national narrative that reminds our fellow citizens how the virtue of enough has shaped our nation's past and best exemplifies our nation's character.

Although often ignored, co-opted, or trivialized in U.S. popular culture and politics, the vision of *Peace as the Enterprise of Justice* has a long tradition in the United States. President John Kennedy, in his famous 1963 commencement speech at American University, spoke eloquently about this vision of peace:

> What kind of peace do I mean and what kind of peace do we seek? Not a *Pax Americana*, enforced on the world by American weapons of war. I am talking about genuine peace, the kind of peace that makes life on earth worth living, and the kind that enables men and nations to grow, and to hope, and build a better life for their children. Not merely a peace for Americans but peace for all men and women. Not merely peace in our time, but peace in all times.⁵

While the stories of those working for distributive justice may not get covered on the evening news or included in our children's history books, we do have models in our nation's past who exemplify the best of our collective commitment to the ethic of the common good. These examples are rooted in the best of our religious and civic traditions. Part of the work of articulating an alternative national narrative based on the vision of *Peace as an Enterprise of Justice* is lifting up these heroes and sheroes of our U.S. story.

## THE PRINCIPLE OF ABUNDANCE

Abundance is the fundamental principle guiding the strategic thinking of those who seek a narrative based on *Peace as the Enterprise of Justice*. The principle of abundance holds that the goods of this earth necessary to support lives that are fully human and fully alive are bountiful. For people of faith, the principle of abundance is rooted in the belief that God created the world as exceedingly fruitful and that the providence of God assures that if we are faithful to God's call to righteousness and justice, all of our needs will be met (Matthew 6:25-34).

At the national level, the principle of abundance is expressed in the ethic of the common good (introduced in Chapter Six). When a nation embraces the principle of abundance (as opposed to the principle of scarcity), competition between people gives way to cooperation. And cooperation makes the ethic of the common good (and thus a sharing of the earth's abundance) possible. Scarcity breeds fear that there is not enough for everyone. An ethic of the common good, born out of the principle of abundance, encourages people to look to their neighbors to ensure that all have what they need. In an age of globalization, this ethic of the common good should be expanded to include our neighbors throughout the world.

However, our dominant national narrative has convinced many citizens that rugged individualism is what has made our country what it is today. Our dominant national narrative prizes independence above all else and tells us that each person should be responsible for self and family only; no one is owed a living and no one has a right to economic security. Our dominant narrative tells us that our nation was built through the hard work of individual achievement: people pulling themselves up by their own bootstraps. This historical telling reminds us that the role of government is to provide order in social relations so that individuals can pursue their own self interests; the government should not concern itself with distributive justice. And what our dominant narrative holds as true for our own nation, it also preaches to the rest of the world.

Unfortunately, while our dominant narrative makes allowances for charity toward those who are poor, distributive justice based on an ethic of the common good is not part of this story. Under the dominant national narrative, we have been socialized into distrusting the concept of distributive justice, viewing it as foreign and alien. Therefore, the ethic of the common good is often viewed as "un-American," a temptation that invites laziness and dependency in others.

To counter this, we can create an alternative based on the vision of *Peace as an Enterprise of Justice*. We can begin by lifting up from our national history the stories of how our forebearers embraced the principle of abundance by living out of an ethic of the common good. In doing so, we need to start by acknowledging that the ethic of the common good was present in many of the nations that inhabited this land long before European immigrants landed on its shores. Many indigenous peoples embodied the principle of abundance and the ethic of the common good in their communal lives. The Iroquois Tribes established their villages so that the land was owned and worked in common. Hunting was done together, and the food was shared with everyone. Even houses were considered common property.[6]

This ethos is not just an artifact of the past. In the face of overwhelming challenges, today many American Indian tribes keep alive this traditional belief in the communal nature of wealth. As American Indian activist Hunter Gray (also known as Hunter Bear) reminds us:

> Despite several centuries of physical genocide, forced removal and relocation, and attempted socio-cultural genocide [all of this designed to secure remaining Indian land and resources] . . . The commitment to a cohesive family and clan, to one's tribe [essentially one big family], remain strong as do the basic values inherent in tribal cultures . . . an essentially communalistic view of land use; democracy; egalitarianism; classlessness.[7]

It is also a concept present in the history of the country we today call the United States. In the political sphere, the ethic of common good based on the principle of abundance is often referred to as the public good. From the beginning of the founding of our republic, the public good was enshrined as an important national value. James Madison stated clearly in the Federalist Papers that "the public good, the real welfare of the great body of the people, is the supreme object to be pursued; and that no form of government whatever has any other value than as it may be fitted for the attainment of this objective." And the preamble to the U.S. Constitution enshrines this notion of the public good: "We, the people of the United States, in order to form a more perfect union, establish justice, insure domestic tranquility, provide for the common defense, promote the general welfare, and secure the blessings of liberty to ourselves and our posterity, do ordain and establish this Constitution of the United States of America."[8]

And while our nation is clearly seduced by the dominant narrative's vision of *Peace as Enforced Order, Peace as the Enterprise of Justice* has always been at work in our collective life. Sometimes it has been in ascendancy in public life and discourse; at other times, it has survived as a minority opinion or prophetic voice crying in the wilderness. One example of this prophetic tradition in U.S. history was Dr. Martin Luther King Jr. Dr. King blended both religious and civic values into a vision of justice. Equally at ease quoting from the Constitution as from the Bible, his greatest appeal was in calling America to live up to its highest ideals and become the nation it was meant to be.

As Dr. King prepared to launch the Poor Peoples' Campaign, shortly before his murder, he appealed to the nation by first recalling the ideals enshrined in the Declaration of Independence: that every person had a right to life, liberty, and the pursuit of happiness. Then he asked the nation to embrace an ethic of the common good by reminding us that we could not lay claim to the ideals of our founders until every person attained these basic rights: "But if a man doesn't have a job or an income, he has neither life nor liberty nor the possibility for the pursuit of happiness. He merely exists." And he linked this civic obligation to a religious call to repentance for collectively failing those left out of the American dream:

> It seems that I can hear the God of history saying, "I was hungry, and ye fed me not. I was naked, and ye clothed me not. I was devoid of a decent sanitary house to live in, and ye provided no shelter for me. And consequently, you cannot enter the kingdom of greatness. If ye do it unto the least of these, my brethren, ye do it unto me."[9]

As King said, echoing the words of Jesus, we cannot live in the Reign of God without taking account of our neighbors. While the principle of scarcity in the narrative of *Peace as Enforced Order* encourages people to strive to obtain as much as they can for themselves, the principle of abundance in the narrative of *Peace as the Enterprise of Justice* can only be realized if people are encouraged to look beyond their needs and the needs of their immediate community in order to address the needs of everyone. This starts by knowing the difference between what we need to live full human lives and what we desire.

## THE VIRTUE OF ENOUGH

While the goods of the earth are abundant, they are not limitless. As the Mahatma Gandhi reminded us, "The earth has enough to meet every one's need but not enough for everyone's greed." Therefore, the highest virtue of *Peace as the Enterprise of Justice* is "enough." Only by recognizing the difference between what is needed and what is merely desired can a person (or nation) understand the virtue of enough.

Implied in this virtue is a constant dialogue between the individual and the community about rights and responsibilities. What rights and responsibilities do individuals have in relationship to the community? What rights and responsibilities does the community have in relationship to its individual members? Or as St. Paul put it in his letter to the Corinthians:

> The body is one and has many members but all the members, many though they are, are one body. . . . If the foot should say "Because I am not a hand I do not belong to the body," would it then no longer belong to the body? If the ear should say, "Because I am not an eye I do not belong to the body," would it then no longer belong to the body? . . . The eye cannot say to the hand, "I do not need you," any more than the head can say to the feet, "I do not need you". . . If one member suffers, all the members suffer with it; if one member is honored, all the members share its joy (1 Corinthians 12:12, 14-16, 21, 26).

St. Paul pointed out that no member of the body can act as if not connected to the whole. The body exists as an interdependent web of relationships that makes each part subject to the whole and makes the whole body subject to each part. This web of mutual relationships, of rights and responsibilities, allows the body to function as a single organism. And this interdependent web of relationships makes it possible to discern the difference between what is needed and what is merely desired. Apart from these mutual relationships, growth cannot be regulated. In fact, unlimited growth of one part without regard to the needs of the whole body has a name: cancer.

Most of us begin to learn the virtue of enough in relationship, often beginning around the family dinner table (especially those of us raised in large families). While the reflexive impulse of a child eying a plate of leftovers is to grab what he/she can before the other siblings, wise parents will use potential dinner table conflicts like this to begin teaching their children the virtue of enough. In these teachable moments, parents remind their children that being a member of a family means negotiating individual needs with the other members of the family.

In addition to dinner table ethics, many children learn the virtue of enough in their faith communities. Often, they are invited to forgo their own wants to meet the needs of those who are poor. In the Catholic tradition, one popular children's Lenten activity is collecting money for Catholic Relief Services in cardboard "rice bowls." Wise religious educators use these teachable moments to encourage children not to ask their parents for money to fill the rice bowls, but to examine ways they might cut back on their own discretionary spending to meet the basic needs of those who are less fortunate.

Unfortunately, sometime between early childhood and adulthood, many of us lose perspective and forget the virtue of enough. Maybe it is because we are so determined to ensure that our own children have a better life that we often forget that having more is not the same as living better. Maybe it is because, as we get older, we tend to compare ourselves with those who have more than we do, so we seldom raise the ethical question, "Do I really need this?" Maybe it is because we are constantly bombarded by so much advertising telling us that we are not whole or happy until we have purchased one more gizmo or consumer experience, that we become seduced into believing that our things define us.

Until the age of mass production, the virtue of enough was always a part of our national character. From the folk wisdom of Benjamin Franklin to the simple living movement of today, people in the United States have often been suspicious of addictive consumerism. U.S. citizens like Henry David Thoreau helped to set a moral tone by writing, "A man is rich in proportion to the number of things which he can afford to let alone."[10] And the first U.S.-born Catholic saint, Mother Elizabeth Seton, set forth the ethical principle, "Live simply that others might simply live."

But with the age of mass production and mass advertising, this virtue has become increasingly disregarded. Elise Boulding, author, peace activist, and co-founder of the Peace Studies program at Dartmouth College, lamented the loss of the importance of frugality in the United States today and questions whether the addictive consumerism that drives so much of our lives is really able to make us any happier: "Frugality is one of the most beautiful and joyful words in the English language, and yet one that we are culturally cut off from understanding and enjoying. The consumption society has made us feel that happiness lies in having things, and has failed to teach us the happiness of not having things."[11]

## EQUITABLE DISTRIBUTION

Given the current inequities of our world, *Peace as an Enterprise of Justice*, unlike *Peace as Enforced Order*, requires fundamentally altering the current economic order. Creating institutional and systemic changes that guarantee all people on this planet the resources they need to develop to their fullest human potentials should become the overriding strategic goal in our efforts to combat terrorism and establish peace and security. Unless and until we can change the culture of acquisition extolled in our dominant narrative into a culture of enough for all, our efforts to end terrorism will amount to little more than trying to put out a raging forest fire with a leaky bucket.

This cultural change can only be accomplished if we successfully challenge our dominant narrative's myth of rugged individualism in pursuit of self-interest. Cultivating the virtue of enough is only possible when people make all their decisions fully conscious of the fact that they are part of a wider community that extends to the whole world. A nation of individual families or interest groups pursing their own self-interests will have no compelling reason to embrace this virtue. Deciding on "enough" is not something an individual can do without looking to his or her neighbor to see if that person's basic needs are met.

The enterprise of justice calls on individuals not to compare their wants and needs to those who live above them in the social order, but to compare themselves to those who live below. Thoughtful discernment about "enough" in a society where the basic needs of some are not met is not only a religious concern; it is at the heart of our republican tradition. As Robert Bellah and his co-authors explain in their book *Habits of the Heart*:

> The litmus test that both the biblical and republican traditions give us for assaying the health of a society is how it deals with the problem of wealth and poverty. . . . Both testaments make it clear that societies sharply divided between rich and poor are not in accord with the will of God. Classic republican theory from Aristotle to the American founders rests on the assumption that free institutions could survive in society only if there were a rough equality of condition and that extremes of wealth and poverty are incompatible with a republic.[12]

## BIBLICAL MODELS

The story of the People of God that runs through the entire Judeo-Christian Scriptures has at its heart a fundamental conviction that we live in a world of great abundance and that we are called to trust in God's providence by practicing the virtue of enough. This principle of abundance—lived out through the virtue of enough—defines what it means to be the People of God. It also requires us to be faithful to the covenant God established with us and to take care of and provide for each other. The biblical story is filled with examples of how God sent prophets to correct the People of God when they failed this covenant, prophets who called them back from the fear-based heresy of scarcity to God's promise of abundance and from the greed-inducing vice of acquisition to the virtue of enough.

Trust in God's providence and practicing the virtue of enough are introduced early in the biblical narrative of God's great work of creating a Covenant People. In Exodus, a newly created community of freed slaves, trying to find their way in the wilderness, provides us with a model of the principle of abundance and the virtue of enough. When these freed slaves left Egypt and began the journey across the wilderness, they faced the ultimate economic challenge: how would they sustain themselves? (Exodus 16:2-3) In addition to religious and ethical laws to guide them (symbolized by the Ten Commandments), God sought to teach them a new set of principles for their economic lives, a set of principles based on abundance and enough for all.

The story of the manna in the desert is often preached as a miraculous feeding story. But, as scripture scholar Ched Myers points out, it is much more. The manna story is also about God testing these newly freed slaves to see "whether they follow my instructions or not" (Exodus 16:4). God instructed the Hebrews to take only what they needed for the day and not to store up any surplus manna, except for the day before the Sabbath (the day they were to rest from work). The story tells us that the Hebrews learned that "those who gathered a large amount did not have too much and those who gathered a small amount did not have too little" (Exodus 16:18). As Myers pointed out, "In God's economy there is such a thing as 'too much' and 'too little.' (This contrasts radically with modern capitalism's infinite tolerance for wealth and poverty.)" God responded to those tempted to horde the manna out of fear of scarcity by causing the horded manna to spoil (Exodus 16:19-20), and God thwarted those tempted to acquire more than others by miraculously distributing the manna in a way that met everyone's needs, but not their wants. In the lessons learned from this manna economy, God established the ethical foundations for the economic lives of the Covenant People.

The book of Exodus also ties the manna story to the establishment of the Sabbath and the requirements of living as a Covenant People. Talking about this link, Myers wrote:

> Torah's Sabbath regulations represent God's strategy for teaching Israel about its dependence upon the land as a gift to share equitably, not as a possession to exploit. . . . Because the earth belongs to God and its fruits are a gift, the people should justly distribute those fruits, instead of seeking to own and hoard them. . . . This primal lesson was so fundamental that the people were instructed to keep a jarful of the manna in front of the Covenant (Ex. 16:32; see Heb. 9:4). Sabbath observation means to remember every week this economy's two principles: the goal of "enough" for everyone, and the prohibition on accumulation.[13]

In this light, we can begin to see the whole of the prophetic tradition in the Jewish Scriptures as a call for Israel to return to the covenantal understanding of "enough" (implicit in the demand for justice for those who are poor) and a condemnation of violations of the Sabbath (i.e., failure to trust in God's providence). The U.S. Catholic Bishops point out in their peace pastoral that in the Jewish Scriptures, "Living in covenantal fidelity with God had ramifications in the lives of the people. . . . When Israel tended to forget the obligations of the covenant, prophets arose to remind the people and call them to return to God." One powerful example of this tradition is from the prophet Isaiah:

> Is not this the fast that I choose: to loose the bonds
> of injustice, to undo the thongs of the yoke, to let the
> oppressed go free and to break every yoke? Is it not
> to share your bread with the hungry and bring the
> homeless poor into your house; when you see the na-
> ked to cover them, and not to hide yourself from your
> own kin? Then your light shall break forth like the
> dawn, and your healing shall spring up quickly; your
> vindicator shall go before you, the glory of God shall
> be your rear guard. Your ancient ruins shall be rebuilt;
> you shall rise up from the foundations of many gener-
> ations; you shall be called the repairer of the breach,
> the restorer of streets to live in (Isaiah 58: 6-8, 12).

In light of the principle of abundance and the virtue of enough, the whole of Jesus' public ministry can be seen as reaffirming this principle of Sabbath economics—equitable distribution, enough for all—in the life of Israel. His mother heralded his coming as a time of great redistribution of wealth, "He has deposed the mighty from their thrones and raised the lowly to high places. The hungry he has given every good thing, while the rich he has sent empty away" (Luke 1:52-53). Jesus began his public ministry by signaling a time of Jubilee, "the year of favor from God" (Luke 4:19), when debts would be canceled, land restored to its original owners, and slaves and debtors set free.

His feeding miracles pivot on conversations with his disciples regarding a perception of scarcity, "Why do you not give them something to eat yourselves? . . . We have nothing but five loaves and two fishes" (Luke 9:13). Yet, when redistributed, everyone had enough. In the Sermon on the Mount, Jesus warns against laying up treasure (Matthew 6:19) and making wealth into a god (Matthew 6:24). Jesus foresees the coming of the Reign of God as a great reversal of economic fortunes, "Blessed are you who hunger, you shall be filled" (Luke 6:20) and "Woe to you who are full; you shall go hungry" (Luke 6:25). In teaching his disciples to pray only for their "daily bread" (Matthew 6:11), Jesus demonstrates the virtue of enough as a sign of trust in God's providence. And when Jesus calls his disciple to witness the charity of the widow at the temple treasury compared to that of the rich and powerful ("They gave from their surplus wealth, but she gave from her want" [Mark 12:44]), he offers an example of living out the principle of abundance. This redistribution, based on God's abundance, is the presence of justice.

In the same way that Dr. Martin Luther King Jr. (prophet of an alternative national narrative of *Peace as an Enterprise of Justice*) wove together a narrative tying our great civic values with the biblical calling to justice, we too are challenged to continue the work of creating an alternative narrative by appealing to both our civic and religious traditions. These biblical stories offer us a rich heritage and source of inspiration.

## WORKING FOR JUSTICE: RECLAIMING U.S. HISTORY

Our dominant national narrative is filled with stories of powerful politicians, generals, and business leaders who came out on top in the zero-sum competition embodied in the principle of scarcity; this telling also celebrates those who manage to acquire more wealth than they could possibly use in a lifetime. Yet our history is also filled with heroic examples of fellow citizens who contributed to the greatness of our nation by dedicating their lives to the pursuit of *Peace as an Enterprise of Justice*. By retrieving the stories of these heroes and sheroes from our past and lifting them up as models for our nation's future, we can effectively challenge the dominant national narrative of *Peace as Enforced Order*.

*Peace as an Enterprise of Justice* has always been a part of the U.S. narrative, although it certainly has never received the attention that our military history of *Peace as Enforced Order* has. In fact, the struggle for economic justice in the United States predates the founding of the republic and is part of the history of many of the indigenous people on this land. For example, in 1676, many in the colonies suffered extreme poverty. Bacon's Rebellion was one attempt by (white) colonists to address the laws and practices that benefited those who were wealthy at the expense of those who were poor. The hopes of those participating in the rebellion were expressed as "leveling," a means of equalizing wealth. In an act that further threatened the social order of the Virginia colony, blacks began to join the rebellion. Anti-racism organizer PaKou Her pointed out that "Black people began joining Bacon in the rebellion against the ruling elite, culminating in approximately 2,000 Black workers and 4,000 White workers burning Jamestown to the ground."[14]

This was but one of the many struggles for economic justice in this country that realized the necessity of building coalitions across the racial lines set in place by the ruling elites to keep poor people divided. In fact, there was a time in U.S. history when citizens, organizing to challenge the accumulation of wealth and power in the hands of the few at the expense of the many who were poor, was not only commonplace, but was also seen as foundational to our national story.

Shay's Rebellion of 1787 is one example: Members of the lower classes, in the spirit of rebellion that launched the War of Independence from Britain, called for distributive justice by appealing to the principles of equality and liberty. In reflecting upon this rebellion for economic justice, Thomas Jefferson, in France at the time, wrote to a friend saying, "I hold it that a little rebellion now and then is a good thing. . . . It is a medicine necessary for the sound health of government. . . . God forbid that we should ever be twenty years without such a rebellion. . . . The tree of liberty must be refreshed from time to time with the blood of patriots and tyrants."[15] Jefferson believed that the struggle for economic justice, born out of an ethic of the common good, was not only patriotic, but absolutely necessary to keep the United States true to its founding principles.

Even members of the ruling elite of this country have recognized the dangers to the public good and the republican ideals of this country that come from inequitable wealth distribution. Speaking to the New York State Legislature in 1788, conservative Alexander Hamilton said, "As riches increase and accumulate in few hands; as luxury prevails in society; virtue will be in a greater degree considered as only a graceful appendage of wealth, and the tendency of things will be to depart from the republican standard." In 1889, Andrew Carnegie wrote in his *Gospel of Wealth*, "The problem of our age is the proper administration of wealth, that the ties of brotherhood may still bind together the rich and poor in harmonious relationship." In 1911, Henry Lee Higginson, a leading member of the Boston establishment, wrote, "I do not believe that, because a man owns property, it belongs to him to do with as he pleases. The property belongs to the community and he has charge of it, and can dispose of it, if it is well done and not with the sole regard to himself or to his stockholders."[16]

## Heroes and Sheroes of U.S. History

But while these proclamations were made by some in the ruling elite, it was usually other individuals who actually did the work of creating justice. One of these heroes is Walter Rauschenbush, considered by many to be the parent of the Social Gospel movement in the United States. This movement, which grew in response to problems associated with industrialization, sought to bring to light the social dimensions of the Gospel and the duty of Christians to participate in transforming the social order so that resources were equitably distributed. Rauschenbush called on fellow Christians in the United States who lived comfortably to see and hear the pain and suffering of those who did not. He once wrote:

> There, do you see that big clothing house on the corner there? Brilliantly lighted; show windows gorgeous; all hum and happiness. But somewhere in that big house there's a little bullet-headed tailor doubled up over the coat he is to alter, and as surely as I know

that my hand is pressing your arm, I know too that he is choking down the sobs and trying to keep the water out of his eyes. Why? Because his little girl is going to die tonight and he can't be there. . . . She's whispering, "Tell my papa to come," but he'll not be there before one o'clock tonight. Saturday night, you know; very busy; sorry, but can't spare him. O, yes, you can say that: ought to go home, permission or none; but that means throwing up a job that he has been hanging to by his fingernails. It will be six months before he gets another. And so he has to sew away and let his little girl die three blocks off. When he gets home he can sob over her corpse; what more does he want? Exceptional case, you think. Not a bit of it. It's the drop on the crest of the wave."[17]

A contemporary of Rauschenbush's, Jane Addams also called the nation to the great republican ideal of social equality and economic parity. Even though she came from a wealthy family, she once wrote, "the good we secure for ourselves is precarious and uncertain, is floating in mid-air, until it is secured for all of us and incorporated into our common life."[18]

Addams did more than call attention to inequality; she directly served people and worked to empower them to change their own lives. Addams co-founded Hull House, a place of refuge and social empowerment in Chicago. In 1893, with a severe depression gripping the country, Hull House served 2,000 people a week. As her charitable efforts increased, Addams's political work grew. She realized that poverty would not end if laws were not changed, so she began to direct her efforts at the root causes of poverty. Addams believed that private charity was inadequate to deal with the vast numbers of people languishing in poverty and that poor people themselves should participate in developing solutions. In appealing to all those in the United States, she wrote, "We have learned to say that the good must be extended to all of society before it can be held secure by any one person or class; but we have not yet learned to add to that statement, that unless all people and all classes contribute to a good, we cannot even be sure that it is worth having."[19]

Dorothy Day also embodied this call to justice. Born in 1897, Day became a social activist and a journalist for progressive newspapers in the 1930s. She championed the cause of people who were poor, hungry, and homeless and languishing in the slums of U.S. cities. After going through a religious conversion and becoming a Catholic, she met Peter Maurin. Together, they founded the Catholic Worker movement, a lay movement dedicated to living out the corporal works of mercy and to calling U.S. Christians to take personal responsibility for those who were poor in their midst. She called on people not to romanticize poverty, but to open their homes to people who were poor: "No, there is nothing particularly holy about dirt and rats and roaches. But there may be something very unholy about the way we regard those who suffer from these things. The safety of the rich lies in almsgiving. We must give until we become blessed. Blessed are the poor. Christ came to make the rich poor and the poor holy."[20]

In work continuing today, Catholic Workers exemplified this call by establishing hospitality houses where they share their lives with the poor. The Worker movement also called for creating solidarity between the low-wage working class and the rest of the Christian community through roundtable discussions and through farming communities where poor and rich people could work and live together. As Day wrote regarding the aims of the Catholic Worker movement, "What we would like to do is change the world—make it a little simpler for people to feed, clothe, and shelter themselves as God intended them to do. And to a certain extent, by fighting for better conditions, by crying out unceasingly for the rights of workers, of the poor, of the destitute—the rights of the worthy and unworthy poor in other words—we can to a certain extent change the world."[21]

Eileen Egan became a good friend of Dorothy Day and the Catholic Worker movement. Egan was a great U.S. citizen ambassador who was moved by the suffering of World War II to help those who suffered the scourge of war. At the same time, she called for an end to all wars. In 1943, she joined Catholic Relief Services, newly established to address the needs of those left homeless by the war. This began a forty-year career of service in countries such as Mexico, Poland, India, and Australia. She helped refugees settle in this country while also calling on her fellow U.S. Christians to open their hearts beyond their national borders to embrace the entire world.

> To his disciples, Jesus addressed an exalted command, to love as he had loved. . . . This was to be the mark of his followers, the mark by which they would be recognized.
>
> Frail human beings were commanded to emulate the limitless love, selflessness, and endurance of suffering of their Lord. . . .
>
> Many theologians have found ways to dismiss this command and the lifestyle that flows from it, as either utopian or irrelevant in the practical world. Yet it has never been rescinded, and those who attempt even to approximate it are convinced that, in the end, evil can only be overcome by good. . . .[22]

Another person who challenges our nation to adopt a world-view of abundance in order to make room for those who are poor is Marian Wright Edelman, whose life represents the best of what we refer to as the "American Dream." Born in South Carolina in 1939, she was one of five children of a Baptist preacher. As a child, she was taught that Christianity required service in this world and that a good education was important to success. Wright Edelman studied at Spelman College and became involved in the civil rights movement which inspired her to study law at Yale. While there, she served on a project to register African-American voters in Mississippi. Later, she became the first African-American woman to practice law in Mississippi, where she also worked on racial justice issues and helped to establish a Head Start program. As she later wrote, "Service is the rent we pay to be living. It is the very purpose of life and not something you do in your spare time."[23]

In 1973, Wright Edelman established the Children's Defense Fund as a voice for poor, minority, and disabled children. The motto of the organization is "Leave No Child Behind." In her role as speaker and activist, she always calls on her fellow citizens to understand the connection between themselves and those who are marginalized. As she once said, "If we think we have ours and don't owe any time or effort to help those left behind, then we are a part of the problem rather than the solution to the fraying social fabric that threatens all Americans." Serving as a conscience to the nation and respected by leaders of both political parties, she lobbies the halls of political power on behalf of children. In calling the United States to live up to its founding principles, she wrote:

> We are living in a time of unbearable dissonance between promise and performance; between good politics and good policy; between professed and practiced family values; between racial creed and racial deed; between calls for community and rampant individualism and greed; and between our capacity to prevent and alleviate human deprivation and disease and our political and spiritual will to do so.[24]

## The U.S. Labor Movement

Like the Catholic Worker movement and the Children's Defense Fund, other groups and movements have made their mark in our nation's struggle for distributive justice based in the common good. At its best, the labor movement in the United States has spoken out not only on behalf of its union members, but for all those marginalized and dispossessed by the economic system.

Many of the success stories in the struggle to establish a more equitable distribution of wealth in the United States come from the thousands of unsung heroes and sheroes that participated in the labor movement.

The dominant narrative of *Peace as Enforced Order* often celebrates war heroes, powerful politicians, and business and industry giants as the primary actors who have shaped our nation's history. To construct an alternative that embraces the vision of *Peace as the Enterprise of Justice*, we should lift up the stories of people like those in the labor movement, such as Mother Jones, A. Philip Randolph, Eugene Debs, and the "labor priests," people whose recognition of economic inequalities led them into struggles that shaped our nation's history as much as any politician, general, or captain of industry. These heroes and sheroes are not just historical figures of the past; they walk among us today in groups like the Coalition of Immokalee Workers and their allies who struggle for economic justice and dignity for migrant farm workers.

Mother Jones, born Mary Harris, married George Jones in 1861. They had four children who all died of yellow fever. After losing her home and dressmaking shop in the great Chicago Fire, she worked as a seamstress. At that time, she became aware of blatant economic and social inequities. Recalling her experiences sewing for a wealthy Chicago family, she stated, "I would look out of the plate glass windows and see the poor, shivering wretches, jobless and hungry, walking alongside the frozen lake front. . . . The contrast of their condition with that of the tropical comfort of the people for whom I sewed was painful to me. My employers seemed neither to notice nor to care."[25]

Mother Jones decided to work on behalf of organized labor, especially the United Mine Workers. She tried at all times to awaken the consciences of her fellow citizens to the plight of those who were poor. In one of her most famous public actions, she led a 1903 "children's crusade" of striking children workers from the textile mills of Kensington, Pennsylvania, on a march to President Theodore Roosevelt's home in Long Island, New York, to call for an end to child labor.

A. Philip Randolph was another union organizer who had a deep commitment to the republican ideals of social equality and economic parity. To reach justice, he also emphasized that people had to be able to participate in the decisions that affected their lives, especially economically. Randolph also connected his work in the labor movement with the struggle for racial justice.

This began with the Pullman Railroad Company, the nation's largest employer of black people. Pullman leased luxury railroad sleeper cars to railroad companies; each car had a trained porter who served the passengers. Many porters were recently freed slaves who worked for very low wages, often depending on tips to survive. In 1925, under Randolph's leadership, the porters formed a union called the Brotherhood of Sleeping Car Porters (BSCP). After a twelve-year struggle, they won their first collective bargaining agreement with the Pullman Company. As Randolph wrote:

> Salvation for race, nation, or class must come from within. Freedom is never granted; it is won. Justice is never given; it is exacted. Freedom and justice must be struggled for by the oppressed of all lands and races, and the struggle must be continuous; for freedom is never a final fact, but a continuing evolving process to higher and higher levels of human social economic, political, and religious relationships.[26]

This labor movement was also tied with struggles for racial justice in this country. Many historians credit the BSCP as the beginning of the modern civil rights era, and many who organized with the union later became involved in the civil rights movement. Additionally, the BSCP broadened the racial scope of the labor movement, as in the 1920s and 1930s, most unions excluded black workers. The triumph of the BSCP and the hard work of A. Philip Randolph eventually led to the union's recognition as a charter member of the American Federation of Labor in 1935. In the *Messenger*, a publication he founded, Randolph wrote:

The history of the labor movement in America proves
that the employing classes recognize no race lines.
They will exploit a White man as readily as a Black
man . . . they will exploit any race or class in order to
make profits. The combination of Black and White
workers will be a powerful lesson to the capitalists of
the solidarity of labor. It will show that labor, Black
and White, is conscious of its interests and power.[27]

Randolph died in 1979, leaving a legacy of concern for both
civil rights and economic justice through worker solidarity.
Speaking on the floor of an AFL-CIO convention, he once said,
"The labor movement traditionally has been the only haven for
the dispossessed, the despised, the neglected, the downtrodden
and the poor."[28]

Eugene Debs was also a labor movement organizer whose
concerns for the working class went beyond the labor movement.
His labor work brought him to the world of politics, as the popular leader of the U.S. Socialist Party in the early 1900s. He opposed U.S. involvement in World War I because he saw it as a war
fought by the working class for the benefit of the rich on both
sides of the conflict. In Debs's view, the rich declared the war,
but the poor did the fighting and dying. After giving an anti-war
speech, he was arrested, found guilty of sedition, and sentenced
to ten years in prison. As a prisoner, Debs ran for President of the
United States in 1920 and received almost one million votes. On
the day of his sentencing, he addressed the court, "Your honor,
years ago I recognized my kinship with all living beings, and I
made up my mind that I was not one bit better than the meanest
on earth. I said then, I say now, that while there is a lower class, I
am in it; while there is a criminal element, I am of it; while there
is a soul in prison, I am not a free man."[29]

The Labor Movement was also blessed to have a number of
religious leaders championing it. In the Roman Catholic Church,
a number of clergy stood in solidarity with workers who struggled for economic justice. They came to be known as the "labor

priests." Among them three stand out: Monsignor Jack Egan and Monsignor George Higgins of Chicago and Monsignor Charles Owen Rice of Pittsburgh.

A Catholic priest for the Archdiocese of Chicago, Monsignor Egan was passionate about fair housing practices, racial justice, support for people who were homeless, and support for worker rights. At a 1972 conference in Toronto on urban and social issues, Egan said it was "the primary responsibility of the church to be on the side of the poor. . . . God places himself with the weak, the sick and the ugly."[30]

Monsignor George Higgins was a contemporary of Egan's from Chicago who later relocated to Washington, DC. A close friend of labor and a passionate advocate of the rights of workers, he directed the U.S. Conference of Catholic Bishops' social action department. In the 1960s and 1970s, he took a leadership role in bringing the Church to support the work of César Chávez and the United Farm Workers union. In 1997, he spoke about the loss of power within organized labor:

> The problem we face is not only a loss of living standards, but a loss of moral standards as well. Increasingly our economy is sending the message that it values accumulated wealth over honest work. In this economy it seems that everything is going up—except the earnings of working people. . . . If you work in the corner offices on the top floors of those glass buildings that tower above our nation's cities, these are the best of times. But if you scrub the floors or wash the windows in those buildings, these times are not so good.[31]

Monsignor Charles Owen Rice from Pittsburgh was known for his decades of activism on behalf of working people. He led marches, stood on picket lines, led labor protests in the 1930s, and participated in the 1960s civil rights movement. In 1998, at a celebration of his 90th birthday, Rice said, "I've only been a parish priest and I haven't tried to be anything else . . . I tried to help the downtrodden."[32]

While the labor movement today has been weakened, we still have success stories to look to and raise up. One success story brings us back to the economic impact of migration in today's globalized world (discussed in Chapter One). As evidenced by the demonization of immigrants today, the ruling elites have continued their pattern of ignoring laws when vulnerable workers who are not U.S. citizens are wanted and then kicking them out when they are no longer needed. But this is not the answer. As long as employers can get away with paying undocumented workers less than minimum wage, forcing them to work in unsafe environments, and avoiding other costly labor regulations, U.S. workers will also be at a disadvantage and the abundance of the earth distributed inequitably.

Instead, the answer is to create legal protections that allow undocumented and low-wage workers to come out of the shadows so they cannot be exploited. If U.S. workers would help those who are undocumented to organize for better wages and benefits, employers would not be able to pit undocumented workers against U.S. citizen workers while keeping economic benefits for themselves.

One such example of U.S. workers standing in solidarity with undocumented and immigrant workers to improve their wages and living conditions is the Coalition of Immokalee Workers (CIW). The CIW organized a successful nationwide boycott of Taco Bell restaurants and successful campaigns against McDonalds and Burger King to get an additional penny-per-pound wage from these multibillion dollar corporations for tomato pickers (including the undocumented) in Florida. U.S. citizens who supported the Immokalee Workers understand that supporting workplace rights for immigrants is not just a matter of compassion for those who are oppressed; it is the best way to preserve job standards and rights for everyone and to work toward a more equitable distribution of wealth.

## U.S. Groups Working for Justice
## on an International Level

As evidenced by the struggle of the CIW, the alternative narrative of *Peace as the Enterprise of Justice* is predicated on abundance and enough for all the world's people, not just those of the United States. Yet while the United States is the largest provider of relief aid to the world, as a measure of Gross National Product or in terms of the amount of aid our government provides per capita, we rank near the bottom of developed nations. Most people mistakenly believe that our government gives a much larger portion of our national budget for foreign aid than it really does. (The United States dedicates less than 1 percent of the federal budget for non-military foreign aid.)[33]

In spite of this, many people in the United States do join together to become international actors on behalf of justice in the world, and there has been a long U.S. tradition of working for justice and the equitable distribution of the world's resources as a crucial component in achieving peace. We can lift up these stories as well and support this work as part of an alternative narrative. This justice work has additional significance. Although none of these U.S. heroes or sheroes probably thinks about his or her work as part of a counter-terrorism strategy, this hard work and the good will it cultivates around the world constitute one of the greatest bulwarks against terrorists' efforts to spread their narrative of hatred and fear against the United States.

One example is the American Friends Service Committee (AFSC), founded in 1917 to provide young Quakers and other conscientious objectors an opportunity to serve those in need instead of fighting during World War I. The AFSC is a practical expression of the faith of the Religious Society of Friends (Quakers). Committed to the principles of nonviolence and justice, it seeks in its work and witness to draw on the transforming power of love. In 1947, it was awarded the Nobel Peace Prize for its work after World War II.

In its international development programs, AFSC ultimately

aims to promote self-sufficiency through education, training, and material resources. Two AFSC initiatives that exemplify the value of its work are their development programs in Vietnam and Laos.

AFSC's work in South Vietnam began in 1966 with aid to refugees and war-injured civilians; AFSC's assistance to North Vietnam started in 1969 in the form of medical aid. After the war, AFSC stayed to help with development work. It developed a Hydrology Project because controlling water with small dams and pumping stations could double village food supplies. Combined with new seed varieties and crops, these innovations made it possible for farm families to meet their basic needs. Through their Community Development Project, AFSC responds to the demand for small-scale credit programs to help poor women become self-sufficient. In 1993, they were the first nongovernmental organization to introduce small-scale credit programs in rural Vietnamese communities. It is now doubling the number of new loans, currently 1,000 per year.

AFSC has been working in Laos since 1974. As population pressures lead to clearing forests for rice cultivation, deforestation has become a serious threat in Laos. Small, reliable irrigation systems are a successful alternative to slash-and-burn farming, as they allow the cultivation of paddy rice twice per year. The AFSC Small-Scale Irrigation Program improves existing irrigation systems and introduces irrigation to new areas, often making a dramatic difference in food production.[34]

Another example of U.S. citizens' commitment to fostering peace through international justice is the Jubilee USA Network. Jubilee USA, an alliance of more than eighty religious denominations, human rights, environmental, labor, and community groups, works to definitively cancel crushing debts owed by poor countries in order to fight poverty and injustice. Taking their inspiration from the Jubilee proclamation in the book of Leviticus and echoed in the life and teachings of Jesus, the Jubilee USA Network has made debt cancellation a moral issue and a political and economic imperative.

Recently, the group testified in Washington, DC, at a House Subcommittee on Africa and Global Health about what they call "vulture funds" (companies that seek to profit by buying heavily discounted debt belonging to countries in serious financial trouble, then trying to recover the original amount and more, often by suing for several times the original investment). Lawsuits against developing-country governments by these funds have increased in the past few years, following recent debt cancellation agreements made by the International Monetary Fund and World Bank. In testifying about this practice, Emira Woods of the Institute for Policy Studies stated:

> The Congress of the United States and the president of the United States took a huge step forward about 10 years ago when they stated that yes, it was a moral imperative to cancel the debts of impoverished nations. Political leaders stated emphatically that it was wrong to ask impoverished citizens to repay the debts of their leaders. Yet today, in Zambia and several other countries, a new set of rich actors is undermining that moral promise. These "vulture funds" are violating Congress' promise of debt cancellation as they enrich themselves.[35]

## EMBRACING THIS ALTERNATIVE NARRATIVE

The stories of such individuals and groups provide the beginning of a story line for our alternative narrative based on *Peace as an Enterprise of Justice*. This narrative, which is largely unknown and underappreciated in our popular culture and political discourse, is built upon the principle of abundance, founded on the virtue of enough and lived out in an ethic of the common good. It is a national story rooted in both civic and religious principles that represent the best of who we are. But more than this, it is a narrative that can move our nation from fear to freedom.

If those consumed by the concept of *Peace as Enforced Order* are always looking over their shoulders for potential threats and enemies, those who embrace *Peace as the Enterprise of Justice* are always looking around to be sure that everyone has a seat at the table. While those compelled by *Peace as Enforced Order* are driven by a fear *of* others, those compelled by *Peace as the Enterprise of Justice* are driven by a fear *for* others.

Embracing the concept of *Peace as an Enterprise of Justice* does not mean rejecting everything that our nation stands for; it means embracing an alternative that is as much a part of our U.S. story as the dominant narrative that now holds sway in our popular culture, our corporate media, and our major political parties. It is still possible to re-vision our U.S. story in a way that will go far beyond the narrow vision of a self-defeating and self-perpetuating "War on Terror." But we need to construct that narrative and begin living out of it in all that we do. This begins by understanding those things that make for true peace.

# CHAPTER NINE

# Re-Visioning the U.S. Narrative: The Things that Make for Peace

Some historians disdain those who are considered historical revisionists. For some scholars, the dominant understanding of history represents a kind of orthodoxy—a dogmatic understanding of our past whose basic contours and timelines have been settled and should not be altered. But many others insist that while the past may be fixed, our understanding of it changes in response to new information that comes to light, new perspectives on information already available, or new situations in which we find ourselves.

As stated previously, those with the power to define our past—those who construct the dominant U.S. narrative—hold the power to shape our future choices. And if the dominant narrative predisposes us to make choices that increase the threat of terrorism and reinforce and validate the narrative of al Qaeda and other terrorist groups, then we need to re-vision our national narrative. We need the freedom to create an alternative that can predispose us to embrace the choices that will create a peace that is the enterprise of justice.

The last chapter outlined the foundational principle, virtue, and ethic of *Peace as an Enterprise of Justice* and lifted up some of the heroes and sheroes throughout U.S. history who have done this work. In this chapter, we will look at the "things that make for peace" (Luke 19:42)—the great challenges facing our nation and our planet that will determine what kind of world we leave to our children. These challenges were articulated by one of this nation's great workers for justice: the Reverend Dr. Martin Luther King Jr. During his famous speech opposing the war in Vietnam, he challenged the nation, saying that unless the evils of poverty, racism, and militarism were defeated, peace would not be possible. Dr. King understood that conflicts at home and abroad have their genesis in these evils. Today, we might also include the evil of environmental destruction to his list. If Dr. King was right, then the task of constructing an alternative narrative will include dealing directly with the evils of poverty, environmental degradation, racism, and militarism. Working to end these evils is the thing that makes for peace; lifting up the voices and stories of those who have gone before us and those who continue to do this work can help to re-vision our U.S. narrative.

## ERADICATING POVERTY

Our dominant national narrative tells us that we are an immigrant people who tamed this continent by the sweat of our brows and the creativity of our inventors and innovators. It tells us that this nation was built through individual initiative and personal achievement. (Inconvenient facts about the wealth and power accrued to this nation through the conquest and theft of lands belonging to the indigenous nations of the Americas and the contribution of hundreds of years of free slave labor from millions of Africans are seldom mentioned in the dominant narrative's mythology of how "we" [mostly white people] built this nation.)

Paralleling this dominant historical account of nation-building is the myth linking worldly success to moral salvation. A central thesis of this myth is that hard work which results in economic prosperity is proof of God's favor. Those who are rich (by virtue of their worldly "blessings") are viewed as morally upright.

The flip side of this myth is that those who are poor are, by virtue of their poverty, morally deficient. As stated in Chapter Seven, our dominant historical narrative casts poverty primarily as a result of bad personal choices and moral inadequacies.

Further, the lives and lifestyles of those who are rich and powerful are celebrated in our dominant narrative as signs of our nation's greatness. Because we as a nation are powerful and wealthy, God has chosen us to play a unique role in world affairs. Because we are God's chosen people, we are blessed with great wealth and power.

Our dominant narrative is filled with stories of heroic individuals who were able to raise themselves out of poverty to attain great wealth and power—their wealth and power attesting to their virtue and moral standing. But for every "virtuous" person who raises him/herself up from poverty, there are millions who, in spite of their hard work, remain in poverty. In the dominant narrative, the fates of these people are accounted for by dividing them into the "deserving poor" and the "undeserving poor." The "deserving"—who through unfortunate circumstances find themselves in poverty—become the objects of charity. The "undeserving"—who by virtue of their moral deficiencies and lack of character are consigned to poverty—become the objects of fear and loathing.

But the dominant historical narrative does not provide a framework for seeing how poverty is often the outcome of the functioning of our systems and institutions. Mahatma Gandhi often insisted that poverty was the worst form of violence. In our dominant narrative, this makes no sense at all. But if we re-vision our national narrative to understand that individual wealth accumulation is not just the result of hard work, but also the result of institutions and systems that distribute power and privilege to some while marginalizing others, then we would begin to see how poverty is not just the result of bad personal choices. Instead, we would see that it may also result from institutions and systems that rob people of their human dignity and consign them to lives of deprivation and marginalization. And if we re-vision our national narrative to include the countless stories of communities working together to change those institutions and systems in order to provide every person with the means to live with human dignity, then we would discover that this great nation of ours was not built by rugged individuals. It was built by communities of mutuality, collaboration, and solidarity, struggling to establish greater justice and "a more perfect union."

The dominant narrative's myth about poverty and wealth has not always held sway in popular culture or public discourse. Times of tremendous social reformation stand as reminders that our nation is capable of doing great things when we look beyond our individual self-interests and work together for the common good. As a nation, we took up the challenge of ending the scourge of poverty through initiatives like the New Deal in the 1940s and the "War on Poverty" in the 1960s.

But beginning in the 1980s, our nation became convinced that our government could not win the "War on Poverty." At the same time, people began to see themselves more as taxpayers and less as citizens. We were told that government (the means by which citizens act together to address political challenges) was the real problem. As a result, the federal government began dismantling and defunding many of President Lyndon Johnson's "Great Society" programs and threatened many of the institutional foundations of the New Deal. Beginning in 1981, the Reagan Administration extracted unprecedented domestic spending cuts from Congress, mostly falling on the backs of people who were poor.[1] Now, in much of popular culture and political discourse, pundits, politicians, and academics talk about a "permanent underclass," consisting of entire communities of U.S. citizens who have been written off as unredeemable and unnecessary to our future.

As we saw in Chapter Seven, the dominant narrative based on *Peace as Enforced Order* requires that people know their places in the economic and social order and be convinced they belong there. Those who are poor and marginalized by the current system are often convinced by a dominant narrative that tells them they are totally to blame for their own economic situations. As

Robert Moroney and Judy Krysik of the School of Social Work at Arizona State University stated, "Despite the evidence that the underclass are victims of an economic system that has little or no use for them, the historical response has been to turn the argument around and suggest that the reason lies not in the economy but in the individuals themselves."[2] And so, in keeping with the philosophy of neoliberalism, those who were poor have been thrown to the mercy of the free market, in a social Darwinian game of survival of the fittest.

In many inner-city communities, this Darwinian game of economic survival of the fittest combined with the illegal drug trade to produce extremely lethal consequences. There have always been illegal drugs in many communities, both rural and inner city. In communities with little or no access to health care (especially mental health care), the illegal drug trade has provided one means of self-medication for those struggling to cope with the hardships of life. And it has provided a method of economic self-sufficiency for communities with few other options. But both have different consequences than elsewhere.

For a time, my wife worked at a mental health clinic in a wealthy suburb of DuPage County, Illinois. The endless stream of people at that clinic who received prescriptions for psychotropic drugs was astounding. And every week, the drug salespeople would stop by with a free lunch for the doctors and new pitches for their drugs. It occurred to me that the difference between the drug trade in DuPage County and the drug trade in the poor, inner-city communities of Chicago (40 miles away) was that in DuPage, the rich can get a diagnosis for their mental stress and illness from their doctors; their drugs are covered by their health care insurance. In addition, these drugs are properly monitored and measured to benefit the users. The poor, on the other hand, cannot get a proper diagnosis from a licensed mental health care provider; they cannot get a prescription to purchase the drugs they need; they can't afford to pay for the drugs; and they don't have professionals to monitor their use. They often find themselves purchasing their drugs on the streets, and attempts at self-medication too often go awry.

For others, the illegal drug market has provided a means of economic self-sufficiency. They have learned the lessons their fellow citizens set out to teach them about the law-of-the-jungle free market. They became entrepreneurs in the only segment of the free market readily available to them: they became drug dealers, the ultimate predatory capitalists. They learned how to manufacture, market, and distribute their products; they learned how to franchise their businesses and how to protect market shares; they learned how to diversify their product line; they learned how to corrupt the political system to protect their enterprises; and they learned how to use violence to protect their profits. And those who promote free markets unrestrained by government interference taught by example not to count the social costs of "doing business," to keep their eyes on the profit margin, and to put the needs of their shareholders (in the case of many in the drug trade, their fellow gang members) first.

While the number of people in the inner city involved in the illegal drug trade may be very small, the impact has been devastating. This form of criminal capitalism has flourished and contributed to the destruction of entire communities, while the suit-and-tie capitalists have fled to the suburbs and gated communities for security.

Through our political and economic institutions, we, through the dominant narrative, have abandoned entire generations of poor people, content to keep them caged in ghettos, barrios, and reservations, and, when necessary, in smaller cages provided by the criminal justice system. As a result, our society has created a form of permanent low-intensity warfare that is fought at street level in communities most middle-class people would never dare to visit, communities that only come to them on the evening news body count of the murdered, the victims of tenement fires, and those killed by drug overdoses.

However, like all of us, most of the people in these communities struggle heroically to provide for their families with courage and dignity. They cling to their faith as an anchor of stability and a source of hope in difficult times. They will do whatever they can to keep their children and neighborhoods whole and healthy. They work harder than most and die earlier than they should. The experiences of those who not only survive but thrive in these communities demonstrates that when people are able to provide for themselves and their families with dignity, social conflicts become less violent and relationships of trust and solidarity across racial and class differences become possible.

While the dominant narrative's myth of rugged individualism has no place for the struggle of communities working to overcome the violence of poverty, our alternative national narrative, based on the principle of abundance and rooted in an ethic of the common good, includes many stories of people coming together to fight for economic justice. A good example of this kind of work is the U.S. Bishops' Catholic Campaign for Human Development (CCHD), which provides grants to community organizations that empower people who are poor. One of the criteria for funding from CCHD is that organizations must be led by poor people. Some of those groups and their empowerment projects include the following:

· **Haley House** is a soup kitchen in Boston's South End. Ten years ago, a group of regular guests asked their hosts to teach them a trade. Haley House responded by offering training in bakery skills after serving the day's last meal. Demand for both the training and the baked goods grew rapidly. Haley House opened a storefront bakery and later expanded its training program.

· **Portland Community Land Trust and the Clackamas Community Land Trust** created the Smart Growth Community Land Trust Homeownership Program, which preserves and renovates homes in the city of Portland and nearby Clackamas County (Oregon), providing low- and moderate-income earners with the opportunity for permanent home ownership.

· **New Road Community Development Group** of Exmore, Virginia, has changed the lives of over 250 poor African-American residents who work in the poultry, agricultural, service, and seafood industries. By banding together around a common concern and lifting up a unified voice, the members of New Road convinced the town to install a community-wide sewer system. Spurred on by that accomplishment, the group set its sights on increasing homeownership. Over twenty families now have keys to their own homes because of New Road's efforts to eliminate substandard housing and replace it with decent, affordable housing that contains indoor plumbing and heating.[3]

Eliminating poverty in the United States and around the world is the one strategy that has the greatest potential for not only reducing the appeal of terrorist groups, but for reducing all kinds of armed struggle. Left unresolved, the violence of poverty will explode with disastrous consequences for everyone, and plenty of people, many of them without altruistic motivations, are willing to light the fuse.

Imagine what might be possible if the U.S. military budget were cut in half and the money instead dedicated to eliminating global and U.S. poverty. (For fiscal year 2008, that would be more than $300 billion.) Ultimately, making a decision of this magnitude would require a tremendous amount of political will. But generating the political will to make this kind of dramatic change in our budget priorities will be impossible so long as we continue to embrace our dominant narrative that predisposes us to believe that peace is only possible through enforced order and that overwhelming military power is the best way to preserve our "way of life."

And so we need to re-vision our U.S. narrative by embracing *Peace as an Enterprise of Justice,* a justice rooted in the belief that God will provide for us if we commit to an ethic of the common good. We need to re-vision our nation's narrative so it will not only include the stories and contributions of those powerful politicians, generals, and corporate titans that currently dominate our history books, but also the stories and contributions of ordinary people acting together to challenge the entrenched interests of the economically and politically powerful in order to bring about a greater degree of economic justice—especially for those who are poor.

---

## PROTECTING THE ENVIRONMENT

People in the United States consume up to twenty-five times more of the world's resources than people from other nations. Our dominant U.S. narrative blesses this arrangement as either ordained by God or as our "just reward" for being more hardworking, smarter, or morally superior. It holds that any who question this economic and social order are acting out of envy. In short, our dominant narrative teaches us that we've earned our way of life and any who challenge it are just too lazy and/or morally defective to do what is necessary to make it on their own. To protect our way of life from the world's malcontents requires that we be willing to go to war anywhere around the world where "our vital interests" are threatened.

However, even the most ardent supporters of the dominant U.S. narrative increasingly recognize that our way of life is rapidly depleting the world's natural resources, destroying many of the planet's ecosystems, and will make it necessary to wage more wars to sustain it over the long haul. As we saw earlier, the problem posed by our dominant narrative is that many of the natural resources we seek to acquire and/or control are in places where many of the world's poorest people live. Our dominant narrative of *Peace as Enforced Order* predisposes us to think of these people as potential threats who need to be controlled. This predisposition often leads to U.S. foreign policies that further marginalize and oppress these communities. The result is that terrorist groups like al Qaeda can find a receptive audience for their narratives and ideologies.

The problem is that we are held captive by a dominant story that makes it difficult to envision or sustain the magnitude of changes necessary to thwart the appeal of the terrorists' narrative to those who are poor or to save our planet. This is why re-visioning our narrative in a way that will enable us to rediscover our national values of frugality, conservation, and simple living is an important step in protecting the environment and in adopting models of sustainable development that are essential to creating a just peace. Adopting sustainable models of development for ourselves and helping other nations to do the same will make it harder for terrorists to appeal to poor people around the world. Developing a foreign policy rooted in a vision of the universal common good will lead us to view our neighbors on this planet not as competitors, but as collaborators in creating a new international economy that serves the needs of everyone. When the poor of the world know that they have a stake in the future of this planet and have a place at the table in setting the rules for how our global economy operates, the nihilistic ideologies of the terrorist will have no appeal.

This long-term view of sustainability and protecting the earth that nourishes us has a rich tradition on this continent. Long before there was a United States of America, the indigenous nations of this land understood the importance of protecting the land, air, and water. In 1854, Chief Seattle, leader of the Suquamish Tribe, responded to an offer made by the U.S. government to buy tribal land:

> we know that if we do not sell, the white man may come with guns and take our land. How can you buy or sell the sky, the warmth of the land? The idea is strange to us. If we do not own the freshness of the air and the sparkle of the water, how can you buy them? . . . This we know, the earth does not belong to man; man belongs to the earth. This we know; all things are connected like the blood which unites one family. All things are connected. Whatever befalls the earth befalls the sons of the earth. Man did not weave the web of life; he is merely a strand in it. Whatever he does to the web, he does to himself.[4]

Carrying on the tradition of Chief Seattle, many American Indian peoples continue the struggle to both defend the earth and their tribal customs and practices. Unfortunately, many traditional environmental groups do not recognize this work. As American Indian activist and anti-racism trainer Robette Ann Dias of the Karuk Tribe of California noted:

> Where ever you find Indigenous peoples active in human rights struggles, you find Indigenous peoples active in environmental struggles, because the two cannot be separated. . . . The problem is that the environmental movement and the larger society do not identify these racialized human rights struggles as also environmental because they don't fit the traditional vision and rhetoric of the environmental movements.[5]

One example of the struggle for human rights and environmental protection is the work being done by Winona LaDuke, a member of the Anishinaabekwe (Ojibwe) Tribe in Minnesota. Located in northwestern Minnesota, the White Earth Reservation encompasses about 1300 square miles, but most of that land is no longer in the hands of the Anishinaabe, due to allotment and tax forfeiture losses in the early twentieth century. Currently, the tribe is legally contesting title to all the government-owned land within the reservation boundaries through the White Earth Land Recovery Project (WELRP) led by LaDuke. WELRP's mission is to facilitate recovery of the original land base under an 1867 treaty, while preserving and restoring traditional practices of sound land stewardship, language fluency, community development, and strengthening spiritual and cultural heritage.

A graduate of Harvard and Antioch Universities and former board member of Greenpeace USA, LaDuke has written extensively on American Indian and environmental issues. In 1998, *Ms.* magazine named her Woman of the Year for her environmental work. In 2000, she ran for vice-president of the United States on the Green Party ticket with Ralph Nader. Speaking about the gifts that Native communities bring to the environmental movement, she stated, "Native communities have an inherent advantage in understanding and creating sustainability. They have cultural cohesion and a land base, and both of these foundations are essential for any sustainable community. . . . Indigenous peoples collectively remember who they are, and that memory creates a cultural fabric that holds us together."[6]

Writing about the need to honor the traditional wisdom of indigenous peoples, LaDuke stated:

> Most indigenous societies are predicated on finding balance. That is how we have continued to live. That is how our ceremonial practice, our spiritual practice, and our day-to-day living is based on finding balance. I believe that balance has to do with our basic concepts of things like reciprocity and of cyclical thinking. . . . I believe that traditional ecological knowledge, the knowledge of indigenous people who have inhabited ecosystems for thousands of years and both observed and been given, through gifts from the Creator and from spiritual practice, that that knowledge is superior to scientific knowledge.[7]

While the original American peoples have been caring for creation for thousands of years, the native peoples were not the only ones who understood the practice of treating the earth as a sacred trust. Throughout U.S. history, a tradition of care for the earth has existed. As early as 1796, the U.S. revolutionary hero Thomas Paine wrote, "Man did not make the earth, and though he had a natural right to occupy it, he had no right to locate as his property in perpetuity, any part of it."[8]

One major figure in the U.S. history of environmental protection is Rachel Carson. Born in 1907, she became a great writer, scientist, and ecologist. After receiving her MA in zoology from Johns Hopkins University, she began a fifteen-year career in the federal service as a scientist and Editor-in-Chief for all U.S. Fish and Wildlife Service publications. She wrote pamphlets on conservation and natural resources and edited scientific articles. But in her free time, she wrote to inspire others to love and respect the natural world. As she wrote in 1954, "The more clearly we can focus our attention on the wonders and realities of the universe about us, the less taste we shall have for . . . destruction. . . ."[9]

Disturbed by the increased use of synthetic chemical pesticides such as DDT, Carson set out to warn the public about the long-term effects of misusing pesticides. In her book *Silent Spring*, she challenged the practices of agricultural scientists and the government, calling for a change in the way we viewed the natural world. Even though the pesticide industry and their lobbyists in government attacked her, she courageously spoke out to remind us that what we do to the earth we do to ourselves.

Rachel Carson died in 1964; her witness on behalf of the beauty of creation continues to inspire new generations of environmentalists. As she wrote to a friend in 1962: "The beauty of the living world I was trying to save has always been uppermost in my mind—that, and anger at the senseless, brutish things that were being done. I have felt bound by a solemn obligation to do what I could—if I didn't at least try I could never be happy again in nature. But now I can believe that I have at least helped a little."[10]

Another great U.S. hero who helped to create the modern U.S. environmental movement was John McConnell. Son of an independent evangelist, McConnell was born in Iowa in 1915. His interest in religion, science, and peace resulted in projects and personal efforts to relieve human suffering and promote the common good. In 1968, John was moved by the first photos of the earth from space. Seeing the planet as a whole, with no boundaries or dividing lines between the human community and nature, he began work to foster the idea of equilibrium in nature and human society. He circulated the first Earth Flag to show support for the idea of the inter-relatedness of all people and the web of relationships that link the human community to the planetary community of all life.

Working to elevate individual and international support for the stewardship of Earth, at the 1969 National UNESCO Conference in San Francisco, McConnell proposed an Earth Day to celebrate Earth's life and beauty and to alert people to the need for protecting the environment. On April 22, 1970, twenty million people across the United States celebrated the first Earth Day. It was a time when cities were buried under their own smog and polluted rivers caught fire. The official proclamation of Earth Day by Mayor Joseph L. Alioto of San Francisco stated, "EARTH DAY is to remind each person of his right and the equal right of each person to the use of this global home and at the same time the equal responsibility of each person to preserve and improve the Earth and the quality of life thereon." On the eve of the new millennium, at the 1999 United Nations Peace Bell Ceremony, McConnell linked the care of the earth to the future of peace on this planet:

> On this last Earth Day before the new millennium, crime and conflict—at home and abroad—threaten our future.
>
> The old failed way of seeking "peace through strength," meaning, "Pennies for Peace and Billions for Bombs," is still with us . . .
>
> As the Peace Bell rings here at the United Nations at the moment Spring begins, let us join in silent prayer and dedication to be responsible trustees of Earth. Strengthened by awareness of the whole human family and of our beautiful planet, our heart will tell our feet to walk each day in the path of peaceful progress.[11]

## DISMANTLING RACISM

The notion of white racial superiority was baked into our dominant U.S. narrative very early on in our history. In fact, the very concept of "whiteness" or the "white race" seems to have been invented in the colonial period. While Europeans recognized differences in skin color, they did not use "white" to identify themselves. "Whiteness" was invented in the colonies to preserve the privilege and power of Europeans in relationship to indigenous peoples and Africans (both slave and free). This was accomplished through the legislative and legal systems. In colonial times, codes of law provided for different treatment for blacks and whites. For instance, the punishment for runaway white indentured servants was considerably less than punishment for black runaway slaves.[12]

Although the new U.S. Constitution enshrined the ideal that all people were created equal and endowed by their Creator with certain inalienable rights, the reality for most of our history has fallen short of this ideal. The Naturalization Law of 1790 first defined citizenship, specifically reserving the right of naturalized citizenship for "any alien, being a free *white* person."[13] (Emphasis added.) This law was the cornerstone of the U.S. system of legal apartheid, remaining in effect until 1952. In the infamous 1857 Supreme Court ruling of *Dred Scott v Sandford*, the nation's highest court affirmed that, under federal law, no Africans residing in the United States, whether slaves or free, could become U.S. citizens.

Defining who was white (and who was not) was not just an academic exercise, nor was it just a matter of keeping track of diversity in the U.S. population. Legally limiting citizenship rights to white people meant that white people legally constituted every institution and system in this country, prior to the modern civil rights movement, for the exclusive purposes of serving their needs. This institutionalization has given power and privilege to white people over hundreds of years and in many ways, continues to this day. Part of the reason is that while laws may have changed, the dominant U.S. narrative about race has been much slower to change—especially when it comes to addressing institutionalized systems of white entitlement and the marginalization of people of color.

Racism and notions of white superiority have also played a major role in the stories constructed to legitimate U.S. wars. To convince U.S. citizens to kill people they have never met, it is necessary to dehumanize the "enemy." Racism has often been useful for this purpose. During World War II, German soldiers were called "krauts"; Japanese soldiers were referred to as "japs." During the war in Vietnam, North Vietnamese soldiers were called "gooks"; in the Gulf wars, Arabs have been referred to as "ragheads." Such terms are used to dehumanize an enemy, a necessary first step in being able to kill them. As Robin Long, a member of the U.S. Army who fled to Canada rather than fight in Iraq, said of his training, "My superiors were telling me, 'You're going to the desert to fight rag heads.' It wasn't like I was going to Iraq to liberate the people. It was like I was going to the desert to kill rag heads. They were trying to make people less human."[14] (Many soldiers in the Armed Forces do not use this language nor approve of this kind of dehumanizing behavior, but most soldiers have heard this kind of language up and down the ranks.)

Promulgating ideologies of racial superiority and inferiority has also provided a noble facade for wars of conquest. In 1847, justifying the Mexican-American War, Congressman Giles of Maryland wrote, "We must march from Texas straight to the Pacific Ocean, and be bounded only by its roaring wave. . . . It is the destiny of the White race; it is the destiny of the Anglo-Saxon race." In 1900, Senator Albert Beveridge stood in the Senate chambers and declared:

> The Philippines are ours forever. . . . We will not renounce our part in the mission of our race, trustee under God, of the civilization of the world. . . . My own belief is that there are not 100 men among them

who comprehend what Anglo-Saxon self-government even means, and there are over 5 million people to be governed. It has been charged that our conduct of the war has been cruel. . . . Senators must remember that we are not dealing with Americans or Europeans. We are dealing with Orientals.[15]

Today, it is unacceptable to use terms like "the manifest destiny of the white race" or "the white man's burden to civilize the world." The Armed Forces are some of the most integrated institutions in the United States, and for some people of color, they provide an avenue for social and economic advancement. But implicit notions of racial superiority and racial inferiority are still embedded in many of the fundamental assumptions forming the basis of U.S. foreign policy.

When President Bush says terrorists are waging war on civilization itself, he is, of course, referring to white, Western civilization. In truth, this planet is home to many civilizations. Making such a claim implies the superiority of white, Western civilization and the irrelevance of all others. When the Administration scares us with warnings of dire consequences should Arabs or Asians acquire weapons of mass destruction, it uses implied racial stereotypes about unstable, untrustworthy, and dangerous people of color. As Nelson Mandela commented prior to the war in Iraq, "What we know is that Israel has weapons of mass destruction. Nobody talks about that. Why should there be one standard for one country, especially because it is black, and another for another country, Israel, that is white?"[16]

It should be no surprise that the racism sustaining foreign wars also intensifies similar expressions of racism at home. In the "War on Terror," race is often intimately linked to assumptions made by citizens and government authorities regarding who is a possible terrorist or a terrorist sympathizer. The consequences of these racist assumptions can be catastrophic for the individuals at whom they are directed.

Only months after the terrorist attacks of 9-11, a teenager

flew a small plane into a building in Florida. In his suicide note, he stated his opposition to the U.S. government and support for Osama bin Laden. However, once it was determined that the 15-year-old boy, Charles J. Bishop, was white, all references to the act possibly being terrorism ended. He was merely a troubled youth. Later that summer, pipe bombs placed in mailboxes in Illinois, Iowa, and Nebraska injured some people. Eventually, the bomber was identified as Luke John Helder, a young, white, male college student. Once the bomber's race was identified, the media described the bomber as emotionally "disturbed." He was not a terrorist.[17]

On the other hand, Mohammed Rafiq Butt was one of over 1,200 Muslims, Arab, and South Asian immigrants rounded up and held without charges in the weeks after September 11. Butt had come to New York to work and send money to his children in Pakistan. After his neighbors called in a "tip," the FBI arrested him and turned him over to the Immigration and Naturalization Service (INS) on September 20. Never charged with a crime, he was held on a visa violation and ordered deported. He died in a New Jersey jail that October.[18] Other prisoners told Butt's relatives that he had complained of chest pains for two days, but officials refused to take him to the hospital. The INS refused to release information about his death.

In September 2006, the Council on American-Islamic Relations (CAIR)—the nation's largest Muslim organization—issued a report stating that complaints involving anti-Muslim discrimination, harassment, and violence jumped over 30 percent from 2005 to 2004. A total of 1,972 such incidents were reported in 2005, the highest number since CAIR began reporting anti-Muslim incidents in 1995. CAIR said it had also received 153 reports of anti-Muslim hate crimes, an increase of nearly 10 percent over 2004, and more than 50 percent over the 93 reports received in 2003.[19]

Wars always bring out the worst racial bigotry and xenophobia in nations. Yet with the increase in hate crimes and discrimination against Muslims, Arabs, and South Asians, there has been an equally powerful witness of U.S. tolerance and respect. Groups of citizens and communities of faith have stood in defense of their Muslim neighbors and have organized talks and discussion groups to bring together Christians, Muslims, and Jews to promote mutual understanding.

For as long as racism has blighted this country, there has been resistance to it. The true history of U.S. racism cannot be told without the stories of those who gave so much (including their lives) to dismantle racism. Too often, this U.S. narrative has been quarantined to one month of the year or limited to celebrations of Martin Luther King Jr. Day. And all too often this narrative has been hijacked, co-opted, and trivialized for narrow political interests.

This parallel history of racism and resistance began in the Americas long before there was a United States. By 1502, only a few pockets of resisting Indians remained in the islands first conquered by Columbus. One young Indian, whose family had been killed by the Spaniards, was raised by missionaries and baptized Enrique. Eventually he was "given" to a debauched young Spaniard named Valenzuela who beat and abused him. When Valenzuela raped his wife, Enrique revolted, escaped, and led a resistance movement in the Bahoruco Mountains. Many Arawak Indians fled their masters and joined this resistance movement that kept the Spaniards at bay. Enrique came to trust one Spaniard—the priest Fray Bartolome de Las Casas (who came to be known as Protector of the Indians). Over time, the priest and Enrique negotiated a truce between the Indians and the government that guaranteed the freedom of all remaining Arawak people.[20]

This has been a familiar pattern: people of color supported by their white allies, struggling against racism and white supremacy. In 1841, Africans who revolted on the slave ship Amistad were tried for murder and piracy. Former President John Adams defended them in front of the U.S. Supreme Court. The anti-slavery resistance led by Frederick Douglass, Sojourner Truth, Harriet Tubman, and others was supported by white allies like William Lloyd Garrison (who founded the New England Anti-Slavery

Movement) and by the abolitionist Liberty Party.

The modern civil rights movements of the 1950s and 1960s also witnessed to the power of social movements led by people of color and supported by white allies. One example was the Freedom Rides, organized in 1961 by the Congress of Racial Equality (CORE) under the leadership of James Farmer and others. This campaign set out to test the enforcement of the Supreme Court decision to desegregate interstate transportation. The original Freedom Riders were seven blacks and six whites. Three years later, the Council of Federated Organizations (COFO) organized Freedom Summer to register black voters in the South.

White activists from the North were encouraged to go to the South to register black voters not out of pity or out of a sense of superiority. Student Nonviolent Coordinating Committee (SNCC) leader Robert Moses told white volunteers not to go south to "save the Mississippi Negro," but to go only if they truly understood that "his freedom and yours are one."[21] Again, whites were invited to stand as allies, side-by-side with people of color in the struggle for racial justice.

That year, three civil rights workers, led by African-American James Chaney and joined by his white coworkers, Michael Schwerner and Andrew Goodman, went to Mississippi to register black voters. They were murdered near Philadelphia, Mississippi. While African Americans and other people of color suffered most of the violent backlash against the march towards civil rights, some white allies were willing to follow the lead of their brothers and sisters of color, even if it meant suffering the same fate.

At the same time the black civil rights movement was exploding onto the national headlines, another under-reported but powerful civil rights movement was taking root in the West and Southwest. The Chicano (Mexican-American) civil rights movement, or El Movimiento, encompassed many political, social, and cultural movements within Mexican-American communities. It began in the land grant movement in New Mexico in the mid-1960s; it was led by Reies López Tijerina, who fought to get the U.S. government to honor the Treaty of Guadalupe Hildago (signed in 1848 at the end of the Mexican-American War). Contrary to that treaty, Mexican Americans found themselves disenfranchised and dispossessed of their lands with no means of redress. The struggle also included the work of Rodolfo (Corky) Gonzales, who founded the Crusade for Justice in Denver in 1966 and worked to instill a sense of cultural pride in the Mexican-American community.

Probably one of the best known leaders of the Mexican-American civil rights movement was César Chávez, who organized farmworkers in the Central Valley of California. Chávez's work was about more than improving working conditions for migrant farmworkers. He emphasized worker self-determination and leadership. He gave people a way of organizing and fighting nonviolently against the much more powerful corporate agribusiness interests in California. Mexican Americans led this movement, which was supported by many white communities and other communities of color across the country. Through pickets, strikes, and especially boycotts, congregations and schools across the country took part in this struggle for human dignity.

Many say that the "race problem" in the United States has largely been resolved as a result of the civil rights movements of the 1950s and 1960s. To some extent, they are right. Most of the legalized racism of the past has been eradicated, and more legal tools are available to combat racist practices and behaviors. However, while the laws changed, much of the institutional and cultural racism that existed before the civil rights movement has stayed entrenched.

To understand why, it is important to remember that the pseudo-scientific notion of racial superiority and inferiority was constructed and institutionalized as part of U.S. legal, religious, and social systems to distribute power and privilege to white Europeans and disenfranchise people of color. That being the case, our efforts at dismantling racism must be judged by how effective we are at redistributing power—especially economic power—in ways that do not continue the practices of white entitlement nor continue the marginalization of people of color.

When assessing whether something is racist, many white people tend to look at intention: whether there was any intent to discriminate against people of color. Most people of color tend to assess if something is racist by looking at the consequences of the action. As noted before, according to the U.S. Census Bureau's 2005 American Community Survey Data, racial disparities in income, education, and homeownership persist forty years after the civil rights movement and, by some measures, are growing. These results are not some statistical anomaly. Even when class and level of education are factored in, studies show that people of color are still discriminated against in access to employment, credit, medical treatment, and a host of other areas. Many white people are not troubled by these statistical trends because they see no proof of overt racist attitudes at play. Others (mostly people of color) conclude that the results themselves are proof of the continuing power of racism.

To truly dismantle racism, we must address institutionalized white entitlement and privilege because understanding racism as race prejudice expressed in individual attitudes and behaviors is inadequate. Organizations like Crossroads Anti-Racism Organizing & Training and the Peoples Institute for Survival and Beyond work directly with institutions and communities to address racism as race prejudice *plus* the misuse of institutional and systemic power. They train anti-racism teams by giving them a common analysis of racism and the skills they need to dismantle white entitlement and privilege within their institutions and communities.[22]

Such organizations insist that power is at the heart of the problem of racism: who has power, how is it exercised, and for whose benefit. The unequal systemic distribution of power in the United States is built into the structures of every institution created before the end of legalized racism (in the 1950s). Therefore, dismantling racism entails transforming these institutional structures to make them accountable to communities of color and to expand who exercises power (e.g., participation in decision-making about policies, procedures, and allocating institutional resources).

Until racism is expunged from hearts and minds and dismantled from institutions and systems, those in power will use it to engender fear and hatred of the other. And it will be used to lead us into war. As a rallying cry to war, racism trumps reason. Like a dangerous narcotic, it can cloud the mind and heighten paranoia. Racism not only makes diplomacy more difficult; it makes it unnecessary because the evil or untrustworthiness of the other is perceived to be endemic and immutable.

## ERADICATING MILITARISM

Militarism can be understood as a set of beliefs and corresponding policies that favor maintaining and using military forces as the best and most reliable means of protecting national interests and achieving political and economic aims. Go to the U.S. history section of any commercial bookstore. You will find that the largest number of books about U.S. history are related to war. Knowing nothing about the United States other than what is on these shelves, one could easily conclude that we are primarily a war-making nation.

War is indeed the central metaphor of the dominant U.S. narrative. When I was in school, we learned to organize our history by wars: the pre-Revolutionary period, followed by the Revolutionary War and the War of 1812. This was followed by the Mexican-American War, which was followed by the pre-Civil War Period and the Civil War. After that, we had the pre- and post-World War One and Two periods, followed by the Cold War period, including the Korean War and the Vietnam War. I assume that we will soon add a new chapter to the history entitled the "War on Terror."

Living in the United States, I can hardly count more than a handful of public monuments that do not have a war theme. In contrast, on my trips to Europe, I have often been surprised to find so many public monuments dedicated to poets, musicians, artists, writers, and statespeople. While it is good to remember soldiers who sacrificed so much for our country, it is also very telling that the service we honor most is military service. Why, for the most part, does a military color guard carry the flag at public events? If we are holding a Labor Day parade, why not have representatives from local unions carry the flag? If we are celebrating a sports event, why not have young people from local sports teams carry the flag? If military service is the only form of patriotic service associated with our nation's most sacred symbols, what does that say about all those who have given their lives representing our country as diplomats, aid workers, teachers, or volunteers around the world?

In spite of protests to the contrary, we are a nation formed by war and characterized by a military mindset. Militaristic language has become standard lexicon in the United States for addressing a whole host of challenges we face. We had the "war on poverty" followed by the "war on drugs" and now a "war on terror." During the Bush-Cheney Administration, the very act of engaging in diplomacy or working through international institutions to resolve conflicts has often been characterized as a sign of weakness or of being "unmanly." This Administration's idea of diplomacy is to issue ultimatums and to refuse to talk to opponents until they capitulate. The art of diplomacy has been reduced to leveling charges and issuing demands.

Since the end of the Cold War, U.S. defense planning has always maintained the need, as then-Secretary of Defense William Cohen stated in 1999, for the United States to be "the only nation in the world able to project overwhelming military power worldwide." This mindset meant that in 2005, the U.S. military budget was almost twenty-nine times as large as the combined spending of the six "rogue" states (Cuba, Iran, Libya, North Korea, Sudan, and Syria), which together spent $14.65 billion. Combined, Russia and China spent $139 billion, only 30 percent of the total U.S. military budget.[23]

While pursuing a mission of global military domination, other means of influencing world affairs and providing for U.S.

national security are neglected. Looking at the federal budget, we find that for every dollar spent on the military, we spend only pennies on diplomacy, foreign aid, and participating in international organizations. For example, for fiscal year 2009, the Bush Administration's proposed budget asks for $711 billion for the military: $541 billion for the Department of Defense and nuclear weapons-related activity of the Department of Energy and at least $170 billion for military operations in Iraq and Afghanistan. In contrast, the request for International Affairs is $39.5 billion. President Bush's fiscal year 2007 budget provided $439.3 billion for the Department of Defense's base budget (not including all of the spending on the wars in Iraq and Afghanistan), but only $31.9 billion for international operations.[24] As the old saying goes, "If the only tool you have in your tool box is a hammer, every problem is going to look like a nail."

Even as we invaded Afghanistan and Iraq with overwhelming military power, our diplomatic corps did not have enough people trained to speak the languages of these countries to be able to communicate with the people we had "liberated." Our soldiers were well trained in exercising the overwhelming firepower at their disposal, but had only the most rudimentary knowledge about the culture or beliefs of the people they were encountering.

While militarism and war have been at the heart of the dominant U.S. narrative, other voices have always sought ways to resolve conflict without military force. This alternative U.S. narrative (which is almost completely silenced during times of war) has a long history. Some of its earliest contributors came from the Quaker tradition in colonial times. In the face of the racist stereotyping of indigenous peoples by other colonists, the theft of native lands, and the religious justification for the wholesale slaughter of entire tribes, the Quakers managed to live peacefully with these original Americans, primarily because the Quakers were committed to treating their indigenous neighbors as equals. Instead of acquiring land by conquest, the Quakers purchased land. They also accorded American Indians the right to trial by a jury of their peers. When disputes and conflicts arose, they sought mediation and resisted the temptation to prejudge the actions of people of other cultures.

Some U.S. military heroes have understood the folly of over-reliance on military force; in fact, those who have faced the heat of battle are often the first to recognize the dangers of militarism. As General Douglas MacArthur put it, "In the evolution of civilization, if it is to survive, all men and women cannot fail eventually to adopt Gandhi's belief that the process of mass application of force to resolve contentious issues is fundamentally not only wrong, but contains within itself the germs of self-destruction."[25]

General David M. Shoup, retired Marine Corps Commandant, also warned the nation of the pitfalls of militarism. Reflecting on the aftermath of the war in Vietnam, he said, "America has become a militaristic and aggressive nation. . . . We have an immense and expensive military establishment, fueled by a gigantic defense industry and millions of proud, patriotic, and frequently bellicose and militaristic citizens." World War II hero General Omar Bradley challenged the nation by framing the issue of war and peace as a question of faith: "We have grasped the mystery of the atom and rejected the Sermon on the Mount. Ours is a world of nuclear giants and ethical infants. We know more about war than we do about peace—more about killing than we do about living."[26]

In times of conflict, are the only choices available to us fight or flight? What would happen if Christians devoted the same discipline and self-sacrifice to nonviolent peacemaking and conflict resolution that armies devote to waging war? Christian Peacemaker Teams (CPT) is a U.S. anti-militarism movement that arose from the challenge posed by these questions. Founded in 1984, CPT was established to encourage Christians to devote the same discipline and self-sacrifice to nonviolent peacemaking that armies devote to war. When invited by local peace and human rights workers, CPT places violence-reduction teams in crisis situations and militarized areas around the world. CPT embraces the vision of unarmed intervention waged by committed peacemakers ready to risk injury and death in bold attempts to transform lethal conflict through the nonviolent power of God's truth and love. Initiated by Mennonites, Brethren, and Quakers and involving broad ecumenical participation, CPT's ministry of biblically-based and spiritually-centered peacemaking is active in conflict areas in the United States and around the world, including Palestine, Iraq, Colombia, and Africa's Great Lakes region (the Congo and Uganda).

CPT initiated a long-term presence in Iraq in October 2002, six months before the beginning of the U.S.-led invasion. For eighteen months following the invasion, the team primarily focused on documenting and calling attention to detainee abuses and the denial of basic legal and human rights. While detainee issues remain the focus, the work has expanded to efforts to end the occupation and militarization of the country and to foster nonviolent and just alternatives for a free and independent Iraq.

Many CPT members face injury and death in such work. On November 26, 2005, CPTers Tom Fox (USA) and Jim Loney (Canada) along with delegation members Norman Kember (UK) and Harmeet Sooden (Canada/New Zealand) were kidnapped in Iraq. Tom Fox was killed on March 9, 2006. The others were freed two weeks later, after 118 days of captivity. Before his abduction Fox wrote:

> As I survey the landscape here in Iraq, dehumanization seems to be the operative means of relating to each other. U.S. forces in their quest to hunt down and kill "terrorists" are, as a result of this dehumanizing word, not only killing "terrorists," but also killing innocent Iraqis: men, women and children in the various towns and villages. It seems as if the first step down the road to violence is taken when I dehumanize a person. . . . Why are we here? We are here to root out all aspects of dehumanization that exist within us. We are here to stand with those being dehumanized by oppressors and stand firm against that dehumanization.[27]

Many U.S. citizens participate in other nonviolent international intervention teams, including the International Fellowship of Reconciliation Nonviolent Peaceforce. Another, the International Solidarity Movement, uses nonviolent, direct-action methods and principles to support and strengthen the Palestinian popular resistance to the Israeli occupation by providing the Palestinian people with two resources: international protection for their nonviolent resistance and avenues for their voices of struggles to be heard around the world.[28]

One U.S. member of the International Solidarity Movement was Rachel Corrie, a 23-year-old college student and human rights activist from Olympia, Washington. On March 16, 2003, an Israeli military bulldozer in Rafah, Gaza, ran over and killed her while she nonviolently defended a Palestinian home from demolition. Corrie represents the U.S. idealism of *Peace as an Enterprise of Justice*. Like many before her, she recognized that the work of peace requires great sacrifice and courage—not the willingness to kill, but the willingness to be killed for what one believes. As she wrote to her parents about her work in the occupied territories:

> This has to stop. I think it is a good idea for us all to drop everything and devote our lives to making this stop. I don't think it's an extremist thing to do anymore. I really want to dance around to Pat Benatar and have boyfriends and make comics for my co-workers. But I also want this to stop. Disbelief and horror is what I feel. Disappointment. I am disappointed that this is the base reality of our world and that we, in fact, participate in it. This is not at all what I asked for when I came into this world. This is not at all what the people here asked for when they came into this world. This is not what they are asking for now. This is not the world you and Dad wanted me to come into when you decided to have me.[29]

## WE HAVE A CHOICE

Not surprisingly, many throughout our history who have been involved in struggles against one of these evils have also been involved in the others. For instance, Henry Clarke Wright, a Congregationalist minister, along with Lucretia Mott, Maria Chapman, and others, founded the New England Non-Resistance Society in the 1830s and were also deeply involved in the abolitionist movement and the women's suffrage movement. Many of these activists in both the North and the South participated in the Underground Railroad for runaway slaves—often at great risk to themselves. Organizations like the Fellowship of Reconciliation and the Women's International League for Peace and Freedom (WILPF), both founded in 1915, moved beyond merely rejecting the violence of war to actively resisting injustice wherever they found it. As the WILPF declared at their 1971 international congress, "The WILPF has a duty to study and work towards developing methods for the effective use of non-violent means; to make the public aware of the problems of the oppressed and the exploited; to analyze the structure of power in society and the use made of it; to engage ourselves actively in non-violent movements for change."[30]

In the last century, Dr. Martin Luther King Jr. learned about the power of nonviolent struggle from members of the Fellowship of Reconciliation like Reverend James Lawson and Glenn Smiley. Dr. King, along with Rosa Parks and others, was trained in nonviolence at the Highlander Folk School founded by Myles Horton. Reflecting what he learned from these teachers of nonviolent direct action, Dr. King later wrote:

> The ultimate weakness of violence is that it is a descending spiral, begetting the very thing it seeks to destroy. Instead of diminishing evil, it multiplies it. Through violence you murder the hater, but you do not murder hate. In fact, violence merely increases

hate. . . . Returning violence for violence multiplies violence, adding deeper darkness to a night already devoid of stars. Darkness cannot drive out darkness; only light can do that.[31]

Our dominant U.S. narrative tells us that competition for scarce resources is inevitable and that violence is an inescapable part of our human condition. This dominant narrative would have us believe that the only response to conflict and violence is through enforced order, domination, and control. But this is not the whole story. We do have one story about the violence of systemic poverty and the growing gap between the rich and the poor, but it is not the whole story. Our nation's story is also about how people have come together across the boundaries of race, class, and gender to eradicate poverty. We have one U.S. story about the constant drive for profits and growth with little regard to the impact on our environment. But we also have the story of the awakening of the U.S. conscience to the human-made dangers to our planet and the struggle of ordinary citizens working together to protect and preserve the natural resources of the earth. On one hand, we have the story of the long legacy of racism in the United States. On the other hand, we have countless stories of people working across the racial divide to purge it from our hearts and dismantle it from our institutions. The story of U.S. militarism is deeply embedded in our popular culture and mythology, but another U.S. tradition addresses conflict without recourse to war.

Within our national story, the vision of *Peace as Enforced Order* is always at play with the vision of *Peace as an Enterprise of Justice*. While it is true that, at this time, our dominant narrative is captivated by the vision of *Peace as Enforced Order*, we know from our history that it has not always been so. We can choose to re-vision our narrative in a way that will unleash our creativity and imaginations, allowing us to move beyond the false choices and either/or thinking of our dominant national narrative.

As we move forward, we can rely on the resources, wisdom, and experiences from our unacknowledged and under-appreciated history to help us through these difficult times. Nothing is set in stone. We are not predestined to always have those who are rich lord it over those who are poor. We are not preordained to a future of false choices between human progress and environmental degradation. We are not eternally bound by our nation's racist past, and we need not be held captive by our addiction to militarism. A different world is possible. At the 2003 World Social Forum people from almost every continent came together in global solidarity to witness to a different, more inclusive world community, one freed from poverty, racism, and militarism and dedicated to protecting the environment. As Arundhati Roy, an Indian activist who spoke at the Forum, reminds all of us, "Another world is not only possible, she is on her way. On a quiet day, I can hear her breathing."[32]

# PART IV

## BACK FROM EMMAUS:
## FROM FEAR TO FREEDOM

*Two of them that same day were making their way to a village named Emmaus seven miles from Jerusalem, discussing as they went along all that had happened. In the course of their lively exchange, Jesus approached and began to walk along with them. However, they were restrained from recognizing him. He said to them, "What are you discussing as you go your way?" They halted in distress and one of them, Cleopas by name, asked him, "Are you the only resident of Jerusalem who does not know the things that went on there these past few days?" He said to them, "What things?" They said: "All those that had to do with Jesus of Nazareth, a prophet powerful in word and deed in the eyes of God and all the people; how our chief priests and leaders delivered him up to be condemned to death and crucified him. We were hoping that he was the one who would set Israel free. Besides all this, today, the third day since these things happened, some women of our group have just brought us some aston-ishing news. They were at the tomb before dawn and failed to find his body, but returned with the tale that they had seen a vision of angels who declared that he was alive. Some of our number went to the tomb and found it to be just as the women said, but him they did not see."*

*Then he said to them, "What little sense you have! How slow you are to believe all that the prophets have announced! Did not the Messiah have to undergo all this so as to enter into his glory?" Beginning then with Moses and all the prophets, he interpreted for them every passage of Scripture which referred to him. . . .*

*When he had seated himself with them to eat, he took bread, pronounced the blessing, then broke the bread, and began to distribute it to them. With that their eyes were opened and they recognized him; whereupon he vanished from their sight. They said to one another, "Were not our hearts burning inside us as he talked to us on the road and explained the Scriptures to us?" They got up immediately and returned to Jerusalem (Luke 24:13-27, 30-33).*

The crucifixion of Jesus was an act of terrorism of the strong. This act was meant to deter would-be resisters to the Roman oc-cupation of Palestine or those who would oppose the authority of the Roman-controlled Temple Chief Priest and religious ruling class. The Romans meant for public crucifixion to terrorize the civilian population. All people witnessing a crucifixion or walk-ing by a corpse on the cross understood that if they stepped out of line, they too could be executed.

The deterrent power of Roman crucifixion was not only in

the act of nailing rebels to crosses. More importantly, it was in the powerful story that the Romans communicated to the people about the executions. That dominant narrative was unchallengeable: no one can stand against Roman power, and any who try will end up a naked corpse hanging from a cross.

In the account of the disciples on the road to Emmaus, we see how this powerful dominant narrative even terrorized Jesus' followers. Their world had collapsed in the face of Roman power colluding with religious authority. Heading out of town, they were no doubt frightened that they might be crucified next—just the kind of thinking that Rome and the Temple were counting on. These disciples were so completely under the power of the Roman/Temple story of Jesus' execution that early reports of the resurrection only confused their minds and hearts.

Ironically, the basic facts were not disputed. The disciples laid out the factual information in a straightforward manner: Jesus was a good man who was delivered up by their religious leaders to be executed; three days later his tomb was empty, and witnesses said he was alive. However, they were interpreting the meaning of these facts through the overpowering narrative of the Roman Empire and the Temple priests. So, instead of expressing Easter alleluias, they slipped out of town in confusion and fear.

Thoroughly terrorized by the dominant narrative about Jesus' execution, the disciples did not even recognize Jesus when he began to walk with them. On that road to Emmaus, Jesus began to help them construct an alternative story of the events of his death and the discovery of the empty tomb. In constructing his alternative, Jesus tied his death and resurrection to the larger Jewish narrative of Moses and the prophets. In his life, passion, death, and resurrection, Jesus consistently rejected Rome's assertion that its narrative was the most powerful story. Jesus rejected *Pax Romana* along with its emperor son-of-god, its kingdom, and its power. Jesus offered an alternative of *Pax Christi*, with himself as the Child of God—the Suffering Servant who came to establish the Reign of God.

The act of communion—the breaking and sharing of

bread—finally broke the spell of the dominant narrative over these disciples. At that point, their eyes were opened. They were free to see Jesus and believe. Through this work of constructing an alternative narrative and coming together in a community of sharing, these terrorized followers of Jesus were transformed into disciples on fire with joy and courage. Immediately, they got up and headed back from Emmaus to Jerusalem.

In many respects, those of us who have felt overwhelmed by the dominant 9-11 narrative of the Bush Administration are like the disciples on the road to Emmaus. The facts of 9-11 are not disputed. But the meaning of these facts put forward by the dominant narrative leaves us terrified and vulnerable. Faced with the enormity of the forces propelling us down the path of this "War on Terror," it would be easy to sink into despair. We could simply try to ignore what is happening, turning off all sources of bad news and sedating ourselves—through distractions like shopping and the latest movies or TV shows. It is equally tempting to want to explode into a rage-driven frenzy of activity scattered in a thousand directions. Or, a more likely and easier route would be to embrace a cynical posture; this would grant us the luxury of knowing that our nation is heading off the edge of a cliff, while excusing us of any responsibility for trying to stop it: "why try, it won't do any good; time to pack it in and head out of town."

Many have come to feel a profound fear for the future of our republic and a deep sadness for our country. As the Bush Administration's 9-11 narrative goes unchallenged and many of our cherished civic and moral values are abandoned, it is getting harder to recognize our own nation. Many feel as if our national story has been hijacked by the traffickers of fear and hatred. Many liberties and rights have been suspended in the name of freedom. National ideals of tolerance and multi-cultural diversity have been imprisoned in secret detention centers; we have no idea if they will ever be set free. At times, a rage wells up within us, while at other times we are filled with terror about what might lie ahead. We find ourselves in a dark place, unable to conceive of the possibility of victory against the forces arrayed against us, hampered, as we are, by the feebleness of those few politicians who claim to speak for us.

But if Martin Luther King Jr., Mother Jones, Eugene Debs, Dorothy Day, Jane Addams, César Chávez, and other heroes of our alternative U.S. narrative were with us on that road to Emmaus, they would remind us that we have been here before. We've been here before during the abolition movement, when runaway slaves and their Underground Railroad supporters faced imprisonment and death. We've been here before when union organizers were jailed, beaten, and killed for demanding an eight-hour workday and humane working conditions. We've been here before when women were jailed and force-fed for demanding the right to vote. We've been here before when freedom-riders in the South were beaten, jailed, and killed for demanding a seat on the bus and access to the voting booth. And we've been here before when anti-war demonstrators were attacked during the police riot in Chicago and killed by the National Guard at Kent State and Jackson State. Yes, we have been here before. And we have never given in to the darkness or despair.

Can we embrace the challenge of our times? Will we follow in the footsteps of those from our past who spoke with the moral clarity of the dispossessed? Can we find the courage to speak from the heart and soul of this nation of lovers, this republic of freedom, this commonwealth of justice, and this community of believers?

The authentic narrative of this country is *not* written only by the generals, the politicians, the corporate CEOs, or the media barons. It is *not* written only by the fear mongers, the war profiteers, or the rich and greedy. The authentic narrative of this great nation is *not* written only by the political pundits, the spin-meisters, or the TV evangelists, rabbis, and mullahs who preach hate.

Our history and the future of our country belong to ordinary citizens who have the power and the right to add their stories and contributions to the larger story of this country. This country is not only the property of those who can afford high-powered lobbyists; it also belongs to those who work the fields and factories;

who raise and educate children; and who clean buildings, cook meals, and bag groceries.

While constructing and proclaiming an alternative narrative is daunting, we have historical and spiritual models for hope. St. Paul speaks of hope as what is not seen but believed. Ruben Alvez, a Brazilian author, explains, "Hope is the hunch that the overwhelming brutality of facts that oppress and repress us is not the last word." Welsh philosopher Raymond Williams reminds us that to be truly radical is to make hope possible rather than despair inevitable. As people of faith, we are called to hope. But hope is more than just wishful thinking about the future. Hope is not a passive state of mind or a spiritual state of being. As political philosopher and peace activist John Schaar reminds us, "The future is not some place we are going to but one we are creating. The paths are not to be found but made and the activity of making them changes both the maker and the destination."[1]

It is time for us to begin the hard work of constructing and proclaiming an alternative U.S. narrative. It is time for us to begin the hard work of re-constituting our constitution. It is time for us to begin the hard work of re-founding this great republic. It is time for us to begin the hard work of restoring that which has been taken from us and of recovering all those ideals and values that have been lost.

In this final section, I focus on ways that each of us can sustain ourselves for the difficult and challenging times we face. The journey from fear to freedom begins in the heart of individuals and is carried forth by communities committed to transforming our world. Transforming the world is an inside job; it begins with our own transformation. But we cannot change ourselves by ourselves. We need the strength that comes from being members of a community. All revolutionary struggles are primarily a work of the heart in communion with the hearts of others. As the anthropologist Margaret Mead so rightly put it, "Never doubt that a small group of people can change the world; indeed that is the only way the world has ever been changed."[2]

# CHAPTER TEN

# A Personal Path

What we have discussed so far about constructing an alternative narrative has been at the macro level of social, political, and economic change. But most of us don't live at the macro level; we live at the level of family and community. While most of us do not hold positions of power that would enable us to reshape U.S. foreign, economic, or social policy, each of us does have the freedom to make choices. And these choices have consequences that can either assist in the birthing of an alternative U.S. narrative or hinder its coming. At times, we may be tempted to retreat from the great responsibilities that come with this freedom by convincing ourselves that our choices are futile, but this does not change the fundamental truth that we always have choices.

So what choices do we need to make? What would a personal response to the Bush Administration's 9-11 narrative of fear look like? How does an individual move from fear to freedom? In raising these questions, I am not suggesting that personal responses apart from community are sufficient. Although we have the power to make personal choices, the role of community is essential; there are no Lone Rangers in the Christian life. In Chapter Eleven, we will look at these community responses.

First, though, we will look at our individual choices and responses. The dominant narrative is dominant precisely because it has the power to shape our perceptions and choices. Therefore, the first step in constructing an alternative is to start changing our perceptions and freeing ourselves to make different choices. In a sense, we create this alternative as we begin living into it; we create the path as we walk it.

This task of building and proclaiming an alternative narrative while learning to live out of it is not primarily an intellectual exercise. It is not primarily an exercise in organizing. It is, above all, a spiritual challenge. Sustaining ourselves for the necessary long haul of challenging the way the dominant narrative has defined our national identity will require immense spiritual resources. The power of narrative does not come from factual accuracy or reasoned argument; its power comes from its ability to tap into the hearts and spirits of its intended audience. To resist the dominant narrative and to construct an alternative is, therefore, primarily a work of spirit and heart. To be successful in this endeavor, we need to do more than simply offer a new political platform or analysis; we need a spiritual revival that is first and foremost a revolution of the heart. As Gandhi once put it, we must *be* the change we wish to see in the world.

Being the change we seek in our nation begins with the commitment to a personal journey from the *fear of others* (the spirit that drives the dominant narrative) to the *freedom to be for others* (the spiritual force of our alternative narrative). I believe the personal journey from fear to freedom encompasses a spiritual path marked by five interrelated virtues: mindfulness, compassion, solidarity, humility, and freedom. The diagram below illustrates the ways these five virtues relate to each other.

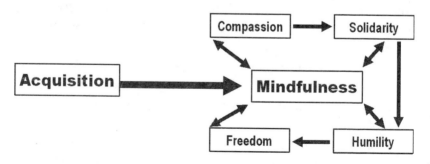

As the diagram illustrates, the primary dynamic requires us to move from acquisition to mindfulness. The other dynamics revolve around mindfulness, which is the engine driving the entire process. Although I write about these dynamics as if they were linear, in truth, they deepen with each turn through the cycle and are augmented by the continuing desire to move from a life of acquisition to a discipline of mindfulness.

## FROM ACQUISITION TO MINDFULNESS

The principle dynamic of this spiritual path out of fear to freedom is the journey from a life focused on acquisition to one centered in mindfulness. Mindfulness, in this model of spirituality, is the ability to see what is real. It is the ability to let go of all the clutter in our lives and to be fully present to each moment. And when we are fully present to each moment, we discover that we don't need the many masks we wear. Living in the moment frees us from the pain and disappointments of the past that cripple us; it frees us from the anxieties and fears of the future that feed our compulsive need for control.

The most important virtue of this spiritual path, mindfulness is also the most difficult. We live in a culture dominated by addictive consumerism that prevents us from seeing and believing the truth about ourselves. And what is that truth? We are sons of God. We are daughters of the Most High Creator. We are not the many labels the world puts on us; we are not defined by the corporate logos on our clothing. We are not members of the "Pepsi Generation." We are more than what we eat, what we wear, what we produce, or what we drive.

As with the struggle to be free of any addictive behavior, our journey from acquisition to mindfulness is best shaped in a community of loving support and forged in the furnace of contemplative prayer. In an age where personal worth is measured by the quantity and quality of what we produce and consume, contemplative prayer stands as a great counter-sign. In prayer, we rest in being, not in doing. Contemplative prayer is radically countercultural because it neither produces nor consumes anything. To sustain the discipline of contemplative prayer, we need the support of fellow seekers who will affirm us and prod us onward when the dominant culture tempts us to surrender to the frenzy.

Until we can find the silence and solitude to clear our vision, we will never be able to see a brother or sister in the eyes of the stranger. As long as we believe that we must always be ready to protect and defend all that we have acquired (whether material, emotional, intellectual, social, or even spiritual wealth), we will live in fear. We will be blind to the humanity of the unknown other. Contemplative prayer has the power to release us from this cycle of fear.

My desire for contemplative prayer was nurtured at New Melleray Abbey, a Trappist Monastery just west of Dubuque, Iowa. I had the great privilege of being a lay associate there many years ago. The motto of New Melleray Abbey describes the goal of contemplative prayer: "*Vacate et Videte*" ("be empty and see"). Many techniques and disciplines can open the door to contemplative prayer.

I tried many of them before finding one that seemed fruitful for me. My contemplative prayer is anchored in a practice known as *Lectio Divina*, or Sacred Reading. This form of contemplative prayer consists of prayerfully reading Scripture. But the purpose of *Lectio Divina* is not to increase one's knowledge of Scripture or to memorize it. Instead, the purpose is to allow the text to be drawn into the heart, to stir the soul. I find Psalms a rich place to practice *Lectio Divina*. I will read a psalm and find my heart and spirit drawn to or touched by a word or phrase. Instead of moving on with my reading, I remain in the hold of that word or phrase, repeating it over and over until it moves from my head into my heart. If I can remain focused and eliminate all distractions of the mind and body, I find that soon the word or phrase disappears and only the silent solitude of the moment remains.

In that moment, which seems to be a fraction of a second while at the same time containing the meaning of a lifetime of study, I find myself in God. In that moment, freed from the daily cares that cause me anxiety and the analytical constructs I hold and protect like treasure, I experience pure existence. And in that moment, I am free to let go of all that binds and blinds me. It does not last for long, and the short-term impact on my daily life is hard to measure. But I believe that it has, over time, begun to transform me. These times of contemplative prayer are like a re-tuning of my spiritual receiver to better pick up God's frequency. I find that I need to do it every day because the world is always broadcasting many competing frequencies that can drown out the voice of God. Every morning when I re-tune to God's frequency, I have a much better chance of hearing the Spirit's whisper throughout the day.

## MINDFULNESS THAT LEADS TO COMPASSION

The journey from a life dominated by acquisition to one centered in mindfulness is a lifelong spiritual quest. But on this journey, we begin to discover another dynamic: how mindfulness leads us to compassion. As we begin to see ourselves and others as we really are, we begin to open to the movement of compassion. In their book *Compassion*, McNeill, Morrison, and Nouwen explain, "Compassion asks us to go where it hurts, to enter into places of pain, to share in brokenness, fear, confusion and anguish. . . . Compassion requires us to be weak with the weak, vulnerable with the vulnerable and powerless with the powerless. Compassion means full immersion in the condition of being human."[1]

This kind of compassion is only possible for those who have nothing to protect or defend. It means relinquishing the posture of having it all together. It means being fully present to a person who is suffering, without pre-conditions or requirements. Genuine compassion becomes possible when, through contemplative prayer and the support of community, we gain the courage to remove our egos from the center of our lives to create a space for the other to enter. If our hearts are full of ourselves, we have no room for anyone else.

Contemplative prayer teaches us that every moment is a sacred invitation from God to become fully human and fully alive. This gives us the grace and courage to live in the present moment, and in the present moment, compassion can be born. Like contemplative prayer, true compassion requires patience. Cultivating patience in our lives and in our prayer is not easy. Patience keeps us from running off to attend to some future anxiety or some past hurt or disappointment. Patience asks us to live in the moment, and only when we are present to the moment can we focus on the other. Compassion requires that we be HERE, not replaying what happened yesterday or thinking about what we need to do tomorrow.

Dorothy Day, co-founder of the Catholic Worker movement, admired the Russian novelist Fyodor Dostoevsky. In explaining the challenge of the Catholic Worker, she once quoted from his novel *The Brothers Karazmov*: "love in action is a harsh and dreadful thing compared to love in dreams." Only when I became part of a Catholic Worker community did I discover the huge chasm between "love in action" and "love in dreams." While contemplative prayer drew me to serve people who were poor, our homeless guests at the Catholic Worker showed me what compassion was really about. They taught me the importance of being present. They challenged me to see them, to hear them, and to be fully present to them. Too often, I preferred the abstract notion of the poor rather than being fully present to those who came through our door. Prayer brought me to the poor, but the poor taught me the true meaning of being human. It is a lesson I still struggle to learn.

## COMPASSION THAT LEADS TO SOLIDARITY

Many of us perform our works of charity and acts of justice out of a sense of compassion. At this point on our spiritual path, we might find it easy to settle into a service model of discipleship, one in which we see ourselves as reaching down to help the "less fortunate," "unenlightened," or "underprivileged." This model of discipleship assumes that we have made it and what we need to do is to pull others up to our level. But this model often leads to a desire to control those we seek to serve. When control becomes our objective, fear is often a byproduct.

We need an entirely different model of service: we need to learn solidarity. To be in solidarity means to stand with others. To be in solidarity means to relinquish our client relationship with those who suffer. It means relinquishing our political, economic, social, cultural, and religious dividing lines in order to walk beside another. It means being willing to learn from those we pity, from those who repulse us, from those who are needy, from those we fear, and from those whom we call our enemies. It means giving up feelings rooted in a sense of our own superiority.

This solidarity is more than a vague feeling of kinship or sense of community. It is the willingness to enter into relationships of accountability with those outside of our comfort zones and to have our lives changed by the encounters. Accountability in relationships means always having the best interests of the other in mind when making choices. Accountability means being willing to be transformed by the other by being open to their truth. Solidarity without accountability is just another form of voyeurism (passing through other's lives without being changed by the experience). Genuine solidarity is evidenced by changes in the way we think and act.

Throughout my life, I have struggled against two tendencies that keep me from moving from compassion to solidarity. The first is my tendency to patronize those who are poor or marginalized. I have spent most of my life as a peace and justice activist, taking account of those who are poor or oppressed, without being accountable to them. Far too often, people who are poor and oppressed have been the objects of my concern, instead of people with whom I am in relationship.

At its most fundamental level, my habitual need to patronize those who are poor and oppressed is about my fear of losing control. I want to always carefully make sure that whenever I go to "help the poor," I am the one who controls my level of commitment and the one who sets the boundaries of my good deeds. More often than not, I set the terms of my service without first putting myself in relationship with those I would serve.

The second tendency that keeps me from being in solidarity is my habit of writing off so many people who wear different political or ideological labels. I find it easier to deal with a complicated world by dividing people up into the good, liberal, peace-loving progressive folks who agree with me and all those greedy, hate-filled, small-minded folks who disagree with me.

But at a more fundamental level, my habitual need to write people off comes from a fear of challenges to my worldview that might force me to change the way I think or the way I divide up the world between those who are "good" and those who "just don't get it." For activists, certitude can be more valuable than gold. It has taken many years of hard study and hard knocks to acquire my certitude, and I am hard-pressed to let it go.

## SOLIDARITY THAT LEADS TO HUMILITY

One of the most painful and humbling results of being in solidarity with those who suffer or those who differ from us is recognizing our own powerlessness to "solve" even some of the smallest of human problems. Through solidarity, we come to truly understand our own limits. We are not the gods we thought ourselves. And, for all the technological wonders spawned from our inexhaustible human creativity, we are still unable to call all the shots.

Humility born of solidarity tends to pull down the dividing lines that we erect to convince ourselves that there are differences between ourselves and those we seek to serve or convert to our way of thinking. The more we move from seeing others as objects of our attention to persons with whom to be in relationship, the more difficult it becomes to rely on pat answers. We can debate the answers to social, political, and economic problems. But when it comes down to trying to help the person sitting across from us, social, political, or economic theory often falls short. We can develop a political and economic critique of a political party or ideology, but when we enter into a relationship with people who belong to that party or hold that ideology, black-and-white analysis gives way to the grays that define most human relationships. If you prefer a clear-cut world, be sure to stay insulated in your own worldview; be sure to keep "those others" at arm's length. And if you must come in contact with those who are different, be sure to seize upon any behavior that confirms your own preconceived notions about them.

Humility, on the other hand, opens us to learning something new about those we consider marginal to ourselves. It makes it possible to hear something new from an enemy or opponent. Humility means being open to the idea that we are as much a product of our environment as are those we pity or despise. As Henri Nouwen put it in his book *With Open Hands*, "In the expression of the oppressor, I recognize my own face, and in the hands of the oppressed, I recognize my own hands which speak of powerlessness and helplessness."[2]

Solidarity has called me to humility through challenges from two different directions. The first direction has come from relationships with people of color. The second direction comes from relationships with upper-middle class, conservative Republicans living in an affluent community.

In 2000, when I was the National Council Chair of Pax Christi USA (PCUSA), our leadership community made a commitment to a twenty-year initiative to transform PCUSA into an anti-racist, multi-cultural Catholic movement for peace with justice. This initiative was born out of the realization that being a national Catholic organization that was over 95 percent white when the U.S. Catholic Church will soon consist of a majority of people of color was increasingly inauthentic. How could we give witness to the "Peace of Christ" if we did not look like the Body of Christ?

To facilitate the goals of this twenty-year initiative, PCUSA mandated forming and training a multi-racial anti-racism team called the Pax Christi Anti-Racism Team (PCART). One of the major elements of this work is learning how, as a largely white organization, to be accountable to people of color in our peace and justice work. This commitment to greater accountability has brought us into relationships with communities that, in the past, were not in our circle of allies.

As a member of PCART, I have been privileged to be in relationships of solidarity with people of color who are committed to this transformational work. At the same time, this new level of solidarity has often been painful and humbling. By being in accountable relationships with people of color, I have had to face some difficult truths about myself.

Prior to involvement with this work, I prided myself in thinking I was a progressive Catholic activist committed to the Gospel of peace and justice and working to build a more just and non-violent world. I was one of the good guys fighting the good fight on behalf of all those who suffer and are oppressed. But I was blind to the ways I exercised white power and privilege in all of this work.

Dr. Peggy McIntosh of Wellesley College has researched and written on white privilege. She compares white privilege to an "invisible weightless knapsack of special provisions, maps, passports, codebooks, visas, clothes, tools and blank checks." This knapsack is given to white people at birth, who draw on its assets throughout their lives. As Paul Kivel writes in his book, *Uprooting Racism*, "Racism is based on the concept of Whiteness—a powerful fiction enforced by power and violence. Whiteness is a constantly shifting boundary separating those who are entitled to have certain privileges from those whose exploitation and vulnerability to violence is justified by their not being White."[3]

The people of color to whom I am accountable have helped me unpack and understand my white power and privilege. Being in accountable relationships with people of color is making it clear to me that, as a peace and justice activist, I often act from within a position of power and privilege in ways that exclude and disempower the very people I pride myself in "helping." My brothers and sisters of color continue to teach me that by refusing to take on racism—particularly in the way I do my peace and justice work—I unconsciously operate as a racist peace and justice activist. As James H. Cone, the father of Black Liberation Theology, makes clear, "No theology . . . can be Christian theology in North America or the world that does not engage White supremacy in society and the Church. To remain silent about the deadly consequences of White racism in the modern world automatically invalidates any theology's claim to Christian identity."[4]

What Reverend Cone says of Christian theology can be applied equally to Christian peace and justice work. Whenever I am tempted to think of racism as tangential or peripheral to my Christian peace and justice work, I risk making that work inauthentic and lacking in integrity. As I enter more deeply into solidarity with people of color, I am humbled by the truths they reveal to me. I am grateful that they don't give up on me, even when I continue, time after time, to fall back into my old patterns of acting out of white power and privilege. It has been painful and humbling, but I feel blessed.

My other growing edge in the work of moving from solidarity to humility has been in my relationships with fellow parishioners at St. Margaret Mary Parish in Naperville, Illinois, where I work as the Justice and Outreach Minister. Naperville is an affluent community in DuPage County, a stronghold of the Republican Party in Illinois. (DuPage County includes part of the district of former Representative Henry Hyde and part of the district of former Speaker of the House Dennis Hastert.)

When I first came to work at the parish, I carried all of the preconceived notions one might expect a former Catholic Worker and long-time peace activist to have regarding the folks I was now called to serve. Coming from Miami, Florida, to Naperville, I first had to adjust to the lack of racial diversity. I also had to adjust to living in a resource-rich environment, not only in terms of the parish's economic resources, but also the social, cultural, and educational assets that people in Naperville could access. I was prepared to sort these people into all the nice "boxes" I had created throughout my life as a way of understanding how "those people" think, act, and believe. Of course, some people fit nicely into the boxes I created, but many others did not.

Nick was one who did not. A lifelong conservative Republican and retired businessman, he is married to Loretta, a PCUSA member at St. Margaret Mary Parish. (They have one of those politically mixed marriages, like Mary Matlin and James Carville.) Loretta's work on the parish peace and justice committee brought Nick into my orbit. Both of them agreed to serve on the committee. Of course, in the beginning I was very leery of Nick. I couldn't tell if he was there to keep an eye on what I was doing, or if he was really interested in promoting Catholic Social Teaching in the parish. In the early days, and even now, we do a good deal of testing each other to see where we stand, but overall, my relationship with Nick is one of my more valued parish relationships.

Being in a relationship of solidarity with Nick, working together to bring Catholic Social Teaching to parishioners at St. Margaret Mary, has been humbling for me. I have been forced to change my political worldview about conservative Republicans. I can no longer write off business owners or people in management. Nick has taught me that people who occupy the political place directly opposed to where I stand can be people of great integrity. They can be deeply compassionate toward those who are poor and oppressed and can be as willing to sacrifice and serve those in need as I am. In addition to Nick, I am learning to see, hear, and work with other political opposites at St. Margaret Mary Parish. Every day, it seems as if old categories are crumbling. Nick and I still don't agree on much of anything (except maybe Notre Dame Football), but he has become an ally in my work at St. Margaret Mary. And he is my friend. I have learned a great deal from him, and I am humbled and grateful.

## HUMILITY THAT LEADS TO FREEDOM

Once we have been humbled by our relationships of solidarity with those outside of our comfort zones, a new dynamic begins to manifest in our spiritual journey. As we relinquish our political, moral, spiritual, social, and economic high ground and give up trying to always be in control, we discover freedom. Freed from the illusions of power, freed from the need to be gods, freed from the need to have a solution to every human problem, we are free to act in faith, without worrying about protecting or defending our self-image, political ideology, or our five-year plan for saving the world. We are free to live in the fullness of the moment without worrying about the crushing demands of tomorrow's problems or the overwhelming weight of regret for yesterday's failures. In short, we are free to seek first the Reign of God and God's righteousness, knowing that all the things we need will come to us as they are needed.

Throughout my entire adult life, I have longed for this land called freedom. Yet even now it is mostly foreign to me. I spend most of my time standing on the riverbank opposite this land. I can feel the breeze blowing from the other side, I can see the green pastures, and I can smell its flowers. But for the most part, my feet are firmly planted on this side of freedom. However, there have been times, brief as they might be, when, finding a shallow crossing, I mustered enough courage to venture onto the opposite shore. These transformative moments continue to have a deep impact upon me.

One of these excursions into the land of freedom taught me that fear wears many faces. As a campus minister at St. Thomas Aquinas Parish and Catholic Student Center at Iowa State University (1976-1983), I had an apartment only a block away from the parish office. Sometimes, after business hours, homeless people would stop by the church asking for help. Because I lived close to the church, I often got calls from the office asking for advice. Normally, I went to the church, met briefly with the person in need, made a sandwich or two, and then sent him or her on with a few dollars.

Over time, I became increasingly uncomfortable with this response. The seeds of my discomfort were planted as I became involved with the Des Moines Catholic Worker community co-founded by my brother Frank. The Catholic Worker operates on the principle of radical personalism: the belief that each Christian is called to take personal responsibility for the corporal works of mercy, even going so far as to offer hospitality to the homeless in her or his own home. I had been taking groups of students from my campus ministry program to the Des Moines Catholic Worker to help with serving meals, painting, and rehabbing houses. I had prayed with this community and had heard them give witness to the students about this call to radical personalism.

This community's witness had lodged itself in my mind and heart like a pebble in my shoe. It irritated my soul, and whenever I found myself face-to-face with a homeless person at the parish office, that pebble felt like a large stone. I felt that responding to them with sandwiches and change was inadequate, but I was afraid to think about going further. This irritation in my soul made its way into my prayer life. Why didn't I just invite these people into my own apartment? Over time, with the grace of God, I became aware of the fear that kept me from dislodging this pebble. In fact, I discovered three different fears.

The first fear was easy to identify and face: I was afraid that if I let a homeless stranger into my home, I could be assaulted and even killed. The second fear, which was a little more difficult to identify, was having my possessions taken from me. In prayer, I became aware that, to a large extent, my possessions owned me. In fact, my attachment to the things I owned set the parameters of my response to these strangers who were homeless. The fear of being taken advantage of was the third and most difficult fear I had to confront in prayer. What if this person was just running a scam? What if I was being played for a fool? I was surprised by how much my own ego and protecting my self-image were at play just beneath the surface.

This pebble in my soul that irritated me so much in prayer was becoming a constant and unwelcome companion. I still felt stuck and unable to move to a different place. That is, until one Friday evening after a hard day's work. I had made plans to go out and was getting ready to leave my apartment when I got a call from the parish office. The receptionist told me that a homeless man was at the office; she wanted to know what she should do. For reasons that I still do not understand, I told her to send him over to my apartment.

The walk from the church office to my apartment took about five minutes. In that time, I went through the apartment and performed what might be called an exorcism. I walked to my stereo and said, "Good-bye stereo!" I then walked to the TV and said, "Good-bye TV set!" I went to every possession that meant anything to me and performed the same ritual. When the doorbell rang, I went to the door and was greeted by a rather timid man in his thirties who said his name was Francis. After welcoming him to my apartment, I made him dinner and set up the couch for him to sleep. I explained to him how the TV worked and then said, "Francis, I have made plans for the evening and so I need to leave. I expect to be back around 10:30 pm. Make yourself comfortable and I will see you in the morning."

When I walked out of the apartment and closed the door behind me, I suddenly felt as if a huge weight had been lifted off my shoulders. It was exhilarating! I was ecstatic! I could not believe how good I felt. It was my first taste of the freedom promised by Jesus to his followers. When I came back that night, Francis was asleep on the couch. In the morning, when I awoke, he had already gone. As far as I could tell, nothing was taken. But at that point, nothing I had mattered. I had tasted freedom, and I was discovering that this freedom was incredibly addictive. Within a year, I had joined with other friends to open our own house for people who were homeless called Loaves & Fishes Hospitality House.

My encounter with Francis changed the trajectory of my life. And even though at this point I am not offering hospitality to those who are homeless, the reverberations of that small experience of freedom still impact me to this day. I have briefly visited the land of freedom. That is why today I still find myself longing to cross back over to it.

## DOING THE INSIDE WORK

Doing the difficult inside work of transforming ourselves is a lifelong process that deepens with each turn through the four spiritual dynamics. But if we want to participate in constructing an alternative narrative that has the power to support and sustain our efforts to build a world of peace with justice, this work is crucial.

The spiritual path that I have described is not the only way; there is no one way. What is most important is that we each find a way to move beyond the trap of addictive consumerism, that we find a way to cultivate the virtues of compassion, solidarity, and humility. Probably most importantly, we must always seek to embrace the freedom that God offers us. We are called to freedom and the fullness of life. But to get to this Promised Land, we have to discard a lot of baggage and treasure. To respond fully to the prompting of the Spirit, we need to learn to pitch tents, not build temples (whether they be temples of wealth, fame, ideology, or certitude).

The good news: we do not have to make this journey from fear to freedom on our own. Many others also seek to live in the freedom offered by God. They too wish to participate in the work of birthing an alternative U.S. narrative. Finding each other and forming communities of support and accountability is important, especially now, when offering an alternative to the Bush-Cheney narrative is still not welcomed by most. In the next chapter, we will explore the communal path from fear to freedom.

# CHAPTER ELEVEN

# A Communal Path

The Constitution of the United States begins, "We the People," and one of its goals is forming "a more perfect union." In this country, this strong ideal of community has always coexisted with the ideal of individualism—"the pursuit of happiness." Our nation is best served when these two ideals are held together in creative tension. However, over the last four decades, the impulse to individualism seems to have overtaken the commitment to community in our U.S. narrative.

The republican virtue of community was once a strong element of our national story. Recapturing this virtue is crucial if we hope to move beyond the paralysis of fear engendered in the Bush Administration's 9-11 narrative and to chart a course toward genuine peace based on justice. In their book *The Quickening of America: Rebuilding our Nation, Remaking our Lives*, Frances Moore Lappé and Paul Martin DuBois talk about the importance of community in responding to the many challenges of this nation:

> The biggest problem facing Americans is not those issues that bombard us daily, from homelessness and failing schools to environmental devastation and the federal deficit. Underlying each is a deeper crisis. . . .

The crisis is that we as a people don't know how to come together to solve these problems. We lack the capacities to address the issues or remove the obstacles that stand in the way of public deliberation. Too many Americans feel powerless.[1]

Unfortunately, in this country, we have come to see national problem-solving as the domain of partisan politics. We no longer think of politics in the way that Lappé and DuBois describe it. Unfortunately, politics—the democratic process—has, for too many citizens, become a spectator sport. We no longer experience politics as something we participate in; we experience it as something we watch others do. Like the TV show *American Idol*, we have come to believe that our only requirement is casting our votes after the "contestants" have been vetted by political pundits and media talking heads who tell us what to think and how to feel. Our role is simply to choose between Tweedledee and Tweedledum, hoping the winner will solve our problems. However, as Lappé and DuBois point out:

Democracy requires a lot more of us than being intelligent voters. It requires that we learn to solve problems with others—that we learn to listen, to negotiate and to evaluate; to think and speak effectively. To go beyond simple protest in order to wield power to becoming partners in problem solving. This isn't about so-called good work; it's about our vital interests. And it isn't about simply running our government; it's about running our lives.[2]

Returning to the virtue of community is not only necessary for revitalizing our national politics; it is crucial to our ability to move from a life based on the principle of scarcity to one based on the principle of abundance. In isolation, no matter how many things we own, we can never fill the void in our souls that longs for meaning. In isolation, we can never realize our full human potentials. In isolation, we will never have enough. But in community, we come to know who we are; in community there is always enough. If we ever hope to move from being a nation compelled by *Peace as Enforced Order* to a nation that embraces *Peace as an Enterprise of Justice*, we will need to build communities that embody the virtue of enough. In other words, to construct the alternative narratives (of both 9-11 and this nation) outlined in the first three sections of this book, we need community.

The concept of community is simultaneously appealing and frightening. At one level, we all want to belong; we all want to be part of a group that will support and nurture us. And yet, on the other hand, community is foreboding because we fear losing our autonomy and independence. In fact, popular notions of autonomy and freedom championed by our consumer society and enshrined in our dominant U.S. narrative make building community more difficult. Yet only in community are we free to actually experience the transformation, support, boundary-crossing, solidarity, and security that make living out of an alternative narrative possible. To begin creating the community necessary to live this alternative (as well as the ideals of our faith), we must understand how the values of the dominant narrative—particularly consumerism, individualism, and the historical development of the concept of the nuclear family—have led to where we find ourselves today.

---

## COMMUNITY: THE ONLY WAY TO BE TRULY FREE IN A CONSUMERISTIC SOCIETY

Advertisers spend billions of dollars trying to convince us that the highest expression of human freedom is being able to produce and/or consume what we want, when we want, where we want, and at the best price we can find. Augmenting the gospel of freedom through consumption and production are the many think tanks who herald the blessings of the "free" market and the "free" enterprise system. As this market mentality comes to dominate more and more of our social lives, freedom is reduced to—as Burger King puts it—having it our way. Freedom is having the car that will get us to the top of mountains or allows us to drive off-road where we escape the inhibiting conformity of the crowd—even though we might only live in Peoria, Illinois.

But social critics as diverse as Bob Dylan and St. Paul remind us that this is an illusion, a myth. In his letter to the Romans, Paul writes, "None of us lives as her own master and none of us dies as his own master" (Romans 7:14). And one of Dylan's songs reminds us, "You're gonna have to serve somebody."[3] In other words, each of us lives in a world of competing forces and influences that seek our allegiances and worship. In this context, no person is autonomous, able to act completely freed from the many cultural, social, economic, and even religious forces in the world.

Having us buy into this myth serves the dominant narrative well. The most docile prisoner is the one who does not know she is living in a cage. The most enslaved person is the one who thinks that the choices he makes are completely free from outside influences. The neediest person is the one who thinks she has made it on her own, who thinks that having consumer choices makes him free. As the poet-environmentalist Wendell Berry put it in his poem, "Manifesto: The Mad Farmer Liberation Front":

> Love the quick profit, the annual raise,
> vacation with pay. Want more
> of everything ready-made. Be afraid
> to know your neighbors and to die.
> And you will have a window in your head.
> Not even your future will be a mystery
> any more. Your mind will be punched in a card
> and shut away in a little drawer.
> When they want you to buy something
> they will call you. When they want you
> to die for profit they will let you know.[4]

Faith calls us to something different. In the struggle for genuine freedom, the fundamental question of Christian discipleship is: which god will we serve? While our consumer society tries to define freedom in terms of commerce, the Scriptures define freedom very differently. Freedom comes from knowing who we are in the context of community and covenant; freedom is the ability to do what we know is right, regardless of the consequences. Everything else is just one of many forms of slavery parading as freedom.

In the Christian view, only in community do we have any hope of achieving freedom from the powerful forces of the dominant narrative that seek to define us primarily in terms of what we produce and consume. If we do not consciously choose whom we will serve, the dominant narrative will choose for us. If we fail to consciously choose our community, we will end up defaulting to a consumer culture to give us meaning, identity, and a sense of belonging. As Laurence Shames, author of *The Hunger for More: Searching for Values in an Age of Greed*, wrote:

> A certain line gets crossed. People look to their goods not just for pleasure but for meaning. They want their stuff to tell them who they are. They ask that inanimate objects serve as stand-ins for deeper qualities. Not just pretty flowers but a built-in serenity is taken to exist in a Laura Ashley wallpaper pattern. Not just style but the character of a person is presumed to be made manifest by a Ralph Lauren blazer. People disappear into their clothes. Their conversation becomes merely a part of the ambience of the restaurants they frequent.[5]

## COMMUNITY: THE ONLY WAY TO BE TRULY FREE IN AN INDIVIDUALISTIC SOCIETY

Another powerful myth of consumer culture is associated with the popular concept of individualism. This myth tells us that wholeness and fulfillment are only possible when individuals break free of the suffocating obligations and limitations of community. Our consumer culture tells us that we can become individuals by buying products that set us apart—even though millions of other consumers are buying the same products in the hopes of creating their own individuality. In this country, we like to talk about being individuals. Yet at the same time, we constantly look to the dominant culture to tell us what it means to be an individual.

We have been so thoroughly socialized into the U.S. narrative of rugged individualism that we've allowed ourselves to be induced into a stupor of selective amnesia about our own family histories. Living in the suburbs, I've run across some affluent people who readily and unabashedly claim that they made it on their own—even though their families are only two or three generations removed from the poverty of ethnic ghetto tenements or subsistence farming. In their idealized and sanitized memories, they think they got where they are simply through their own hard work and the hard work of their parents and grandparents. They choose to forget that survival for their families in those ethnic ghettos and poor rural communities was never an individual family struggle; it was a community struggle, assisted by extended families and neighborhoods, societal institutions, and governmental programs.

### Made it on Their Own?

Have they simply forgotten that not long ago, families depended on their neighbors and extended families to make it through times of crisis? When families fell on hard times, meals came to the back door from the kitchens of women who provided not only for their own children, but for all the neighborhood's children. Have these "self-made" men and women conveniently forgotten what it meant to have a neighborhood grocery store or family doctor's office where credit was readily available when a parent was out of work?

## Made it on Their Own?

When they wag their heads disapprovingly at the youth crime rate today (which has actually dropped in recent decades), have they forgotten the neighborhood cop of the past, who was as likely to take a child in trouble back to the neighborhood pastor or to a family patriarch or matriarch as to haul him or her off to jail? Don't they remember that for their grandparents, churches were not just places for Sunday services, but literal lifelines, providing not only education, but social services, legal advice, counseling, and even medical care? Can those who are Catholic bring themselves to acknowledge that the quality parochial education their parents or grandparents received—that put their families on the road to success—was subsidized through the nearly free labor of women religious? Have some of these "self-made" professionals considered that the unions they now castigate were instrumental in helping their families make living wages that enabled them to move out of the squalor of tenement life?

## Made it on Their Own?

Have they simply forgotten the accrued social and financial capital that came to their families directly or indirectly because of government social programs? Is it possible that some of these rugged individuals don't remember the GI Bill that enabled a family member, likely for the first time, to get a college education? Can they be ignorant of the fact that this GI Bill made it possible for their families to move from being blue-collar wage earners to being white-collar career professionals, with the attendant rise in income? (Over two million men received higher education benefits from the GI Bill after World War II; by 1947, one-half of all college students were veterans.)[6] Don't they realize that those government college benefits that gave their grandparents the opportunity to get jobs with generous pensions are still taking care of them today?

Have some of these "self-made" workers forgotten the impact of Social Security and Medicare on the quality of their lives because of the added financial security these programs provide for their parents or grandparents? (Of course, many families of color were initially excluded from the Social Security system because they made too little to qualify or because Social Security did not cover agricultural or domestic workers. These families don't get a government subsidy to help care for their grandparents.)

Have many of these self-made, never-asked-anyone-for-a-handout suburbanites ever considered the financial capital accrued to their families through the government's Federal Housing Authority (FHA) or the Veterans Administration (VA) Housing Authority low-interest loans that made homeownership (often in the suburbs, where housing values rose dramatically) possible for their parents or grandparents? (Most families of color were not afforded this entitlement because the FHA channeled loans away from the central city to the suburbs where "restrictive covenants" kept out families of color. The FHA and the VA financed more than $120 billion worth of new housing between 1934 and 1962, but less than 2 percent of it was available to families of color.)[7]

An honest appraisal of our family histories would show that very few of us can genuinely claim to have made it on our own. In each family history, we would find key moments where the intervention of someone outside of the family—a neighbor, a church, a charitable organization, a government program, or a sympathetic employer—made all the difference in the world and changed the course of the entire family. If those interventions had not taken place, our families would not be where they are today.

While the idealized notion of the rugged individual or the self-made person is at the center of our dominant cultural narrative in the United States, we won't find it in the Bible, just as we cannot find identity based in consumption in the Bible. On the contrary, the testimony of the sacred Scriptures tells us that we cannot be fully human as individuals. The Scriptures tell us that only in the context of community do we receive our identity and personhood. In every book of the Bible, individuals are always identified in relationship to their family, their tribe, or their ancestors. In fact, the vast majority of Scripture is addressed to communities, not individuals. God speaks to a people, not to individuals. Even when God does speak to individual leaders or prophets, God speaks to them as leaders of a people.

## CHANGING NOTIONS OF "FAMILY"

The corollary myth of the individual presented in the dominant U.S. narrative is the concept of the nuclear family. In less than seventy years, we have seen the common understanding of family radically redefined. Four generations ago, if you asked six-year-old children to draw pictures of their families, they would have drawn their parents, siblings, and most likely some aunts, uncles, grandparents, and cousins. Now, if you ask a child to draw a family picture, she or he would most likely draw siblings and maybe two parents. In a relatively short time period, the norm of family life—the extended family—has been replaced by a new concept: the nuclear family.

Many historians agree that the most crucial changes in the role of families occurred with the birth and evolution of the industrial age. During that time, many of the functions typically done by families began to be transferred to other institutions. In an agricultural society, extended families were self-contained economic units that had primacy in the socialization process. Moving from family farms and trades to a society of wage earning meant that a large amount of family members' time belonged to their employers. This resulted in a host of institutions to provide services once thought of as the sole responsibility of families.

The rise of the wage earner as the predominant form of family economic participation also required that families become more mobile to meet the demands of production. Extended families began to break down because it became increasingly difficult to keep a clan together in one geographic location. Families moved to where the jobs were (and to where affordable housing was being built in newly designed suburbs). As a result, extended families began playing a reduced role.

The move from the extended family to a new concept of nuclear family was supported by both economic and social forces. The new age of mass production and planned obsolescence required families to be dependable and frequent consumers in order to keep the economy growing. Extended families tended not to buy as much because of the practice of mutual sharing and a more communal sense of ownership. In an extended family living in the same neighborhood, every household did not need a lawnmower or washer and dryer. In extended families, women came together to can their own fruits and vegetables, and at the same time, younger women learned the art of raising children and got advice on strengthening their marriages. These kinds of shared economic activities also gave extended families an inexpensive way of putting food on the table and meeting other needs of life.

The nuclear family, on the other hand, proved to be the ideal unit for the consumption of whole new categories of goods (like frozen vegetables and dinners) and services (like self-help books and videos on the art of raising children or strengthening marriages). Popular culture also supported this shift in family structure, especially through TV and movies. Shows like the *Beverly Hillbillies* and *The Real McCoys* conveyed a rather negative stereotype of extended families—they were charming but backward and unsophisticated. At the same time, shows like *Father Knows Best* and *The Adventures of Ozzie and Harriet* expounded on the virtues of the nuclear family living in the suburbs. Can anyone recall a grandparent, uncle, aunt, or cousin making regular appearances on these shows?

## THE IMPORTANCE OF CREATING COMMUNITY TO OUR ALTERNATIVE NARRATIVE

Today, the extended family, as a functioning economic and social unit, has all but disappeared, except in immigrant communities and some communities of color. Most of us cannot go back and reknit our extended families. We must find other ways of creating supportive intentional communities that help us forge identities that are alternatives to the powerful consumer culture and dominant U.S. narrative that envelop us.

The dominant U.S. narrative is called dominant because it is embraced and promulgated by most of our social, cultural, political, economic, and even religious institutions. Its power comes from its ability to provide rewards and punishment. Those who accept it are designated as patriotic true believers; they are rewarded with access to the community of consumption. But those who question the dominant narrative are often labeled social and political heretics; they are often considered unpatriotic, and their lifestyle choices put them outside of the community of consumption. As individuals, we will find it extremely difficult to stand alone against the power of this dominant narrative. The myth of the heroic individual standing against the forces of evil is just that—a myth.

Moving away from the addictive consumerism of the dominant culture may start as an individual choice, but only a community can sustain it. In fact, when we decide to begin this journey, we often find that genuine community becomes possible. For Katy Butler, writing in the magazine *Mother Jones*, the path to a more meaningful, simple life began with a personal conversion: "I thought of my own life—my constant conversations with myself about wanting a child, a new couch, a weekend cottage, a bigger house on a quieter street—and realized my discontent was cheating me of the life I had." As Butler began to simplify her life, she started to recycle more, walk more, and eat less meat and more beans. But the unexpected surprise on her journey toward simple living was discovering genuine community:

> I began facing the life I had, not the life I dreamed of
> having or thought I deserved to have. I turned off lights.
> I started to cut the link between consumption and plea-
> sure, between consumption and self worth. And that
> paved the way for some unexpected things. . . . Having
> less money forced me to get to know my neighbors
> and a network of borrowing emerged. My next-door
> neighbor Mack, a salesman, lost his job and borrowed
> my computer to type resumes; when my husband's
> car broke down, Mack lent us his. My husband, Bob,
> helped Jay, a carpenter, change his clutch. Jay brought
> us wood scraps for kindling and his wife, Gloria, fed
> us dinner.[8]

But for a community to be Christian, it must do more than
support a countercultural lifestyle. A Christian community is
also an agent for social transformation. Christian community is
more than a coping mechanism; it is more than a rejection of the
addictive consumer values of the individualistic dominant U.S.
narrative. Christian community is where we can face our fears
and together work to create a better world.

Engaging in the work of constructing an alternative narrative is risky and difficult. To overcome our fears in this age of
terrorism and violence, we will need to strengthen the bonds of
community that give us hope and sustain us in the darkness. Pri-
oress Christine Vladimiroff, OSB, of the Benedictine Sisters of
Erie (Pennsylvania), shares how her community offers a countercultural witness to the importance of community as the antidote
to fear:

> Building community is a radical activity in an alien-
> ated society. It is a prophetic statement to our domi-
> nant culture of isolation and individualism. We af-
> firm by our lifestyle that God is the God of gathering.

It is an alternative vision of reality that contradicts society's fear of the stranger. It replaces the paranoid suspect of the foreigner amongst us with acceptance and love. It is a clear affirmation that the human family is one. . . . Benedictine hospitality tells us not to close our doors in fear, not even with the threat of terrorism in our midst. It moves us not to shutter our windows as to appear unapproachable, but to welcome the poor. The gospel clearly calls us to not close our borders to those refugees who seek a new home among us. It is a national tragedy, a betrayal of the American experiment, to now have a mindset that is hostile to immigrants. Hospitality is never easy, but as Abraham welcomed into his tent the three visitors, it will also be for us a blessing and a revelation of God in our midst.[9]

Unless we find each other, we will never find our way. And if our communities are to become more than just a coping mechanism to help us survive, we will need to build them around the principle of crossing boundaries. Communities capable of transforming the world have the courage to reach across the boundaries of race, class, gender, nationality, sexual orientation, and the other dividing lines that the dominant U.S. narrative uses to keep us from connecting to one another. Genuine Christian community is not exclusive; its identity is not based on the rejection of others; it is not content with the notion of insiders and outsiders; it always seeks to make connections.

These communities of transformation eagerly reach beyond their neighborhoods, their regions, and their nations. Communities of transformation understand that constant change and adaptation are the norm; they realize that faith, hope, and life are found at the margins and on the borders, not at the center. By their very nature, communities of transformation do not allow fear to paralyze them or to set limits on their caring. Communities of transformation will not be satisfied until they are in solidarity with every other community on the planet.

There are dozens of resources and models for overcoming isolation and forming genuine communities of support and transformation. Some use a *community organizing* model, bringing people together around common concerns and issues in order to exercise political power for change. A *small faith-sharing community* model brings people together to support and deepen their faith and to act together to live out their faith values. Still others use an *intentional community* model in which people share their lives by living in the same household, forming joint ownership of land and resources, and/or working in a joint business venture around a common vision or set of values. Community organizing, small faith-sharing groups, and intentional communities are just a few models of community that can be explored and adapted to one's personal needs and abilities.[10]

But while many resources are available to help form communities of support and transformation, most people who have actually tried to create communities will tell you that the key to creating community is not a matter of technique or having the right information. Communities that persist over time do so because the people who belong to them understand that being in community is crucial to their quality of life and their survival as countercultural agents of transformation.

If community building is nothing more than an optional activity we engage in (like belonging to a health club or social club), chances are that community will not last very long. Personality clashes and conflicts are also a part of community building. And everything in our dominant culture is designed to make community unnecessary and unachievable. Over time, our dominant culture will provide us with a thousand reasons to walk away from trying to build genuine communities of support and transformation. The only thing that can sustain a community over time is its members' recognition that if they do not continue struggling to make community work, something essential to their identity will die. When living in community becomes a matter of survival, communities have a better chance of surviving.

Community-building has implications beyond the personal or small-scale. Hand-in-hand with a return to our communitarian roots as a guiding principle for our future work, many also call for an inclusive understanding of security that moves beyond "national" security. A fear-based understanding of security sees potential enemies everywhere. An understanding of security that is based on the pursuit of justice sees potential allies everywhere. In addition, security based on the pursuit of justice is rooted in the conviction that no one community or nation can attain true security apart from others; each part is connected to the whole, and instability resulting from injustice in one nation is a threat to the stability of all nations. As Marie Dennis, Director of the Maryknoll Office of Global Concerns, stated:

> Inclusive human security, as opposed to national security, guarantees access to food, clean water, healthcare, education and employment. It recognizes the right of people to participate in important decisions that affect their lives and respects the integrity of creation. Inclusive human security would emerge from a "globalization of solidarity" that promotes international cooperation to preemptively address root causes of terrorism and to manage deep grievances and conflicts before they turn violent.[11]

Together in community, we can face and forge a new future. Fighting terrorism is not just about improving military technology or building better security walls. Regardless of how much of our treasure we invest in these things, we will still only be as strong as our covenants with one another. In the end, it is our relationships that will save us. And it is the quality and strength of our relationships that will enable us to preserve the sometimes-ignored values and principles of our republic.

# EPILOGUE

# Be Not Afraid

In a recent sermon, Rabbi Stuart Dauermann reminded his congregation, "The command 'fear not' or 'be not afraid' is the most frequently repeated command in both the Hebrew Bible and the B'rith Chadasha. It is found 122 times in the Hebrew Bible and another couple hundred times in the B'rith Chadasha."[1] Many of these exhortations address misplaced fear: fearing the wrong things. The testimony of Scriptures reminds us that fearing the wrong things often leads to slavery. In contrast, learning to value what is most important is the beginning of wisdom and overcoming fear. What we should fear most is being cut off from God, the source of all life. To live in the fear of God, in overwhelming awe of God's power and love, is to live unafraid of anything else that may enter our lives.

The Christian Scriptures also recount Jesus' many exhortations to his followers to "be not afraid." If the disciples had remained hostage to fear, they never would have dared go out to the world to preach Christ crucified and risen. Maybe the greatest challenge we Christians face in this age of terrorism is finding the courage to come out from behind the security and comfort of our locked doors. The potential risks and costs to our relationships and even our lives are substantial: the testimony of Scripture and our Christian tradition tells us that many of those disciples who left the security of their locked doors to preach the Good News also lost their lives. Yet as Christians, we also live with the promise of the resurrection, a narrative that gives us the courage to let go of all fear.

## LETTING GO OF FEAR: OUR RELATIONSHIPS

For many of us, the risks and costs are not just a matter of being willing to put ourselves in danger, or giving our lives for the sake of the Gospel. Many of us have not only been called to discipleship, we have also been called into relationships with our spouses, children, and other significant people. Even if we wanted to sell everything and follow Christ, we could not make that choice for our families. People depend on us; we cannot be so cavalier with our lives.

I love my wife Brigid; she and I have been together for a long time. But from the beginning, we understood our relationship as part of our call to work for peace with justice. We were not just a couple; we were a couple with a sense of mission to the world. We even wrote this commitment into our marriage vows. Both Brigid and I entered into our marriage aware of the risks and the costs of this kind of commitment. As such, we have tried to be prepared for those risks for the sake of the Gospel. We have marched together, we have risked arrest, and we understand that, if faced with a situation where either of us might have to act out of conscience, we would support each other, whatever the cost.

However, it is no longer just the two of us. I remember the birth of my daughter Angela. In the delivery room, I cut the umbilical cord, freeing her from her mother's womb and sending her on her journey through life. Since then, my heart and soul have had an ongoing conversation. The love I have for Angela has become so strong that it frightens me. It frightens me because it makes me feel so vulnerable. When Angela was born, it was as if my heart leapt from my chest and took on a life of its own. She is my heart walking in the world, and that makes me want to be very protective. On the other hand, what God has revealed to my soul is that Angela does not belong to me. She belongs to God first and to herself second. God has made clear to me that my role is to care for Angela, but that she is only entrusted to my care for a short time.

In my relationship with Angela, I have experienced a thousand deaths. Every stage of her life has meant that I had to let go and let die a daughter whom I loved more than my own life. I wept over the loss of the five-year old Angela who played with me for hours; the Angela who thought I was a superhero; the Angela who almost knocked me to the ground when she jumped into my arms. I remember weeping while driving alone during those difficult times in her early teens, when relating with her was never easy.

But now, I find the 19-year-old edition of Angela a fascinating, intelligent, and extremely delightful young adult. The more I fall in love with this Angela, the more forlorn I become at the thought that this Angela will die one day to become the adult woman she is destined to be. And when this happens, I will weep again. Always, this dying occurs. Always there is a renegotiating of our relationship, and always I find myself falling in love again.

Life has taught me the truth that God revealed to my soul when Angela was just a baby. Over time, my heart has learned what the soul has revealed. As much as we would like to keep the ones we love, we always lose them—if not in physical death, than in the many deaths we call human development. We cannot protect our loved ones from these deaths any more than we can protect them from life. And if we were to try, we would deprive them of both.

Yes, we have the responsibility to care for our children. But are we always able to distinguish between what they really need and what we think they should have? I think of how much some parents go through to give their children what they think they need, only to discover later how much of their lives they wasted on things that proved useless to their children. I recall the wisdom of the prophet Isaiah: "Why waste your money on what really isn't food? Why work hard for something that doesn't satisfy?" (Isaiah 55:2)

What do our children most need from us? From what must we protect them? Maybe what Angela needs the most is for her father to show her what it means to be true to herself, to live without abandoning her values or principles. Maybe what Angela needs to be protected from is the cynicism that comes from watching adults in her life "sell out" their beliefs for financial security or for social acceptance. What Angela needs—maybe what all our children need—are adults whose lives witness to something bigger than themselves. In addition to meeting their basic needs and lavishing unconditional love upon them, maybe our children need adults who are willing to risk it all for something more than personal gain. Maybe our children need a reason to believe that life is more than a competition to see who can get the most stuff.

Often, I find that when I use my daughter or my wife as an excuse for not taking such risks on behalf of the Gospel, it has more to do with my own fears than my concerns for them. Sometimes I find it easy to hide behind my role as responsible parent or responsible spouse or responsible community member. As poet-priest-activist Daniel Berrigan, SJ, puts it in his rendition of Psalm 32:

> Because of duty and law and responsibility and obligation
> and so on and so on; how I weary myself (and undoubtedly
>     you)
> and lose your gracious gesture, and tie myself in knots
> because "law" is a cover for my lawlessness, not the freedom
>     you offer
> and "duty" gets along with my deviousness
> and "obligation" is hand in glove with my laxity
> and "responsibility" is a cover for childishness.
> So I carry about these heavy absurd words, a beast's burden
> because in fact I wish to be burdened, dread to be free
> which is to say, I dread to be your friend and brother.[2]

## LETTING GO OF FEAR:
## DEATH AND DARING TO BE FREE

Finally, at the end of things, we fear not only for the lives of those whom we love, but for our own lives. In her 1969 book *On Death and Dying*, psychiatrist Elisabeth Kübler-Ross outlined five stages of grief discovered in her research on people who were dying. The first stage is denial: "This is not happening to me." Then anger: "How could this happen to me!" The third stage is bargaining: "If I stop smoking or if I start eating right, then maybe I can beat this." The next stage, depression, is the dark night of the soul: "I can't bear this." And finally, acceptance: "I'm ready; I don't want to struggle anymore."[3]

In this final stage, many of the dying report a sense of serenity and peace. At the same time, life becomes much more vivid. Everyday experiences become more intense. In a way not possible before, they see clearly those things that really matter. People in this stage of dying focus on important people in their lives. Things like career, wealth, power, and popularity become trivial. And most importantly, they begin to lose their fear. They begin speaking more truthfully. They stop wearing masks and start being real. At this stage, the dying commonly seek to bring closure and, if possible, reconciliation and healing to broken relationships.

As Christians who have died with Christ in Baptism and live in the hope of the resurrection, should we not already be living in this last stage of death and dying? If we truly believed in the resurrection of the dead, shouldn't this give us the courage to live free from fear and in complete acceptance of death? In St. Paul's famous chapter on the promise of the resurrection in the First Letter to the Corinthians, he concludes his declaration of faith by writing, "O death where is your victory? O death, where is your sting?" (1 Corinthians 15:55). Can we make a similar declaration?

What would it mean if Christians lived as if they really believed in the resurrection? Imagine an entire people who no longer fear death, who no longer need to protect their image, their ego, their social standing, their wealth, or their power. Imagine an entire people who live each moment as if it were a gift of God, given one breath at a time. Imagine if Christians lived unafraid of death—not only the final death of the body, but all those little deaths we so often hide from because they challenge us to abandon our certitudes and our carefully constructed worldviews.

What if Christians lived in acceptance of death—not in morbid fascination or fixation—but acceptance of death as part of the mystery of life? What might this acceptance of death mean for our freedom? Imagine being free to risk loving where others hate. Imagine forgiving where others harden their hearts. Imagine giving without a desire for repayment. Imagine speaking the truth in love without worrying about our reputations or standing in the community. Imagine having nothing to protect. Imagine being free enough to give it all away. Imagine being so alive to every moment of every day that every person we meet becomes an epiphany of the divine, every tree or plant becomes a messenger of God, and every sky becomes a lesson in wonder.

To be sure, such people would greatly threaten any social, political, religious, or economic institution that relies on fear to keep people in their places. (St. Paul refers to these institutions as the "powers and principalities.") These institutions would have no power over those who have conquered their fear of death. Yes, these institutions could take away our wealth or our political rights; they could take away our freedom of movement and even put us to death. But if we were truly free in Christ, none of that could really touch us. As St. Paul assures us, "For I am sure that neither death, nor life, nor angels, nor principalities, nor things present, nor things to come, nor powers, nor height, nor depth, nor anything else in all creation, will be able to separate us from the love of God in Christ Jesus" (Romans 8:38-39).

Living without fear of losing our reputations, our wealth, and even our lives is the most radical form of freedom. The closer we come to this freedom, the more daring and creative we can be in confronting our fears. St. Francis of Assisi exemplified this freedom and creativity. When Pope Innocent III called for a fifth crusade to recapture the Holy Land, Francis journeyed to the regions of Syria, constantly exposing himself to dangers, unarmed, and without the protection of rank or privilege. He went armed only with the freedom gained from his faith in Jesus, to preach the Good News to the Sultan of Egypt in an attempt to make peace. In addition, for Francis, embracing poverty was not just an ascetic or spiritual discipline. It was a way of life that allowed him and his followers the freedom to respond fully to Jesus' call to love and serve even those who were considered dangerous. G. K. Chesterton writes of Francis' argument for poverty that the dedicated person might go anywhere, among any kind of person, even the worst, so long as there was nothing by which the others could hold that person.[4]

This freedom does not mean that we will not die, but it will change the way we live. Jesus never promised us a long life; he promised us the fullness of life. Martin Luther King Jr. posed the dilemma of this freedom in a speech shortly before his assassination: "Like anybody, I would like to live a long life. Longevity has its place. But I'm not concerned about that now. I just want to do God's will."[5]

My real fear is not just that someday I will die—we all must die. My real concern is whether I will have the courage to live as a fully alive human being before I die. Can I, even for a brief moment, live with open hands and open heart to the world before me? Can I be fully present to both the pain and joy that life gives me? In short, can I dare to be free?

---

## LETTING GO OF FEAR:
## THE PROMISE OF RESURRECTION
## AND THE TRIUMPH OF GOD'S NARRATIVE

As Christians, we must also keep in mind that our lives—and even our freedom—are part of a much greater narrative. The Scriptures make clear that at the end of history, good will triumph over evil, and peace with justice will come to all of God's creation. As Dr. King summarized in his 1967 address to the Southern Christian Leadership Conference, "let us remember that there is a creative force in this universe, working to pull down the gigantic mountains of evil, a power that is able to make a way out of no way and transform dark yesterdays into bright tomorrows. Let us realize the arc of the moral universe is long but it bends toward justice."[6]

My brother Frank once wrote a poem using the metaphor of Merlin the Magician (advisor, prophet, and magician to King Arthur) as a model for the Christian understanding of the Reign of God at the end of history. One of the legends about Merlin was that his gift of prophecy was possible because he lived time backward. In essence, he remembered the future. Frank's poem picks up on this gift and posits it as a component of Christian discipleship:

A backward looking people,
backwards that is from the End of Time,
where victory assured has fully arrived.
Merlin's each one of us with a future sense in the present
    tense.[7]

We are called to live as Merlinian Christians. Like Merlin, we Christians claim to know the future; it has been revealed to us through Jesus. The full flowering of the Reign of God at the end of history is our destiny. A Merlinian Christian lives each day as if the fullness of the Reign of God had already arrived; in a sense, we project the future back into our present. Because we know the end of all things, we can live without fear in the present, because in the end, death is conquered. Because in the fullness of the Reign of God, at the end of history, the lion will lie down with the lamb, we refuse to participate in killing our enemies. Because in the fullness of the Reign of God those who are hungry will be fed, we can give from our sustenance as well as from our surplus. Because in the fullness of the Reign of God those who are oppressed will be liberated, those of us from privilege can choose to be in solidarity with those who are disenfranchised or marginalized. Because in the fullness of the Reign of God death is defeated, we can lay down our lives in the cause of justice, without desiring to harm others.

But how can we let go of the life we have to embrace the unknown? Isn't it better to make peace with the demands of fear? Wouldn't accepting the slavery we know be better than risking it all on an uncertain future, a promised resurrection, or a dream of justice fulfilled? Wouldn't it be safer to just stay where we are and hope for the best? A Sufi tale tells of a stream working itself across the country, experiencing little difficulty until it arrived at a desert.

> Just as it had crossed every other barrier, the stream tried to cross this one, but it found that as fast as it ran into the sand, its waters disappeared. After many attempts it became very discouraged. It appeared that there was no way it could continue the journey. Then a voice came in the wind, "If you stay the way you are you cannot cross the sands, you cannot become any more than a quagmire. To go further you will have to lose yourself."
>
> "But if I lose myself," the stream cried, "I will never know what I'm supposed to be."
>
> "Oh, on the contrary," said the wind, "if you lose yourself you will become more than you ever dreamed you could be." So the stream surrendered to the drying sun. And the clouds into which it was formed were carried by the raging wind for many miles. Once it crossed the desert, the stream poured down from the skies, fresh and clean, and full of the energy that comes from storms.[8]

In the end, it is all about the choices we make and which narrative will guide those choices. We can choose the dominant narrative (and the "official" 9-11 narrative), knowing how they operate in our nation and in our world. Or we can construct an alternative capable of empowering us to make choices that can free us from fear, effectively reduce all forms of terrorism, and bring about a genuine peace founded in justice.

At the same time, we must remember that as Christians, we are invited to embrace one narrative above all others. It is the story of how one man and his company of disciples challenged the one dominant narrative that was laying waste to every other known narrative of the time. Jesus and his followers came preaching an alternative that was new and vibrant, yet ancient in wisdom and power. It was a narrative that directly challenged the dominant narrative of *Pax Romana*, and Jesus was willing to stake his life on the power and promise of his alternative story. And he who came to reveal God's story showed us the way to conquer the power of the dominant narrative by overcoming the very power of death itself. God raising Jesus from the dead undid all the powers and principalities, all of the institutions and systems of the dominant narrative. To those who are willing to die to all that today's dominant narrative demands of us, Jesus promises new life. All we have to do is let go and allow ourselves to be transformed. There is no telling what we might become.

# ENDNOTES

---

## NOTES FOR CHAPTER ONE:
## GLOBALIZATION: A FRAMEWORK
## FOR UNDERSTANDING OUR TIMES

1. In his farewell speech on January 17, 1961, President Dwight D. Eisenhower warned the nation about the dangers of what he called the military-industrial-complex: "This conjunction of an immense military establishment and a large arms industry is new in the American experience. The total influence—economic, political, even spiritual—is felt in every city, every state house, every office of the Federal government. We recognize the imperative need for this development. Yet we must not fail to comprehend its grave implications. . . . In the councils of government, we must guard against the acquisition of unwarranted influence, whether sought or unsought, by the military-industrial complex. The potential for the disastrous rise of misplaced power exists and will persist." www.eisenhower.archives.gov/speeches/farewell_address.html

2. Pax Christi USA, "Towards a Globalization of Solidarity" (Erie, PA: Pax Christi USA, November 2001).

3. Elizabeth Martínez and Arnoldo García, "What is 'Neo-Liberalism'?: A Brief Definition," (updated February 26, 2000). www.globalexchange.org/campaigns/econ101/neoliberalDefined.html

4. William M. Adler, "A Job on the Line," *Mother Jones*, March/April 2000. www.motherjones.com/news/feature/2000/03/job.html

5. David Cay Johnston, "Income Gap Is Widening, Data Shows," *New York Times*, 29 March 2007.

6. Paul Vallely, "UN Hits Back at US in Report Saying Parts of America Are as Poor as Third World," *The Independent*, 8 September 2005. www.independent.co.uk/news/world/politics/un-hits-back-at-us-in-report-saying-parts-of-america-are-as-poor-as-third-world-505967.html   United Nations Development Programme, "Human Development Report 2005: International Cooperation at a Crossroads: Aid, Trade and Security in an Unequal World" (New York: UNDP, 2005).

7. UN Department of Economic and Social Affairs, Population Division, "International Migration Facts & Figures" (New York: UN, June 2006).

8. Carlos Salas, Bruce Campbell, and Robert Scott, "NAFTA Revisited: Still Not Working for North America's Workers" (Washington, DC: Economic Policy Institute, 28 September 2006).

9. Nina Bernstein, "100 Years in the Back Door, Out the Front," *New York Times*, 21 May 2006. www.nytimes.com/2006/05/21/weekinreview/21bernstein.html?scp=1&sq=100+Years+in+the+Back+Door&st=nyt

10. Evan Osnos, "The Price We Pay for China's Boom," *Chicago Tribune*, 17 December 2006.

11. Editorial, "The Other Side of the Bargain," *Chicago Tribune*, 21 December 2006.

12. Pax Christi USA, "Towards a Globalization of Solidarity."

13. Lydia Polgreen and Marlise Simons, "Global Sludge Ends in Tragedy for Ivory Coast," *New York Times*, 2 October 2006. Available at www.truthout.org/cgi-bin/artman/exec/view.cgi/65/22882

14. Richard Perez-Pena, "Study Finds Asthma In 25% of Children in Central Harlem," *New York Times*, 19 April 2003.

15. Janet A. Phoenix and Nsedu Obot Witherspoon, "Childhood Asthma Policy and Housing," presented at the Second National People of Color Environmental Leadership Summit, 23 October 2002. www.cehn.org/cehn/policy/ChildhoodAsthma.pdf

16. Janet Wilson, "State Has Most Minorities Near Toxic Facilities, *Los Angeles Times*, 12 April 2007. 2007 study conducted at four universities by the United Church of Christ. Newspaper article available at www.truthout.org/issues_06/041207HB.shtml

17. Pax Christi USA, "Towards a Globalization of Solidarity."

18. Benjamin R. Barber, *Jihad vs. McWorld: How Globalism and Tribalism Are Reshaping the World*, reprint edition (New York: Ballantine Books, 1996), 17.

19. Jihad is a Muslim religious term that means struggle. It is associated with believers' efforts to improve themselves and deepen their commitments to God. As used in the Quran, jihad refers to the obligation of believers to strive to live out the tenants of Islam. A person engaged in living out this struggle to be faithful is called a *mujahid* (the plural is *mujahideen*).

Some radical Islamists, like al Qaeda, believe that jihad also includes an obligation to defend the faith and Muslim lands against non-Islamic influences by violent means.

20. Guy F. Tozzoli, addressing the 1989 WTCA General Assembly in Geneva, Switzerland. Found at www.ericdarton.net/a_living_archive/html/ideobite.html

21. CNN World News, 17 December 2004. Recording refers to attack in Jeddah. www.cnn.com/2004/WORLD/meast/12/16/bin.laden.tape/index.html

## NOTES FOR CHAPTER TWO: WHAT IS TERRORISM?

1. Code of Federal Regulations, 28CFR0.85, revised 1 July 2007.

2. From Susan Tiefenbrun, "A Semiotic Approach to a Legal Definition of Terrorism," ILSA Journal of International & Comparative Law, Vol. 9:357, 2003, 372. Citation: Terrorism and the Law, U.S. Code. Vo. 22, section 2656f(d), supra note 29, at 4. www.pegc.us/archive/Journals/tiefenbrun_terroism_def.pdf

3. "Iraq Faces Massive U.S. Missile Barrage," CBSNews.com, 24 January 2003. www.cbsnews.com/stories/2003/01/24/eveningnews/main537928.shtml?source=search_story

4. Benjamin Netanyahu, ed., How the West Can Win, reprint edition (New York: Avon Books, 1987), 9.

5. Barton Gellman, "Allied Air War Struck Broadly in Iraq: Officials Acknowledge Strategy Went Beyond Purely Military Targets," Washington Post, 23 June 1991. Available at www.globalpolicy.org/security/issues/iraq/history/0623strategy.htm

6. Wolfgang Kluge, "Iraqi Sanctions: A Crime Against Humanity," Doctors for Global Health, October 1999. www.dghonline.org/nl5/iraqisanctions.html

7. Paul Lewis, "After The War; U.N. Survey Calls Iraq's War Damage Near-Apocalyptic," New York Times, 22 March 1991.

8. Ibid. Matthew Hay Brow, "Iraqi Sanctions: Without Medicine and Supplies, The Children Die," Hartford Courant, 23 October 2000.

9. CBS 60 Minutes, 12 May 1996.

10. David Pilgrim, Dr., "What Was Jim Crow?" (Big Rapids, MI: Ferris State University Museum of Racist Memorabilia, September 2000). www.ferris.edu/jimcrow/what.htm

11. Ibid.

12. UN Special Envoy on Human Settlement Issues in Zimbabwe, "Report of the Fact-Finding Missions to Assess the Scope and Impact of Operation Murambatsvina," 22 July 2005. www.un.org/News/dh/infocus/zimbabwe/zimbabwe_rpt.pdf

13. Human Rights Watch, "Clear the Filth: Mass Evictions and Demolitions in Zimbabwe," 11 September 2005. hrw.org/backgrounder/africa/zimbabwe0905/zimbabwe0905.pdf

14. Ibid.

15. Suzy Price, "Despatch: Tamil Tigers Bomb Buddhist Shrine," *BBC News*, 26 January 1998. news.bbc.co.uk/1/hi/despathces/50820.stm

16. Maximilien Robespierre, "On the Moral and Political Principles of Domestic Policy," 1794. Available at www.fordham.edu/halsall/mod/robespierre-terror.html

17. Amnesty International, "AFRICA In Search of Safety: The Forcibly Displaced and Human Rights in Africa," AI Index: AFR 01/05/97. web.amnesty.org/library/print/ENGAFR010051997

18. Ibid.

19. Stefan Lovgren, "Liberia's President Taylor's Life of Crime," *National Geographic News*, 25 July 2003.

20. Amnesty International, "Liberia: Submission to the Truth and Reconciliation Commission," 4 September 2006. AI Index: AFR 34/006-2006

# NOTES FOR CHAPTER THREE:
# LIVING IN AN AGE OF FEAR AND TERRORISM

1. Quoted in Rev. Bryan Massingale, "The Vision of Shalom Counters the Self-Interest of the U.S. Push for Homeland Security," *Catholic Peace Voice*, July/August 2003.

2. Office of the Press Secretary, "President Discusses War on Terror at National Endowment for Democracy," Ronald Reagan Building and International Trade Center, Washington, DC, 6 October 2005, www.whitehouse.gov/news/releases/2005/10/20051006-3.html

3. David Keene, "Ashcroft: Good Intentions on a Bad Road," *The Hill*, 31 July 2002.

4. Donald Rumsfeld, interview with Sam Donaldson, *ABC News*, 16 September 2001. Transcript available at www.defenselink.mil/transcripts/transcript.aspx?transcriptid=1886 Edward L. Morse and Amy Myers Jaffe,

"Strategic Energy Policy Challenges for the 21st Century: Report of an Independent Task Force," James A. Baker III Institute for Public Policy of Rice University and the Council on Foreign Relations. www.rice.edu/energy/publications/docs/TaskForceReport_Final.pdf

5. Robin Buckallew, "The American Way of Life is Not Negotiable," FaulkingTruth.com. www.faulkingtruth.com/Articles/GlobalWarning/1024.html

6. Ernest Berker, *The Denial of Death* (New York: Simon & Schuster, Inc., 1973).

7. Gene Weingarten, "Fear Itself: Learning to Live in the Age of Terrorism," *Washington Post*, 22 August 2004. www.washingtonpost.com/wp-dyn/articles/A15004-2004Aug19.html

8. John L. McKenzie, SJ, *The New Testament Without Illusions* (Chicago: Thomas More Press, 1980).

9. Edward W. Goodrick and John R. Kohlenberger III, *The NIV Exhaustive Concordance* (Grand Rapids, MI: HarperCollins Publishers, 1990).

10. John L. McKenzie, SJ, *Dictionary of the Bible* (New York: Simon & Schuster, 1995), 97.

11. U.S. Conference of Catholic Bishops, *Catechism of the Catholic Church*, English translation (New York: Doubleday Publishing, 1995), #2148.

12. Chris Hedges, *War is a Force That Gives Us Meaning* (New York: Perseus Books Group, 2002), 89.

13. Richard Rhodes, *The Making of the Atomic Bomb* (New York: Simon & Schuster, 1995), 676.

14. Bill Moyers, "9-11 and the Sport of God," address at Union Theological Seminary, New York, NY, 9 September 2005. Adaptation available at www.truthout.org/article/bill-moyers-911-and-sport-god

## NOTE FOR PART II:
## CREATING AN ALTERNATIVE TO THE "WAR ON TERROR": CONSTRUCTING A NEW 9-11 NARRATIVE

1. David Randall and Emily Gosden, "62,006—The Number Killed in the 'War on Terror,'" *Independent*, 10 September 2006. www.independent.co.uk/news/world/politics/62006--the-number-killed-in-the-war-on-terror-415397.html

2. Frank D. Macchia, "Terrorists, Security, and the Risk of Peace: Toward a Moral Vision," *PNEUMA: The Journal of the Society of Pentecostal Studies*, Spring 2004.

## Notes For Chapter Four:
## Narrative Creation and 9-11

1. Office of the Press Secretary, "President Bush Addresses American Legion National Convention," Salt Palace Convention Center, Salt Lake, UT, 31 August 2006. www.whitehouse.gov/news/releases/2006/08/20060831-1.html "President Bush Discusses Global War on Terror," Wardman Park Marriot Hotel, Washington, DC, 29 September 2006. www.whitehouse.gov/news/releases/2006/09/20060929-3.html

2. Office of the Press Secretary, "President Bush Reaffirms Resolve to War on Terror, Iraq and Afghanistan, Remarks on Operation Iraqi Freedom and Operation Enduring Freedom," The East Room, White House, 19 March 2004. www.whitehouse.gov/news/releases/2004/03/images/20040319-3_do31904-1-515h.html  Office of the Press Secretary, "President Bush Addresses American Legion National Convention." Office of the Press Secretary, "President Bush Reaffirms Resolve to War on Terror, Iraq and Afghanistan." Office of the Press Secretary, "President Bush Discusses Global War on Terror," 29 September 2006.3. Office of the Press Secretary, "President Bush Addresses American Legion National Convention." Office of the Press Secretary, "President Discusses War on Terror at National Endowment for Democracy," Ronald Reagan Building and International Trade Center, Washington, DC, 6 October 2005.  www.whitehouse.gov/news/releases/2005/10/20051006-3.html

4. Office of the Press Secretary, "President Bush Reaffirms Resolve to War on Terror, Iraq and Afghanistan." Office of the Press Secretary, "President Discusses War on Terror at National Endowment for Democracy."

5. Office of the Vice President, "Vice President's Remarks at a Rally for the Troops," Hanger One, Andersen Air Force Base, Guam, 22 February 2007. www.whitehouse.gov/news/releases/2007/02/20070222-4.html  Office of the Press Secretary, "President Bush Discusses Global War on Terror," 29 September 2006.

6. Office of the Press Secretary, "President Bush Reaffirms Resolve to War on Terror, Iraq and Afghanistan."

7. Fiona Symon, "Analysis: The Roots of Jihad," BBC News, 16 October 2001. news.bbc.co.uk/2/low/middle_east/1603178.stm

8. Al Qaeda Training Manual. Available at www.au.af.mil/au/awc/awcgate/terrorism/alqaida_manual/

9. Osama bin Laden, taped remarks, translated by USAToday.com, 7 October 2001. Osama bin Laden, "Letter to American People," BBC News, 12 November 2002. news.bbc.co.uk/1/hi/world/middle_east/2455845.stm

10. World Islamic Front Statement, "Jihad Against Jews & Crusaders, " 23

February 1998. Available at www.library.cornell.edu/colldev/mideast/wif.htm

11. Al Qaeda Training Manual.

12. World Islamic Front Statement, "Jihad Against Jews & Crusaders."

13. Osama bin Laden (audiotape attributed to), "Bin Laden Accuses West," *Al-Jazeera*, 23 April 2006. english.aljazeera.net/English/archive/archive?ArchiveId=22235

14. Osama bin Laden, speech released 29 October 2004, as broadcast by Al-Sahab Institute for Media Productions. www.memri.org/bin/articles.cgi?Page=subjects&Area=jihad&ID=SP81104

15. Ayman al-Zawahiri, letter to Abu Musab al-Zarqawi, 9 July 2005. Available from the Office of the Director of National Intelligence, www.dni.gov/press_releases/20051011_release.htm

16. World Islamic Front Statement, "Jihad Against Jews & Crusaders."

17. Al-Zawahiri letter.

18. Osama bin Laden (audiotape), text of TV station *al-Jazeera* broadcast, translated by BBC Monitoring, 19 January 2006. news.bbc.co.uk/2/hi/middle_east/4628932.stm

19. Office of the Press Secretary, "President Discusses Global War on Terror," Capital Hilton Hotel, Washington, DC, 5 September 2006. www.whitehouse.gov/news/releases/2006/09/20060905-4.html

20. Hedges, *War Is a Force That Gives Us Meaning*, 22.

21. Joseba Zulaika and William A. Douglass, *Terror and Taboo: The Follies, Fables, and Faces of Terrorism* (New York: Routledge, 1996), 26.

22. James Stengold, "Cheney's Grim Vision: Decades of War," *San Francisco Chronicle*, 15 January 2004. Office of the Vice President, "Vice President's Remarks at a Rally for the Troops."

23. George W. Bush, interview by Katie Couric, *CBS Evening News*, 6 September 2006. www.cbsnews.com/stories/2006/09/06/five_years/main1979933.shtml

24. Office of the Press Secretary, "President Discusses Global War on Terror," 5 September 2006.

25. Hillary Rodham Clinton, remarks at John Jay College of Criminal Justice, New York, NY, 24 January 2003. http://clinton.senate.gov/news/statements/details.cfm?id=233779 Joseph R. Biden, Jr., "Biden Blasts Administration For Failing to Put Forth a Chemical Plant Security Plan," Press Release, 22 March 2006. http://biden.senate.gov Robert C. Byrd, "Regain the Focus on the War on Terrorism," remarks on 10 September 2003. http://byrd.senate.gov/speeches

26. Zbigniew Brzezinski, "Terrorized by "War on Terror," *Washington Post*, 25 March 2007.

27. Primetime Torture, Human Rights First, www.humanrightsfirst.org/us_law/etn/primetime/index.asp#problem Colin Freeze, "What Would Jack

Bauer Do?" *The Globe and Mail*, 16 June 2007. www.theglobeandmail.com/
servlet/story/LAC.20070616.BAUER16/TPStory/TPNational/Television/rss

---

## NOTES FOR CHAPTER FIVE:
## MOVING BEYOND THE POLITICS OF FEAR
## TO CHALLENGE THE AL QAEDA NARRATIVE

1. Irving Kristol, "Now What for U.S. Client States?" *Wall Street Journal*,
3 March 1986. Charles Krauthammer, "The Unipolar Moment," Henry Jackson Memorial Lecture, 18 September 1990.
2. Project for the New American Century, "Statement of Principles," 3
June 1997. Available at web.archive.org/web/20021014084203/http://www.
newamericancentury.org/statementofprinciples.htm  Charles Krauthammer, "The Bush Doctrine," *Time*, 5 March 2001. Available at http://edition.
cnn.com/ALLPOLITICS/time/2001/03/05/doctrine.html
3. Project for the New American Century, "Letter to President Clinton on
Iraq," 29 May 1998. Available at http://web.archive.org/web/20060101093120/
http://www.newamericancentury.org/iraqclintonletter.htm  William Kristol and Robert Kagan, "Bombing Iraq Isn't Enough," *New York Times*, 30
January 1998.
4. Thom Shanker and Eric Schmitt, "Secretary Rumsfeld Interview with
the New York Times," *New York Times*, 12 October 2002. White House, "The
National Security Strategy of the United States of America," September
2002. www.whitehouse.gov/nsc/nss/2002/nss.pdf
5. Quoted in Elizabeth Drew, "The Neocons in Power," *New York Review of Books*, 12 June 2003. www.nybooks.com/articles/16378 Julian Borger, "Guardian Interview: Richard Clarke," *Guardian*, 23 March 2004. www.
guardian.co.uk/world/2004/mar/23/usa.september11
6. Steven G. Calabresi and Kevin H. Rhodes, "The Structural Constitution: Unitary Executive, Plural Judiciary," *Harvard Law Review*, Vol. 105, No.
6, April 1992.
7. Dick Cheney, "The Vice President Appears on ABC's *This Week*," interview with Sam Donaldson, ABC News, 27 January 2002. Available at www.
whitehouse.gov/vicepresident/news-speeches/speeches/vp20020127.html
8. David L. Altheide, "Notes Towards a Politics of Fear," *Journal for
Crime, Conflict and Media Culture*, Vol. 1, No. 1, December 2003. www.jc2m.
co.uk/Issue1/Altheide.pdf
9. Dana Milbank, "In Cheney's Shadow, Counsel Pushes the Conservative Cause," *Washington Post*, 11 October 2004. www.washingtonpost.com/
wp-dyn/articles/A22665-2004Oct10.html

10. Charles C. Krulak and Joseph P. Hoar, "It's Our Cage, Too: Torture Betrays Us and Breeds New Enemies," *Washington Post*, 17 May 2007. www.washingtonpost.com/wp-dyn/content/article/2007/05/16/AR2007051602395.html

11. R. W. Behan, "The Surreal Politics of Premeditated War," CommonDreams.org, 3 December 2006, www.commondreams.org/views06/1203-21.htm

12. Ibid.

13. Judicial Watch, "Maps and Charts of Iraqi Oil Fields," www.judicialwatch.org/iraqi-oil-maps.shtml

14. The National Security Archive, "New State Department Releases on the 'Future of Iraq,'" 1 September 2006. www.gwu.edu/~nsarchiv/NSAEBB/NSAEBB198/index.htm

15. Special Investigations Division, U.S. House of Representatives Committee on Government Reform–Minority Staff, "Iraq on the Record: The Bush Administration's Public Statements on Iraq," 16 March 2004, 30. http://oversight.house.gov/IraqOnTheRecord/pdf_admin_iraq_on_the_record_rep.pdf

16. LeMoyne College/Zogby International, "U.S. Troops in Iraq: 72% Say End War in 2006," Zogby International, 28 February 2006. www.zogby.com/news/ReadNews.dbm?ID=1075

17. Dwight D. Eisenhower, "Farewell Address to the Nation," 17 January 1961. www.eisenhower.utexas.edu/farewell.htm

18. Ibid.

19. Henry A. Waxman, "Fact Sheet: Halliburton's Iraq Contracts Now Worth over $10 Billion," Committee on Government Reform, House of Representatives, 9 December 2004. Available at www.truthout.org/article/waxman-halliburton-iraq-contracts-pass-10-billion-mark

20. Robert Greenwald, "The Madness of the War Profiteering in Iraq," testimony to the House Appropriations Committee, Subcommittee on Defense, 10 May 2007. Available at www.truthout.org/article/robert-greenwald-the-madness-war-profiteering-iraq

21. Mark Fineman, "Arms Buildup Enriches Firm Staffed by Big Guns," *Los Angeles Times*, 10 January 2002. Available at www.globalsecurity.org/org/news/2002/020110-attack01.htm

22. Greenwald, "The Madness of the War Profiteering in Iraq."

23. Peter Spiegel, "Tank-Size Defense Request," *Los Angeles Times*, 5 February 2007.

24. Jim Wallis, "Don't Be Afraid," Sojo.net, 21 May 2003. www.sojo.net

25. Hedges, *War Is a Force That Gives Meaning*, 10.

26. Ibid., 145. Original source: Elias Canetti, *Crowds and Power* (New York: Viking Books, 1962). Please note that non-gender-inclusive language

in orginal quotations has not been changed throughout the book.

27. Ibid., 145.

28. Ann Coulter, *Godless: The Church of Liberalism* (New York: Random House, Inc., 2006), 103.

29. John Paul Lederach, "Breaking the Cycle of Violence," *UU World*, January/February 2002. www.uuworld.org/2002/01/feature2.html

30. James Fallows, "Declaring Victory," *The Atlantic Monthly*, September 2006.

31. Ibid.

32. Editorial, "Bush Policy Brings the Worldon his Back," *Agence France Press*, 21 September 2004. Available at www.truthout.org/docs_04/092304Z.shtml

33. David Clark, "This Terror Will Continue Until We Take Arab Grievances Seriously," *Guardian*, 9 July 2005. www.guardian.co.uk/politics/2005/jul/09/world.july7

34. Kim Sengupta and Patrick Cockburn, "How the War on Terror Made the World a More Terrifying Place," *The Independent*, 28 February 2007. www.independent.co.uk/how-the-war-on-terror-made-the-world-a-more-terrifying-place-438190.html

35. Riverbend, *Baghdad Burning II: More Girl Blog from Iraq* (New York: The Feminist Press at CUNY, 2006).

36. Mark Mazzetti, "Spy Agencies Say Iraq War Worsens Terror Threat," *New York Times*, 24 September 2006. www.nytimes.com/2006/09/24/world/middleeast/24terror.html

37. Lederach, "Breaking the Cycle of Violence."

38. Zbigniew Brzezinski, "Terrorized by 'War on Terror,'" *Washington Post*, 25 March 2007.

---

# NOTES FOR CHAPTER SIX:
## PRINCIPLES AT THE FOUNDATION
## OF AN ALTERNATIVE 9-11 NARRATIVE

1. Fallows, "Declaring Victory."

2. Justice Robert Jackson, "Opening Statement for the Prosecution,"21 November 1945. Part 04, in *Trial of the Major War Criminals before the International Military Tribunal*. Volume II. Proceedings: 11/14/1945-11/30/1945. [Official text in the English language.] (Nuremberg: IMT, 1947), 98-102. Available at www.law.umkc.edu/faculty/projects/ftrials/nuremberg/Jackson.html

3. Jane Sutton, "Guantanamo Trials Unfair Says Nuremburg Prosecutor,"

Reuters, 12 June 2007. Available at www.alertnet.org/thenews/newsdesk/
N6B384799.htm

4. Ann Wright, "*Guantanamo's Cost to Our Humanity*," Truthout, 4 January 2007. www.truthout.org/docs_2006/010407N.shtml

5. Martin Luther King Jr., "I Have a Dream," speech at the Lincoln Memorial, Washington, DC, 28 August 1963. Available at www.americanrhetoric.com/speeches/mlkihaveadream.htm

6. Ann Coulter, "Drop Bombs, Take Names Later," *Mansfield News Journal*, 17 September 2001.

7. David Michael Green, "Bush Is at War with Americanism," *Albany (NY) Times Union*, 28 January 2006.

8. Blue Triangle Network, "Mission Statement." Blue Triangle Network, P.O. Box 7451, Dearborn, MI 48121. www.bluetrianglenetwork.org/old/index.html Blue Triangle Network, "*Blue Triangle Network Condemns U.S. Torture of Prisoners*," 6 May 2004. www.bluetrianglenetwork.org/old/statements/iraq-torture.html

9. Ariel Dorfman, "Are We Really So Fearful?," *Washington Post*, 24 September 2006.

10. It is important to sharply distinguish between political spin and rhetoric and the process of creating authentic narrative. Genuine narrative is meant to help us make sense of the events in our lives and to reveal their meaning; with political spin, words are used not to reveal, but to conceal, not to clarify but to confuse.

11. Michael Klare, "*Asking "Why?*," The Nautilus Institute Special Forum 09, 20 September 2001. www.nautilus.org/archives/fora/Special-Policy-Forum/09_Klare.html#sect2

12. Robert Fisk, "Protestors Beaten as Egypt Votes on Electoral Reform," *The Independent*, 26 May 2005.

13. Robert Parry, "Bush's Failed Policy of Kill, Kill, Kill," *Consortium News*, 6 October 2006. www.consortiumnews.com/2006/100506.html

14. Martin Luther King Jr., "Letter from a Birmingham Jail," 16 April 1963. Available at www.africa.upenn.edu/Articles_Gen/Letter_Birmingham.html

15. Protestants for the Common Good, "Principles Statement." www.thecommongood.org/principles.asp

16. Pope John Paul II, "*Pacem in Terris:* A Permanent Commitment," World Day of Peace Message, 1 January 2003. www.vatican.va/holy_father/john_paul_ii/messages/peace/documents/hf_jp-ii_mes_20021217_xxxvi-world-day-for-peace_en.html

17. Agence France Presse, "CIA Concerned US War on Terror is Missing," 29 October 2002. Available at www.commondreams.org/headlines02/1029-01.htm Karen De Young, "World Bank Lists Failing Nations That Can Breed

Global Terrorism," *Washington Post*, 15 September 2006.

18. David Cortright, "Nonviolence and the Strategy against Terrorism," Sojomail, 28 August 2006. www.sojo.net/index.cfm?action=sojomail.display&issue=060828. Also at kroc.nd.edu/media/nonviolence_cortright.shtml

19. Pope John Paul II, "Address to the New Ambassador of the United Kingdom to the Holy See," 7 September 2002. www.vatican.va/holy_father/special_features/tragedies/20010911_index_en.html

20. Peter Ford, "Injustice Seen as Fertile Soil for Terrorists," *Christian Science Monitor*, 28 November 2001. Available at www.commondreams.org/headlines01/1128-01.htm

21. Karen Armstrong, *The Battle for God* (New York: Random House, 2001). Karen Armstrong, "Transcript: Bill Moyers Interviews Karen Armstrong," *NOW* with Bill Moyer, Public Broadcasting System, 1 March 2002. www.pbs.org/now/transcript/transcript_armstrong.html

22. Dick Cheney, "Meet the Press: Dick Cheney," with Tim Russert, NBC News, 16 September 2001. Available at www.fromthewilderness.com/timeline/2001/meetthepress091601.html

## NOTES FOR CHAPTER SEVEN:
## PEACE AS ENFORCED ORDER:
## AT THE HEART OF THE DOMINANT U.S. NARRATIVE

1. George Kennan, "Review of Current Trends, U.S. Foreign Policy, Policy Planning Staff, PPS No. 23," U.S. State Department Policy Planning Staff, 28 February 1948, declassified 17 June 1974. Available at www.geocities.com/athens/forum/2496/future/kennan/pps23.html   Jack Nelson-Pallmeyer, *Brave New World Order* (Maryknoll, NY: Orbis Books, 1992), ix.

2. Project for the New American Century, "Rebuilding America's Defenses: Strategic Forces and Resources for a New Century," September 2000. http://newamericancentury.org/RebuildingAmericasDefenses.pdf

3. Michael T. Klare, *Blood and Oil: The Dangers and Consequences of America's Growing Dependency on Imported Oil* (New York: Henry Holt & Company, 2004), 7.

4. Walter Brueggemann, "The Liturgy of Abundance, The Myth of Scarcity," *The Christian Century*, 24-31 March 1999. Available at www.surfinthespirit.com/environment/liturgy-of-abundance.html

5. Editorial, "Poor and Rich - The Facts," *The New Internationalist*, March 1999. www.newint.org/features/1999/03/01/poor-rich-the-facts/

6. Water Brueggemann, *The Prophetic Imagination*, revised edition (Minneapolis, MN: Augsburg Fortress Publishers, 2001), 63.

7. United Nations Development Programme, *Human Development Report 1999: Globalization with a Human Face* (New York: UNDP, 1999), 104.

8. Bernie Sanders, "A Budget for the Middle Class," *Mother Jones*, 30 January 2007. www.motherjones.com/news/update/2007/01/sanders_oped.html

9. Jack Nelson-Pallmeyer, *War Against the Poor: Low-Intensity Conflict and Christian Faith* (Maryknoll, NY: Orbis Books, 1989), 15.

10. Jonathan Kozol, *Amazing Grace: The Lives of Children and the Conscience of a Nation* (New York: Crown Publishers, 1995), 39.

11. Ibid., 41.

12. Stephen Ohlemacher, "Race Still Divides U.S., Census Says," *Chicago Tribune*, 14 November 2006. See also U.S. Census Bureau: www.census.gov

13. School of the Americas Watch, Press Release, "Colombian Paramilitary Leader Confirms Collusion with U.S. Trained Colombian Generals," 16 May 2007. www.soaw.org/pressrelease.php?id=133

14. "New Evidence in February 2005 Massacre Investigation," *Colombia El Tiempo*, 26 April 2007.

15. Hiram Monserrate, "NYC Fact-Finding Delegation on Coca-Cola in Colombia," Councilman, City of New York, 250 Broadway, New York, NY, www.cwa1180.org/solidarity/COLOMBIAcokeREPORT.pdf

16. Lesley Gill, "Coca-Cola in Colombia: Increased Profits, Downsized Workforce," *Colombia Journal Online*, 26 July 2004. www.colombiajournal.org/colombia190.htm

17. Joshua Goodman, "U.N.: Colombia's Army Killed Civilians," Associated Press, 16 March 2007.

18. Bryan Bender, "U.S. Is Top Purveyor on Weapons Sales List," *Boston Globe*, 12 November 2006.

19. Ched Myers points out that while the media acknowledged poverty as a cause of the uprising, no attempt was made to understand the cause of the poverty: "What was never mentioned was the systematic de-industrialization of South Central Los Angeles over the past two decades, which has destroyed the economic base of the working class. The corporate interests that for the sake of profit have exported tens of thousands of jobs from Los Angeles to the Third World have contributed more to the devastation of South Central than all the arsonists of 1965 and 1992 combined. Similarly, economic and social tensions attributed to the massive influx of immigrants to Los Angeles over the last decade were identified as a 'cause' of the spring violence. But again, little attention was given to the structural shifts—specifically the human displacement resulting from the global migration of capital and the long-term effects of U.S. military intervention." Myers, *Who*

*Will Roll Away the Stone?: Discipleship Queries for First World Christians* (Maryknoll, NY: Orbis Press, 2003), 52.

20. U.S. Conference of Catholic Bishops, "Rehabilitation and Restoration: A Catholic Perspective on Crime and Criminal Justice" (Washington, DC: United States Conference of Catholic Bishops, November 2000). www.usccb.org/sdwp/criminal.shtml U.S. Department of Justice, "One in Every 31 U.S. Adults was in a Prison or Jail, or on Probation or Parole at the End of Last Year," 5 December 2007. www.ojp.usdoj.gov/bjs/pub/press/po6ppuso6pr.htm The Pew Center on the States, Public Safety Performance Program, "One in 100: Behind Bars in America," February 2008.

21. U.S. Conference of Catholic Bishops, "Rehabilitation and Restoration." Darnell Little, "Drug War Enforcement Hits Minorities Hardest," *Chicago Tribune*, 22 July 2007.

22. Meredith Koldner, "Immigration Enforcement Benefits Prison Firms," *New York Times*, 19 July 2006. www.nytimes.com/2006/07/19/business/19detain.html

---

# NOTES FOR CHAPTER EIGHT:
## PEACE AS THE ENTERPRISE OF JUSTICE:
## AT THE HEART OF AN ALTERNATIVE U.S. NARRATIVE

1. Second Vatican Council, "*Gaudium et Spes* (Pastoral Constitution on the Church in the Modern World)," Rome, October 1962.

2. Pope Paul VI, "Papal Address to the United Nations," 1 January 1972. Rev. Gregory Boyle, SJ, et al, "After the Simi Valley Verdict: A Christian Confession of Conscience," in "America's Original Sin: A Study Guide on White Racism" (Washington, DC: Sojourners, 1992).

3. U.S. Conference of Catholic Bishops, "Economic Justice for All" (Washington, DC: United States Conference of Catholic Bishops, 13 November 1986). www.usccb.org/sdwp/international/EconomicJusticeforAll.pdf

4. Benjamin R. Barber, *Jihad vs. McWorld: How Globalism and Tribalism are Reshaping the World* (reissue, 2001), xxv.

5. John F. Kennedy, "American University Commencement Speech," American University, Washington, DC, 10 June 1963. www.american.edu/media/speeches/Kennedy.htm

6. Howard Zinn, *A People's History of the United States: 1492–Present* (New York: Harper Collins Publishers, 1980), 20.

7. Hunter Gray, "Native American Struggle: One Century Into Another," *Democratic Left*, Spring 2002. www.dsausa.org/antiracism/editorials/

editorials2.html

8. James Madison, "The Federalist Papers: No. 45," 26 January 1788. Available at www.yale.edu/lawweb/avalon/federal/fed45.htm "Constitution of the United States of America," written 1787, ratified 1788. Available at www.archives.gov/national-archives-experience/charters/constitution.html

9. Martin Luther King Jr., "Remaining Awake Through a Great Revolution," Washington, DC, 31 March 1968. Available at www.stanford.edu/group/King/publications/sermons/680331.000_Remaining_Awake.html

10. Joseph Wood Krutch, ed., *Thoreau: Walden and Other Writings*, Bantam edition (New York: Bantam Books, 1971), 166. (From *Walden*, "Where I Lived and What I Lived For.")

11. Sy Safransky, ed., *Sunbeams: A Book of Quotations* (Berkeley, CA: North Atlantic Books, 1990), 18.

12. Robert N. Bellah et al., *Habits of the Heart: Individualism and Commitment in American Life* (New York: Harper & Row Publishers, 1986) 285.

13. Ched Myers, *The Biblical Vision of Sabbath Economics* (Washington, DC: Tell the World Publishing, Church of the Savior, 2001), 13.

14. PaKou Her, "Racism, Classism and Worker Injustice: A Historical Wagging Tail," *At the Crossroads*, Vol. 13, Issue 3, Fall 2007.

15. Zinn, *A People's History of the United States*, 94.

16. Bellah, *Habits of the Heart*, 253. Andrew Carnegie, "Wealth," *North American Review*, June 1889. Available at www.swarthmore.edu/SocSci/rbannis1/AIH19th/Carnegie.html Bellah, *Habits of the Heart*, 260.

17. Gary J. Dorren, *Reconstructing the Common Good: Theology and the Social Order* (Maryknoll, NY: Orbis Books, 1990), 20.

18. Jean Bethke Elshtain, ed., *The Jane Addams Reader* (New York, Basic Books, 2002), 17.

19. Jane Addams, *Democracy and Social Ethics* (London: Macmillian Company, 1905), 220.

20. Helen Caldwell Day, *Not Without Tears* (New York: Sheed and Ward, 1954). Text available at www.catholicworker.com/hcd03.htm

21. Robert Ellsberg, ed., *By Little and by Little: The Selected Writings of Dorothy Day* (New York: Knopf Publishing, 1983), 98.

22. Eilgeen Egan, *Peace Be With You: Justified Warfare or the Way of Nonviolence* (Maryknoll, NY: Orbis Books, 1999), 19.

23. Wendy J. Deichmann Edwards and Carolyn De Swarte Gifford, eds., *Gender and the Social Gospel* (Champaign, IL: University of Illinois Press, 2003), 226.

24. Jone Johnson Lewis, "Marian Wright Edelman Quotes," Women's History About.com. womenshistory.about.com/od/quotes/a/marian_edelman.htm Marian Wright Edleman, "Standing Up For The World's Children:

Leave No Child Behind," State of the World Forum, October 1996. Available at http://gos.sbc.edu/e/edelman.html

25. Mary Harris Jones, *The Autobiography of Mother Jones* (Charles Kerr, 1925, Mineola, NY: Dover Publications, 2004).

26. A. Philip Randolph, "80th Birthday Dinner," Waldorf Astoria Hotel. New York, 6 May 1969. Available from the Kansas Workbeat, Wichita/Hutchinson Labor Federation, www.ksworkbeat.org/Resources/Black_History_Month/A__Philip_Randolph/a__philip_randolph.html

27. A. Philip Randolph Institute, "Biographical Notes on A. Philip Randolph 1889 – 1979," Washington, DC. www.apri.org

28. Ibid.

29. David Karsner, *Debs: His Authorized Life and Letters from Woodstock Prison to Altanta* (New York: Liveright Publishers, 1919), 48.

30. Mary Claire Gart, "Gone Back to God," *Catholic New World*, 21 May 2001.   www.catholicnewworld.com/archive/cnw2001/052701/cover-story_052701.html

31. George G. Higgins, "We All Benefit From a Strong Labor Movement," AFL-CIO Convention, 3 October 1997. Available at www.catholiclabor.org/higgins/higgins-8.html

32. Nate Guidry and Jon Schmitz, "'Labor Priest' Msgr. Rice Dies at 96," *Pittsburgh Post-Gazette*, 14 November 2005. www.post-gazette.com/pg/05318/606197-122.stm

33. Anup Shah, "U.S. and Foreign Aid Assistance," Global Issues: Sustainable Development, 8 April 2007. www.globalissues.org/TradeRelated/Debt/USAid.asp

34. American Friends Service Committee, 1501 Cherry Street, Philadelphia, PA, 19102. www.afsc.org

35. Jubilee USA Network, "Africa Subcommittee Holds Hearings on Vulture Funds," Jubilee USA Network, 23 May 2007. Jubilee USA Network, 212 East Capitol Street NE, Washington, DC 20003. www.jubileeusa.org

## NOTES FOR CHAPTER NINE:
## RE-VISIONING THE U.S. NARRATIVE:
## THE THINGS THAT MAKE FOR PEACE

1. Shelly Lynne Tomkin, *Inside OMB: Politics and Process in the President's Budget Office* (Armonk, NY: M.E. Sharpe Publishing, 1998).

2. Robert M. Moroney and Judy Kirysik, *Social Policy and Social Work: Critical Essays on the Welfare State* (New York: Aldine De Gruyter Publishing, 1998), 245.

3. Catholic Campaign for Human Development, 3211 Fourth St. NE, Washington, DC 20017. www.usccb.org/cchd

4. Robert Cooney and Helen Michalowski, eds., *The Power of the People: Active Nonviolence in the United States* (Philadelphia, PA: New Society 1987), 6.

5. Robette Ann Dias, personal communication, 14 August 2007.

6. Sonya Paul and Robert Perkinson, "Winona LaDuke—Native American Ecological Activist—Interview," *The Progressive*, October, 1995. See more at the Web site www.nativeharvest.com

7. Winona LaDuke, "Social Justice, Racism and the Environmental Movement," speech, University of Colorado at Boulder, 28 September 1993. http://zena.secureforum.com/Znet/zmag/articles/barladuke.htm

8. Michael Foot and Isaac Kraminck, eds., *The Thomas Paine Reader* (New York: Penguin, 1987), 476. From *Common Sense* by Thomas Paine.

9. Rachel Carson, *The Sense of Wonder* (Rachel Carson National Wildlife Refuge: U.S. Fish & Wildlife Service, 1965). www.fws.gov/northeast/rachelcarson/writings.html

10. Wendy Jewell, "Earthkeeper Hero: Rachel Carson," 1999. www.myhero.com/myhero/hero.asp?hero=rcarson

11. Joseph L. Alioto, "Earth Day Proclamation," 21 March 1970. www.wowzone.com/eday70.htm   John McConnell, "Trustees of Earth," at United Nations Peace Bell Ceremony, 20 March 1999. www.wowzone.com/oneearth.htm

12. Judy Helfand, "Constructing Whiteness," The University of Dayton School of Law, 29 April 2006. http://academic.udayton.edu/Race/01race/White11.htm Ronald Takaki, *A Different Mirror: A History of Multiculturalism in America* (Boston, MA: Little Brown and Company, 1993), 56.

13. George M. Fredrickson, "The Historical Construction of Race and Citizenship in the United States," the United Nations Research Institute for Social Development, 1 October 2003. www.unrisd.org/unrisd/website/document.nsf/0/8A0AE7EACD11F278C1256DD6004860EA?OpenDocument

14. Rachael Daigle, "Interview with Robin Long on his Reasons for Deserting the US Army and Seeking Refugee Status in Canada," unedited transcript, *Boise Weekly*, 10 May 2006. www.couragetoresist.org/x/content/view/53/27/

15. Albert J. Beveridge, speech in the *Congressional Record*, 56th Congress, 1st Session, Vol XXXIII, 704-712.

16. Nelson Mandela (interview), "The United States of America is a Threat to World Peace," *Newsweek*, 10 September 2002. Available at www.

wagingpeace.org/articles/2002/09/10_mandela-interview.htm

17. Kathleen Koch, "Police: Tampa Pilot Voiced Support for bin Laden," CNN.com/U.S., 7 January 2002. http://archives.cnn.com/2002/US/01/06/tampa.crash/index.html "Pipe-Bomb Suspect Is Ruled Incompetent," *New York Times*, 31 May 2007. http://query.nytimes.com/gst/fullpage.html?sec=health&res=9F00EFDA1239F931A35757C0A9629C8B63

18. Melissa August et al., "Milestones," *Time*, 5 November 2001. www.time.com/time/magazine/article/0,9171,1001159,00.html

19. Council on American-Islamic Relations, "The Struggle for Equality: Annual Civil Rights Reports," September 2006. Council on American-Islamic Relations, 453 New Jersey Ave, SE, Washington, DC.

20. Alvin M. Josephy, Jr., *500 Nations: An Illustrated History of North American Indians* (New York: Alfred A. Knopf, 1994), 125-129.

21. Clayborne Carson, consultant, *Civil Rights Chronicle: The African-American Struggle for Freedom* (Lincolnwood, IL: Publications International, Ltd., Lincolnwood, IL 2003), 266.

22. Crossroads Anti-Racist Organizing & Training offers education, training, and organizing to dismantle racism and build anti-racist multicultural diversity. P.O. Box 309, Matteson, IL 60443-0309. www.crossroadsantiracism.org People's Institute for Survival and Beyond is dedicated to training and organizing to dismantle racism. 601 N. Carrollton, New Orleans, LA 70119. www.pisab.org

23. William S. Cohen, "Annual Report to the President and Congress" (Washington, DC: Department of Defense, 1999). www.dod.mil/execsec/adr1999/index.html Christopher Hellman and Travis Sharp, "The FY 2009 Pentagon Spending Request—Global Military Spending," Center for Arms Control and Non-Proliferation, 22 February 2008. www.armscontrolcenter.org/policy/securityspending/articles/fy09_dod_request_global/ Christopher Hellman and Travis Sharp, "The FY 2009 Pentagon Spending Request—Discretionary," Center for Arms Control and Non-Proliferation, 4 February 2008. www.armscontrolcenter.org/policy/securityspending/articles/fy09_dod_request_discretionary/

24. Condoleezza Rice, "FY 2007 State Department Budget Request," remarks before the House Appropriations Subcommittee on Foreign Operations, Export Financing, and Related Programs, 4 April 2006. www.state.gov/secretary/rm/2006/64120.htm Office of Management and Budget, "FY 2007 Department of Defense Budget Request." www.whitehouse.gov/omb/budget/fy2007/defense.html

25. Jeanne Larson and Madge Micheels-Cyrus, eds., *Seeds of Peace* (Philadelphia, PA: New Society Publishers, 1987), 176.

26. J. William Fullbright, *The Pentagon Propaganda Machine* (Vancouber, WA: Vintage Books, 1971), 13. Larson and Micheels-Cyrus, *Seeds of*

*Peace,* 26.

27. Tom Fox, *"Why Are We Here?,"* Electronic Iraq, 3 December 2005. http://electroniciraq.net/news/2212.shtml Christian Peacemaker Teams, P.O. Box 6508, Chicago, IL 60680. www.cpt.org

28. International Fellowship of Reconciliation, Spoorstraat 38, Alkmaar, 1815 BK, The Netherlands. www.ifor.org International Solidarity Movement, www.palsolidarity.org/main

29. Rachel Corrie, "'I Am in the Midst of a Genocide': E-Mails from Gaza," *Monthly Review,* May 2003. www.monthlyreview.org/0503corrie.htm

30. Cooney and Michalowski, eds., *The Power of the People,* 43.

31. Martin Luther King Jr., *Where Do We Go from Here: Chaos or Community?* (Boston, MA: Beacon Press, 1968), 62.

32. Arundhati Roy, "Confronting Empire," World Social Forum, Porto Alegre, Brazil, 27 January 2003. www.ratical.org/ratville/CAH/AR012703.html

## NOTES FOR PART IV:
## BACK FROM EMMAUS:
## FROM FEAR TO FREEDOM

1. Larson and Micheels-Cyrus, *Seeds of Peace,* 255.

2. Margaret Mead, edited by Robert Textor, *The World Ahead: An Anthropologist Anticipates the Future* (New York, Oxford: Berghahn Books, 2005), 12.

## NOTES FOR CHAPTER 10:
## A PERSONAL PATH

1. Henri Nouwen, Donald P. McNeill, Douglas A. Morrison, *Compassion: A Reflection on the Christian Life* (New York: Image Books, 1983), 4.

2. Henri J. M. Nouwen, *With Open Hands* (Notre Dame, IN: Ave Maria Press, 1972), 46.

3. Peggy McIntosh, "White Privilege: Unpacking the Invisible Knapsack," Wellesley College Center for Research on Women, 1989. Available at www.ssc.wisc.edu/~rturley/Soc134/WhitePrivilege.pdf Paul Kivel, *Uprooting Racism: How White People Can Work for Racial Justice* (Gabriola Island, BC: New Society Publishers, 2002), 15.

4. James H. Cone, "Black Liberation, Theology and Black Catholics: A Critical Conversation," *Theological Studies*, Vol. 61, No. 4, December 2000. Available at www.accessmylibrary.com/coms2/summary_0286-28729956_ITM

---

## NOTES FOR CHAPTER 11:
## A COMMUNAL PATH

1. Frances Moore Lappé and Paul Martin DuBois, *The Quickening of America: Rebuilding Our Nation, Remaking Our Lives* (San Francisco, CA: Jossey-Bass Inc, 1994), 9.

2. Ibid., 15.

3. Bob Dylan, "*Gotta Serve Somebody: The Gospel Songs of Bob Dylan*," Sony, 25 March 2003. Song written by Shirley Caesar.

4. Wendell Berry, *The Country of Marriage* (New York: Harcourt Brace Jovanovich, 1973), 16. Used with permission of the author.

5. Laurence Shames, *Hunger for More: Searching for Values in an Age of Greed* (New York: Vintage Books USA, 1991), 146.

6. Kivel, *Uprooting Racism*, 28.

7. George Lipsitz, *The Possessive Investment in Whiteness: How White People Profit from Identity Politics* (Philadelphia, PA: Temple University Press, 1997).

8. Katy Butler, "The Great Boomer Bust," *Mother Jones*, June 1989. Available at http://americanpublicmedia.publicradio.org/programs/giving_thanks/archive/2001/gtbutler.shtml

9. Christine Vladimiroff, OSB, "Prophet Sharing," *U.S. Catholic*, October 2002.

10. One excellent book on the principles of community organizing is Lappé and Moore's *The Quickening of America: Rebuilding Our Nation, Remaking Our Lives*. A few good resources for starting small faith-sharing communities are BuenaVista and the North American Forum for Small Christian communities. BuenaVista (www.buenavista.org) has supported small Christian Communities and faith-sharing groups since 1987. They encourage, collaborate, and network small communities and the people and groups working with them through regional and national gatherings. North American Forum for Small Christian Communities (www.nafscc.org) is a network of Catholic diocesan leaders and organizations working with North American Catholic communities. The Fellowship for Intentional Communities has a Web site (www.ic.org) serving the growing intentional community movement, including ecovillages, cohousing, residential land trusts, communes, student co-ops, urban housing cooperatives, alternative communi-

ties, and other projects where people strive together with a common vision. One intentional community model in the Catholic tradition is the Catholic Worker Movement. A good resource about the Catholic Worker Movement is Rosalie Riegle Troester, *Voices from the Catholic Worker* (Philadelphia, PA: Temple University Press, 1993).

11. Marie Dennis, "Solidarity for the 21st Century: Remembering the Martyrs of El Salvador," National Council of Church News Service, 3 December 2005. www.ncccusa.org/news/051206MarieDennis.html

## NOTES FOR EPILOGUE: BE NOT AFRAID

1. Stuart Dauermann, "Having a Fear—Not Faith," sermon, Parashat Toldot, 25 November 2006. http://rabbenu.blogspot.com/2006/12/having-fear-not-faith.html

2. Daniel Berrigan, SJ, *Uncommon Prayer: A Book of Psalms* (Maryknoll, NY: Orbis Books, 1978), 30. Used with permission of the publisher.

3. Elisabeth Kübler-Ross, *On Death and Dying* (New York: Simon & Schuster, 1997).

4. G. K. Chesterton, *St. Francis of Assisi* (New York: Doubleday Books, 1957).

5. Martin Luther King Jr., "I've Been to the Mountaintop," speech, Memphis, TN, 3 April 1968. Available at www.stanford.edu/group/King/publications/speeches/I've_been_to_the_mountaintop.pdf

6. Martin Luther King Jr., "The Southern Christian Leadership Conference Presidential Address," 16 August 1967. Available at www.hartford-hwp.com/archives/45a/628.html

7. Frank Cordaro, "The Reign of God (St. Luke's Beatitudes)," written at Holden Village, 5 June 1987. Personal copy of author.

8. Mary Lou Kownacki, OSB, ed., *Peacemaking Day by Day*, Vol. I (Erie, PA: Pax Christi USA, 1985, reprint 2003), 133.

# OTHER RESOURCES FROM PAX CHRISTI USA

**Personal Nonviolence:**
**A Practical Spirituality for Peacemakers**
By Gerard Vanderhaar, Ph.D.
In this post-humously published book, Vanderhaar explains how a spirituality of nonviolence provides methods and guidance in everyday activities, helps peacemakers recognize both their gifts and shortcomings, and guides them in dealing with the challenges of life in the twenty-first century. Understanding nonviolence can guide peacemakers to a practical spirituality based on the nonviolent Christ, our guide and inspiration.
Item No. 550-001          $12.00 + s/h

**Imagine a World: Poetry for Peacemakers**
Compiled by Peggy Rosenthal, Ph.D.,
full-color artwork by Mary Ann Lederer

This collection includes poems about injustice and war; poems about celebrating life, the nonviolent spirit, and refreshing the soul; and poems for rallies, vigils, or prayer services. Poems by poets such as Daniel Berrigan, Wendell Berry, Lucille Clifton, Martín Espada, Thich Nhat Hanh, Barbara Kingsolver, and Alice Walker are great resources for peacemaking and justice-seeking, in personal meditation or reflection, in small groups, or in meetings.
Item No. 529-432          $14.00 + s/h

**The Way of Peace:**
**Exploring Nonviolence for the 21st Century**
Revised and expanded by Shannon McManimon
An updated and expanded classic (based on text by Gerard Vanderhaar, STD, and Mary Lou Kownacki, OSB). This manual introduces the spirit and practice of nonviolence in recent decades. Includes stories, prayers, reflection questions, action ideas, and exercises. If you're searching for another way, use this book to learn about the spirit and practice of nonviolence. Perfect for classroom or parish study groups!
Item No. 533-054          $15.00 + s/h

**Love Beyond Measure: A Spirituality of Nonviolence**
By Mary Lou Kownacki, OSB

A full and powerful expression of insights on the spirituality of nonviolence, this profound book begins with the groundbreaking essay, "Doorway To Peace." Sister Mary Lou then offers five sessions to help readers reflectively and prayerfully digest the essay's insights and challenges. Each session begins with a prayer service, contains reflection questions, suggests related readings, and includes questions based on Scripture from the prayer service. Equally suited to the individual reader or to a group process.
Item No. 523-239          $12.00 + s/h

## Peacemaker Pamphlet Series

Small paperbacks with the stories of holy and heroic figures, for younger and older readers alike. These books are long enough to give readers a thorough portrait of the lives and messages of these revered individuals, but short enough to be read quickly. Perfect for classroom use, confirmation study classes, daily reflection, and more!

### Mohandas Gandhi and Lifelong Peacemaking
Excerpted/adapted from a book by Eknath Easwaran
This 28-page booklet outlines Gandhi's early life and influences; his search for truth and justice through the practice of satyagraha in South Africa; British colonial rule in India; the salt march and campaign; Gandhi's "experiments in truth"; and Gandhi's thoughts on nonviolence. Based on Eknath Easwaran's book *Gandhi the Man*.
Item No. 537-004          $3.00 + s/h

### Martin Luther King Jr.: The Dream of a Just Community
By J. Milburn Thompson, Ph.D.
Provides an overview of Dr. King's work for a just community and the meaning of his life, including the formation of his views and conscience, the Montgomery Bus Boycott, the Birmingham and Selma campaigns, his time in Chicago, the emergence of Black Power, his stance on the war in Vietnam, and the Poor Peoples' Campaign.
Item No. 537-050          $3.00 + s/h

### Others in the Series:

Jean Donovan: The Call to Discipleship (By John Dear, SJ):
    Item No. 537-049   $3.00 + s/h
Oscar Romero and the Nonviolent Struggle for Justice (By John Dear, SJ):
    Item No. 537-175   $3.00 + s/h
Dorothy Day and the Permanent Revolution (By Eileen Egan):
    Item No. 537-005   $2.50 + s/h
Franz Jaegerstaetter: Martyr for Conscience (By Gordon Zahn, Ph.D.):
    Item No. 537-009   $2.50 + s/h
Thomas Merton's Struggle with Peacemaking (by Jim Forrest):
    Item No. 537-006   $2.50 + s/h
Complete Set of Seven (with discussion guide): Item No. 537-010   $15.00 + s/h

### Peacemaking Day by Day
Our bestseller of all time, these original books of daily quotes for peacemakers are lively, practical, educational, and inspirational. A great resource for teachers who want to introduce students to peacemakers and justice-seekers from around the world.
Volume I, bound edition: Item No. 532-028  $7.00 + s/h
    (no further discount)
Volume I, stapled edition: Item No. 532-027  $6.00 + s/h
Volume II, stapled edition:  Item No. 532-130   $6.00 + s/h
Peacemaking Day by Day, (Original) Volumes I & II:  $10.00 + s/h

## Pax Christi USA Prayer Cards

Prayers printed on card stock (3.5 x 5.5 inches), often with action suggestions. Perfect for including in correspondance, church bulletins, for use at prayer services, and more! $0.50 each; $10/100; $80/1000 + s/h (of any one card)

### Prayer in a Time of Terrorism (By Mary Lou Kownacki, OSB):
English-language Item No. 540-471; Spanish-language Item No. 540-469
This prayer gives us the opportunity to recommit to nonviolence, to cast out fear, and to renounce hatred and revenge as weapons of war.

### Prayer for Global Restoration (By Michelle Balek, OSF):
Item No. 540-291
A prayer of reverence for all creation, an invocation asking that we may know we are irrevocably part of the web of life, asking for forgiveness for our ignorance, asking for our own radical transformation into God's kin-dom.

### Prayer for Unity in a Time of War (By Kathy Kelly): Item No. 540-440
The war in Iraq wages on, with thousands killed. This prayer asks God to grant us the grace to hear deep in our hearts our Muslim brothers' and sisters' daily call to prayer: "O God you are peace. From you is peace and unto you is peace. Let us live our lives in peace. Bring us into your peace. . . . Grant us your forgiveness God, and unto you be our becoming."

### Jesus Our Tortured Brother Today (By Dianna Ortiz, OSU):
Item No. 540-480
This prayer calls on Jesus, tortured more than 2000 years ago, to be with those tortured today and to help us "to look into the secret prisons—the unmarked graves—the hearts and minds of torture survivors," to embrace their wounds and give us the will to end torture.

### Prayer for a New Society: Item No. 552-244
This prayer calls for order and beauty to emerge from chaos and violence, and for opening narrow hearts to people who are suffering or poor.

### Prayer for Dismantling Racism
### (Created by the Pax Christi USA Anti-Racism Team): Item No. 540-285
This prayer asks God to "create in us a new mind and heart" to help us see that we are all part of the same family. It asks for the grace to rid ourselves of our racial stereotypes, so that we can help create a Church and nation that embraces all people.

### Prayer for a Globalization of Solidarity (By Jim Hug, SJ):
English-language Item No. 540-472;
Spanish-language Item No. 540-470
This prayer asks for God's help in freeing ourselves from the "idolatry of wealth" that blinds us to the poverty of others and the degradation of the Earth for the sake of profit.

### Muslim, Jewish, Christian Prayer for Peace
English-language Item No. 536-236; Spanish-language Item No. 536-237
This prayer calls forth the deepest shared beliefs of the three traditions that affirm they are followers of one God, children of Abraham, brothers and sisters who need to join hands to seek peace together. This prayer asks for the "understanding that puts an end to strife. . . Forgiveness that overcomes vengeance."

## The Cost of Peace T-Shirt (made in Bethlehem)

Natural-colored, 100% organic cotton t-shirt with brown printing. Front: a peace dove and "Pax Christi USA." Back: "Peace is costly, but it is worth the expense. ~ Kenyan proverb" These shirts are made in a Palestinian-owned, union factory in Bethlehem. This endeavor has the active support of both the Israeli and Palestinian foreign ministries and is helping the economic development of the West Bank. More information on our Web site. Design by Zach Whitney.
*NOTE: Sizes run at least one size smaller than most U.S. shirts.*

Small Item No. 530-00S      Medium Item No. 530-00M

Large Item No. 530-00L XL Item No. 530-0XL XXL Item No. 530-XXL

$18.00 + s/h (maximum discount: 20%)

## Pax Christi USA: A Journey of Faith and Hope
### Introductory DVD or VHS

Introduce your friends, family, or parish to Pax Christi USA! This DVD or VHS features two parts: a 5-minute overview outlines what Pax Christi USA is and a 20-minute section explores the roots and history of Pax Christi USA. Uses video and stills of Pax Christi events and members. Produced by Redwoodproductions.net.

DVD Item No. 547-002; VHS Item No.547-001

$10.00 + s/h    (maximum discount: 20%)

## Order Form

**Name**

**Address**

**City**                     **State**                     **Zip**

**Telephone**                     **Email**

| Qty. | Item No. | Description/Size | Unit $ | Total $ |
|------|----------|------------------|--------|---------|
|      |          |                  |        |         |
|      |          |                  |        |         |
|      |          |                  |        |         |

|  |  |
|---|---|
| | Subtotal* |
| | Shipping/Handling* |
| | *PA residents only 6% sales tax |
| | TOTAL |

**Shipping**: Please see our Web site for current rates or call 814-453-4955, ext. 231.
***Bulk Orders:*** 10 or more, deduct 10%; 25 or more, deduct 20%; 100 or more, deduct 40% (DOES NOT apply to certain products)
***Special Discounts:*** Bookstores, Parish Sponsors, Corporate Sponsors, and Local Groups: A maximum 40% volume discount is available on select items. Please contact our sales department for details. We also offer products on consignment.
***Delivery Info:*** Please allow 2-3 weeks for product shipping and delivery. Rush shipping is available upon request; contact our sales dept. for details.
*Prices valid as of July 2008.*

**Payment:**

O Check      O Visa      O MasterCard

Name:_____

Card #:  _____

Exp. Date:_____

Signature: _____

*Full-line catalog available at www.paxchristiusa.org/fullcatalogo6.pdf*

# ABOUT PAX CHRISTI USA

## Statement of Purpose:

Pax Christi USA strives to create a world that reflects the Peace of Christ by exploring, articulating, and witnessing to the call of Christian nonviolence. This work begins in personal life and extends to communities of reflection and action to transform structures of society. Pax Christi USA rejects war, preparations for war, and every form of violence and domination. It advocates primacy of conscience, economic and social justice, and respect for creation.

Pax Christi USA commits itself to peace education and, with the help of its bishop members, promotes the gospel imperative of peacemaking as a priority in the Catholic Church in the United States. Through the efforts of all its members and in cooperation with other groups, Pax Christi USA works toward a more peaceful, just, and sustainable world.

Pax Christi USA is a section of Pax Christi International, which has representation status at the United Nations in New York and Vienna, the UN Human Rights Commission and Sub–Commission in Geneva, UNESCO in Paris, and UNICEF in New York.

## Who We Are:

Pax Christi USA is a national Catholic peace and justice movement reaching over one half-million U.S. Catholics. Our membership includes: 650 religious communities; 800 parishes; 130 bishops; 400 Pax Christi local and campus groups; 20 regions that coordinate activities in their geographic areas; and tens of thousands of individual members.

Pax Christi local groups offer opportunities to join with others in a community setting to deepen their understanding of the gospel call to peace and justice. Pax Christi USA's nearly 400 local chapters meet regularly in neighborhoods, parishes, religious congregations, high schools, and on college campuses to pray, study, and act for peace with justice on local, national, and global issues.

## The Four Priority Areas of Our Work:

- Spirituality of Nonviolence and Peacemaking
- Economic and Interracial Justice
- Human Rights and Global Restoration
- Disarmament, Demilitarization, and Reconciliation
       with Justice

For more information, please visit www.paxchristiusa.org

# Sustainers' Circle for Peace with Justice

More than ever, we need people who are willing and able to sustain the work for peace with justice over the long haul. Pax Christi USA's "Sustainers' Circle" allows you to make safe and convenient monthly donations directly through your credit card. By committing to becoming a Sustainer, you provide Pax Christi USA with important monthly support on which we rely, you help us to be more eco-friendly (less paperwork equals more trees), and you help to build the base from which to make our work even more prophetic, effective, and stronger.

Use the form below or contact us (see next page for contact information) to set up a monthly contribution by credit card.

Please select a monthly donation amount:

_____ $10                    _____ $20

_____ $50                    _____ $100

$ _____ other ($10 minimum)

This payment will repeat monthly on an ongoing basis. You may cancel at any time.

MC/Visa _____

Exp. Date _____

Signature _____

Name _____

Address _____

_____

City _____ State _____ Zip _____

Phone _____

Email _____

## GENERAL MEMBERSHIP CONTRIBUTION

I believe "peace is possible" and want to join Pax Christi USA:

Name _____

Address _____

City _____ State _____ Zip _____

Phone _____

Email _____

**(If you would like to join the "Sustainers' Circle," please fill out the previous page.)**

The regular membership fee for Pax Christi USA is $35 a year, more if you are able or whatever you can afford. We rely on the generosity of our members. Please consider enclosing a membership contribution to Pax Christi USA for:

_____$35 _____$50 _____ $100 _____$500 _____ other

At this time I can only contribute_____.

MC/Visa _____

Exp. Date _____

Signature _____

Check any of the following:
_____ I would like more information about joining or starting a local group in my area or school.
_____ I would like more information about the Parish Sponsorship Program.
_____ I would like information on making a will/bequest.
_____ I would like to receive a publications catalog.
_____ Please do not give my e-mail or phone number to local Pax Christi group leaders.

***Send this form to:***
Pax Christi USA
532 West Eighth Street
Erie, PA 16502
814-453-4955
Fax: 814-452-4784
info@paxchristiusa.org
www.paxchristiusa.org

# ABOUT THE AUTHOR

Over the past thirty years, Tom Cordaro has worked as a professional speaker, writer, organizer, and national leader in the faith-based peace and justice movement. During his career as an activist, Mr. Cordaro has organized anti-war, disarmament, and economic justice campaigns at the local, regional, and national levels.

He has served both as a national staff person and the National Council Chair of Pax Christi USA (a Catholic peace organization) and was named a Pax Christi USA Ambassador of Peace in 2002. Mr. Cordaro has authored many Pax Christi USA publications and has contributed articles for the *National Catholic Reporter*, *Sisters Today*, and *Blueprint for Social Justice*. He has also written for the *Catholic News Service*.

Mr. Cordaro has also served as Co-Chair of Crossroads Anti-Racism Organizing & Training and is a founding member of the Pax Christi Anti-Racism Team. In this capacity, he has co-led anti-racism training for church groups around the country.

Mr. Cordaro was awarded the 2008 Pax Joliet Peace Award from the Catholic Diocese of Joliet for his work on peace and justice issues as the Justice & Outreach Minister at St. Margaret Mary Catholic Church in Naperville, Illinois. He has a Masters Degree in Pastoral Studies from St. Thomas University in Miami, Florida.